Globe Law and Business

ESG in Mining and Minerals

Consulting Editor **Ted Rhodes**

Consulting editor
Ted Rhodes

Managing director
Sian O'Neill

ESG in Mining and Minerals
is published by

Globe Law and Business Ltd
3 Mylor Close
Horsell
Woking
Surrey GU21 4DD
United Kingdom
Tel: +44 20 3745 4770
www.globelawandbusiness.com

Printed and bound by CPI Group (UK) Ltd, Croydon CR0 4YY, United Kingdom

ESG in Mining and Minerals

ISBN 9781837230402
EPUB ISBN 9781837230419
Adobe PDF ISBN 9781837230426

Table of contents

Introduction: environmental, social and governance in mining and minerals

Ted Rhodes
CMS Cameron McKenna Nabarro Olswang LLP

1. A new focus on mining and minerals

In much of the developed world, the mining and minerals industry is currently the focus of more government policy, press scrutiny and general public interest than at any time since the UK miners' strike of the mid-1980s. That is because it will play a fundamental role in the outcome of two of the most critical societal issues of our times: climate change; and a profound geopolitical shift back to a multi-polar and more volatile world.

2. Energy transition drivers

Considering current levels of greenhouse gas emissions, global temperatures are expected to rise 1.5°C above pre-industrial levels between 2030 and 2052 if they continue to increase at the current rate[1] (with recent studies suggesting that that temperature increase could occur as early as 2029, condemning the world to warming of 1.5°C).[2] That is expected to result in the irreversible melting of ice sheets, higher sea levels, an increase in extreme weather events and stresses on food production, water supply and many natural habitats, among other impacts. There is broad (although perhaps no longer unanimous) global consensus that drastic action is required to avert those consequences. For example, at the COP28 climate summit, more than 100 countries agreed to triple global renewable power capacity by 2030. With current technology, all realistic scenarios for significant reductions to greenhouse gas emissions require the substitution of fossil fuel electricity generation with renewables and increased electrification of industry and particularly transportation, both rapidly and on a massive scale. Those changes are commonly referred to as the 'energy transition'.

Both renewable generation and electrification require significant mineral inputs. For example, nickel, cobalt, graphite, manganese and lithium are found in modern batteries; certain rare earth elements are crucial for wind turbines and EV

---

1 IPCC, *Global Warming of 1.5°C: An IPCC Special Report*, 2019, www.ipcc.ch/site/assets/uploads/sites/2/2022/06/SR15_Full_Report_HR.pdf.

2 Robin D Lamboll *et al*, "Assessing the size and uncertainty of remaining carbon budgets", *Nature Climate Change*, 30 October 2023, www.nature.com/articles/s41558-023-01848-5.

motors; and electricity networks need large quantities of copper and aluminium. As economies pivot from fossil fuels to renewable energy, governments are belatedly waking up to the strategic imperative for secure supply chains for solar panels, wind turbines, batteries and similar technologies. Those supply chains have come to be controlled by China, which dominates many of the technologies not just for manufactured products, but also for the processing of minerals to produce intermediate materials. Chinese companies, with state support, have moved upstream to acquire equity in or offtake rights from some of the most important suppliers of lithium, cobalt and rare earths. Also, supply of energy transition minerals often comes from a small number of lowest cost producers such as Indonesia for nickel or the Democratic Republic of Congo for cobalt.

UN Trade and Development (UNCTAD) has identified a critical global shortfall in investment in key energy transition minerals, predicting that current mineral production levels are insufficient to limit global warming to 1.5°C in accordance with the Paris Agreement. UNCTAD estimates that approximately 250 mines, including around 80 new copper mines, 70 new lithium and nickel mines each, and 30 new cobalt mines are needed to achieve the 2030 net zero emissions targets, yet only 110 new projects have presently been identified. The investment needed between 2022 and 2030 to achieve that number of projects ranges from $360 billion to $450 billion. With the value of new developments currently sitting at around $39 billion, there is a potential funding shortfall of $180 billion to $270 billion, with the most significant investment gaps in copper and nickel, accounting for 36% and 16% of the total gap, respectively.[3]

The International Energy Agency[4] has estimated that mineral demand for clean energy technologies will double between 2020 and 2040 based on its Stated Policies Scenario,[5] and will quadruple in that period based on its Sustainable Development Scenario.[6]

3. Resource competition

Over recent years, as relations have deteriorated between western developed economies and China and Russia, the former have realised how fragile their

---

3 UNCTAD, "Critical minerals boom: Global energy shift brings opportunities and risks for developing countries", 26 April 2024, https://unctad.org/news/critical-minerals-boom-global-energy-shift-brings-opportunities-and-risks-developing-countries.

4 International Energy Agency, *Global Energy and Climate Model: Documentation 2023*, https://iea.blob.core.windows.net/assets/ff3a195d-762d-4284-8bb5-bd062d260cc5/GlobalEnergyandClimateModelDocumentation2023.pdf.

5 This scenario takes into account relevant policies and implementation measures adopted as of the end of August 2023, together with relevant policy proposals, even if the specific measures needed to put these proposals into effect have yet to be fully developed.

6 This scenario considers the contribution needed from clean energy technology innovation for a clean energy transition to net zero CO_2 emissions by 2070. The Sustainable Development Scenario describes the broad evolution of the energy sector that would be required to reach the key energy-related goals of the United Nations, including the climate goal of the Paris Agreement (SDG 13), universal access to modern energy by 2030 (SDG 7), and a dramatic reduction in energy-related air pollution and the associated impacts on public health (SDG 3.9).

Figure 1. Total mineral demand for clean energy technologies by scenario, 2010–2040

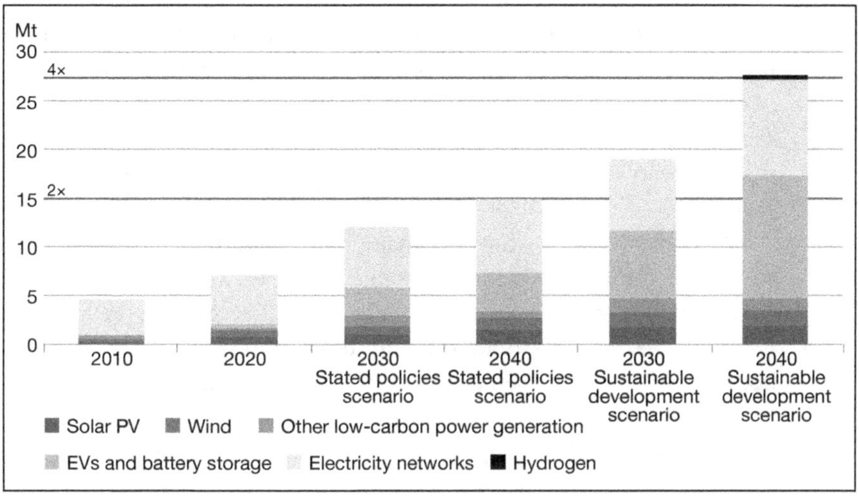

Source: International Energy Agency (under licence CC BY 4.0)

energy transition supply chains are and how dependent they are on China in particular, a country which dominates the global supply and processing of critical minerals. In 2022, China produced 70% of the world's rare earth minerals,[7] 61% of the natural graphite and 98% of the final processed materials used to make battery anodes.[8] China's processing power is even stronger than its production capabilities. In 2022 China refined 89% of the world's neodymium and praseodymium, the key metals for EV magnets[9] and processed 100% of the world's graphite supply, 74% of its cobalt, 90% of its rare earth minerals[10] and 60% of its lithium.[11] This dominance gives China a huge head start in the race to develop supply chains for energy transition technologies.

Over recent years, Western governments have woken up to this, and have

7 *Financial Times*, "Can Europe go green without China's critical minerals", 19 September 2023, https://ig.ft.com/rare-earths/#:~:text=Even%20in%20areas%20of%20technology,to%20power%20a%20greener%20future.

8 Eric Onstad, "Auto firms race to secure non-Chinese graphite for EVs as shortages loom", Reuters, 21 June 2023, www.reuters.com/business/autos-transportation/auto-firms-race-secure-non-chinese-graphite-evs-shortages-loom-2023-06-21/?utm_source=Sailthru&utm_medium=Newsletter&utm_campaign=Daily-Briefing&utm_term=062123.

9 Mai Nguyen and Eric Onstad, "China's rare earths dominance in focus after it limits germanium and gallium exports", Reuters, 21 December 2023, www.reuters.com/markets/commodities/chinas-rare-earths-dominance-focus-after-mineral-export-curbs-2023-07-05/.

10 Will Daniel, "China has a 'near monopoly' on many critical minerals. JPMorgan says it could be the next battleground with the US", *Fortune*, 10 June 2024, https://fortune.com/2024/06/10/china-near-monopoly-many-critical-minerals-jpmorgan-says-next-battleground-usa/.

11 Alex Scott, "Challenging China's dominance in the lithium market", *Chemical and Engineering News*, 29 October 2022, https://cen.acs.org/energy/energy-storage-/Challenging-Chinas-dominance-lithium-market/100/i38.

been belatedly scrambling to deploy policies, regulation, incentives and even direct government funding to promote alternative supplies of critical minerals. Examples include the Minerals Security Partnership (a collaboration of 14 countries and the European Union to promote public and private investment in responsible critical minerals supply chains globally), the US Inflation Reduction Act (which includes a commitment to increasing the domestic US supply of critical minerals) and the EU Critical Raw Materials Act (which aims to ensure the European Union has access to a secure and sustainable supply of critical raw materials).

We do not yet know how successful these measures will be in securing access to critical minerals for the economies that need them. But as the energy transition gathers pace and the global economy becomes more reliant on these minerals, resource nationalism and protectionism, combined with supply bottlenecks, could exacerbate international tensions and conflicts. Shortages may also push countries to compete for resources in new, remote and so far untouched areas, including international waters, polar regions or even space; each of which presents very serious and specific environmental, social and governance (ESG) challenges.

4. The importance of ESG in mining and minerals

Much of the current buzz in mining is around the opportunities to supply this emerging demand for critical minerals and other inputs to the energy transition. As there is an environmental driver to the demand, consumers want to know that they are not just replacing one set of ESG concerns with different ones. In many cases, consumers want their consumption choices to make a positive difference, especially if they are willing to pay a premium for an electric car or green electricity. That gives an extra dimension to the headlines about deforestation for nickel in Indonesia, child labour in cobalt mining in Central Africa or pollution associated with copper mining.

Electric vehicle companies and other original equipment manufacturers (OEMs) are increasingly becoming directly involved in the sourcing of raw materials for their production lines, and even taking equity in upstream mining companies or mineral processing operations. That allows them to ensure they have robust supply chains despite fierce competition for resources and geopolitical tensions, but also to ensure better ESG standards so they can stand behind their products' green credentials.

As governments take a more direct role in supporting the mining industry to develop new supplies of critical minerals, they also assume a share of the ESG risk. They will not want to see subsidies funded by their taxpayers syphoned off by corrupt host governments or used to fund projects that will unfairly displace indigenous communities or destroy the habitats of endangered species.

So, the increased involvement of governments, OEMs and conscious consumers has thrown a new spotlight on the mining and minerals industry – which is not used to this kind of scrutiny.

5. Historic neglect of ESG considerations

Mining and heavy industry have been in decline in much of Europe and the United States since the 1970s and 1980s. In 1970 the United Kingdom mined 147.2 million tonnes of coal, but this figure has fallen drastically to only 0.5 million tonnes in 2023. Coal mining in the rest of Europe has experienced similar declines. While mining for other minerals has not necessarily declined in the same way, nothing else comes close to replacing coal in terms of volumes and new sources of production have been concentrated outside of Europe and the United States.[12]

The relatively wealthy populations in these economies, which are dominated by the services sector, were generally happy to outsource these disruptive, polluting industries to China and other developing economies with lower production costs, importing the intermediate or end products they needed to supply voracious consumption. Even in developed economies with important mining industries like Canada and Australia, mining activities tend to be distant from major population centres, so they often remain 'out of sight, out of mind'.

Consumers generally gave little thought to why costs of imported products were lower. In some cases, energy for mineral processing was generated using cheap, dirty coal. Other projects would be more competitive because of a relative lack of labour standards, health, safety or environmental protections or because there was little transparency or public scrutiny of revenues in the host country. Better governed, more sustainable projects had to compete on price with less well governed, less sustainable projects, often creating a race to the bottom.

6. Emergence and evolution of ESG

Thankfully, local communities and non-governmental organisations have been working hard to shine a light on the industry, and many mining companies have invested heavily in improving ESG standards over recent decades. Over that time, we have seen an evolution in mindset. Initially, ESG investments were limited to what was required to comply with laws and regulations of the host state. Or they were seen, and justified to shareholders, as a way of mitigating ESG risks. For example, if investments were not made in mine safety, there was increased risk of injury, liability, downtime and lost productivity.

12 UK Department for Energy Security and Net Zero and Department for Business, Energy & Industrial Strategy, "Historical coal data: coal production, availability and consumption 1853 to 2023", 30 July 2024, www.gov.uk/government/statistical-data-sets/historical-coal-data-coal-production-availability-and-consumption.

Towards the end of the last century, the mining industry was an early adopter of the concept of a 'social licence to operate', which recognises the need for 'buy-in' or acceptance of a project by different stakeholder groups and the general public. Again, this began as a response to the economic risk presented by disgruntled communities who might blockade, sabotage or otherwise disrupt and protest against mining operations that ignored their interests. Faced with such opposition, mining projects could see their licences delayed, suspended or revoked, or encounter regulatory changes that would significantly impact their project economics; not to mention the serious reputational risks and consequences for attracting investment. This concept developed in response to those challenges, being used to support mining companies' investing in community infrastructure and social programmes, local supply chains and training of the workforce, environmental conservation and compensation measures.

But the mining and minerals industry has evolved beyond that concept to a business model that sees ESG measures as a potential source of competitive advantage. Industry associations like the International Council on Mining and Metals (ICMM), the World Gold Council or the International Copper Association have been increasingly active in promoting ESG best practices, developing and adopting standards and certifications such as ICMM's Mining Principles, the Responsible Gold Standards or the Copper Mark.

These industry standards have helped to set a new baseline for sustainable mining practices, and to draw a distinction between those miners that are investing in better ESG practices and those that are not, including producers in underregulated mining provinces and the many informal and even illegal miners operating globally. New critical minerals policies are now promoting these standards, not just for their intrinsic value, but also for their ability to distinguish new sources of production that they are promoting from lower cost competition in less regulated markets.

7. The brighter future for ESG

Industry standards have proliferated to form a patchwork of different norms required by different industry participants, which can be hard to navigate. Mining companies have been calling for harmonisation or consolidation of these norms and there are initiatives in that direction, including a collaboration that has been announced between the Copper Mark, the Mining Association of Canada, ICMM and the World Gold Council to work towards consolidating their voluntary standards into a single global responsible mining standard, and multi-stakeholder oversight system. The 'UN Secretary-General's Panel on Critical Energy Transition Minerals', has also been recently established by a number of important mining and consumer nations, international organisations, non-governmental organisations, mining standards and governance bodies and other non-state actors. It is intended to draw up new guidelines to address issues relating to equity, transparency, investment, sustainability and human rights abuses associated with mining.

There are hopes that products certified to have better environmental or ESG credentials, and particularly lower carbon intensity, may attract a premium in commodities markets, although there is relatively little evidence of this so far. In many cases, the emissions associated with mining itself are dwarfed by those from the downstream processing or consumption of those minerals; ie, the Scope 3 emissions of mining. Climate change efforts have tended to focus on those parts of the supply chain with the highest emissions intensity, targeting the displacement of coal-fired power, green steel and low-carbon aluminium, as well as recycling as a less energy-intensive alternative to new primary mineral production. As new climate regulations like the EU Carbon Border Adjustment Mechanism (CBAM) impose costs linked to carbon content in these supply chains, that pressure is likely to be passed downstream, economically incentivising ore beneficiation and grade control, for example.

Besides risk management and commodity premiums, there are other emerging drivers for improved ESG performance. Industry ESG certifications are increasingly being required by investors and lenders, particularly government-backed funds, multilateral development banks and export credit agencies, and similar standards are applied to determine access to green or sustainability-linked finance. So, although compliance may be voluntary, it may be a practical requirement for many mining projects, or at least a source of advantage in the competitive capital markets.

These industry standards are also guiding a new wave of ESG regulation, which is intended to produce extra-territorial effect throughout supply chains, typified by the EU Corporate Sustainability Due Diligence Directive, Germany's Supply Chain Due Diligence Act and the US SEC Climate Disclosure Rules. As well as promoting the ESG objectives in themselves, these measures all aim to level the playing field between more and less heavily regulated mining companies, which compete in a global commodities market.

The trends have added to an already bewildering array of different laws and standards for different ESG topics. Some are binding, while others are voluntary or required only in relation to specific certifications or categories of industry participants. There are international treaties and norms with varying levels of binding force, national legislation and regulation (including, for these purposes, EU regulation), which may have purely domestic or extra-territorial application, as well as different provincial, state or municipal laws and by-laws depending on the place of operation. The appendix, which you will find at the end of this introduction, illustrates this point by reference just to the national and international norms referred to in this book, which are by no means exhaustive.

That proliferation of norms and standards goes some way to explaining the increase in number and importance of ESG and sustainability professionals within the mining and minerals industry over recent years. Thankfully though, most of these standards are pulling in the same direction most of the time, aiming to 'do the right thing' in relation to a business's stakeholders generally and the environment it is operating in. So, much can be achieved by building a corporate culture around a set of values, policies and procedures that take due account of those broader societal interests.

Fortunately, where combined with emerging technologies, there is also a certain alignment between ESG considerations and business economics, particularly in terms of climate. That is because many new technologies, including artificial intelligence, increased automation, better imaging, modelling and monitoring can result in reduced energy consumption, which is associated with both reduced costs and reduced greenhouse gas emissions. To the extent these technologies can reduce the footprint or labour demands of a mining operation, they may also help to reduce other negative environmental and social impacts.

Many modern mining companies already go well beyond the ESG investments required to comply with industry standards or emerging regulation. They are exploring new business lines and potential revenue streams associated with ESG objectives. Mining companies often control areas of land far larger than are being used for mineral extraction at any given moment, and are capitalising on those holdings to generate renewable energy or develop conservation or reforestation projects that allow them to earn carbon credits or provide other nature-based solutions. By returning mine sites to productive economic use after closure, they can maximise their residual value, while minimising safety and environmental risks.

8. Potential headwinds

If you were to attend one of the many mining conferences with no background knowledge of the industry, you could be forgiven for believing that mining is the world's greenest and most sustainable sector. Often an overwhelming majority of the panel sessions will be dedicated to ESG-related topics and mining companies will be vocally promoting their environmental credentials and latest ESG projects. That is positive, because it does show how central ESG considerations have become to the industry, but it is also misleading.

Of course, mining companies want to talk about the progress they have made, and it is important that they do raise awareness of the industry's positive contributions, as mining will need to compete for talent and investment if it is to supply society's mineral needs, particularly for the energy transition. On the other hand, they should be careful not to distort the truth regarding their overall ESG impact, particularly as we are seeing a tightening of anti-greenwashing regulation and increased enforcement action, especially in Europe.

In that respect, this book will present some of the many positive trends we are seeing in terms of mining's ESG performance, but we must also acknowledge the significant risks and negative impacts that continue to plague the minerals industry and often dominate the popular narrative. Progress on ESG metrics has been widespread, but there is still much work to be done.

In particular, we should not let the focus on critical minerals obscure the reality of the global mining industry. The vast majority of mined volumes and values are attributable to fossil fuels and industrial use, with only a small portion of demand linked to low carbon energy. For example, while 7 million tonnes of minerals for renewable technologies are mined each year, that is a tiny fraction of the 8.5 billion tonnes of coal mined each year. That volume continues to grow.

Although coal demand has peaked in the United States and Europe, that is not the case globally, with countries like China and India yet to reach peak demand. Besides thermal coal for power generation, demand for metallurgical coal and iron ore remains strong. Indeed, steel is a critical input to many energy transition technologies, including wind turbines, electric cars and electricity pylons, so that demand is unlikely to reduce significantly any time soon. While the western world has turned its back on coal, Asia has more than filled that gap. China is now responsible for more than half of global supply and India and Indonesia are the next largest producers. Their domestic miners may not always follow the industry ESG best practices that are promoted by ICMM and similar organisations, so it is important to keep in mind this diversity in the global mining industry.

Even in the West, there is a significant risk of backsliding on ESG, with much recent discussion of a backlash or having reached 'peak ESG'. That backlash is partly political, with ESG becoming caught up in America's culture wars. Over the last few years, Republican-controlled states have introduced a growing number of bills intended to limit ESG-focused business practices, for example, by requiring fund managers to prioritise profits over ESG considerations in their investment decisions. That was partly prompted by opposition to the Democrats' intended Green New Deal and the climate objectives of the Inflation Reduction Act.

There is also an important economic motive for this backsliding. Having reached fever pitch around the beginning of the 2020s, the clamour for ESG investing inevitably created something of a bubble. The proliferation of ESG-linked funds chasing a limited pool of appropriate projects pushed up valuations in the short term, but became disconnected from the underlying economics. Some companies were relying on ever-decreasing costs and sustained government subsidies to underpin investments in new, green technologies. Those assumptions were scuppered by a period of much higher global inflation and, in some countries, the impacts of the COVID-19 pandemic on government spending priorities. In this regard, the ESG slow-down may be seen as a return to more rational and sustainable decision making, rather than anything that undermines the fundamentals of ESG.

9. Beyond ESG: sustainability and responsibility

In one sense, it may indeed be correct to talk about having passed 'peak ESG', and in that sense this book may be seen as one of its last bastions. But that is a question of terminology, rather than the importance of ESG as a concept. In 2023, Larry Fink, CEO of BlackRock, said that he had stopped using the term because it had been "weaponized" in the US political debate. Elsewhere, political objections may be less strong, but use of the term may still be on the wane.

Use of the term ESG is usually traced back to a United Nations report entitled *Who Cares Wins* that was published in 2004,[13] and it grew in prominence until it became a buzzword of global business by the early 2020s, with ESG policies, professionals and conferences proliferating. However, ESG is just another iteration of a much older concept. Before that, there was SRI – socially responsible investing and CSR – corporate social responsibility. Buzzwords, by their nature, have a limited lifetime and are liable to fall out of fashion, a process that is likely to be accelerated by ESG's current political connotations.

The term ESG is useful for its simplicity and ability to pull together and facilitate action on a number of related objectives. However, it should not be forgotten that it encompasses a complex web of different considerations, which are not always aligned. Treaties, regulations and policies dealing with environmental concerns are often separate and different from those dealing with social factors or governance. Just taking 'social' as an example, that encompasses fundamental human rights, workers' rights and labour conditions, the rights of indigenous communities and the needs of society more widely, including economic development considerations and cultural heritage.

ESG is a very broad group of topics, but there is some sense in considering them together, specifically because of those interfaces and potential conflicts. Mining and minerals companies (like companies in any other sector of the economy) need to be able to form a holistic view of their impact on the environment, society and the economies in which they operate, so that they can take decisions that best reconcile the needs of their multiple stakeholders. The term ESG seems to have evolved to encompass those considerations for a business that may not directly impact its bottom line, but which are important

---

13 The Global Compact, *Who Cares Wins: Connecting Financial Markets to a Changing World*, https://documents.worldbank.org/en/publication/documents-reports/documentdetail/280911488968799581/who-cares-wins-connecting-financial-markets-to-a-changing-world.

for society more broadly, and that seems to have prompted a reaction from the political right, who argue that companies should act in the interests of their shareholders, rather than taking decisions about what is best for society.

That may go some way to explaining the recent shift in terminology towards 'sustainability'. That term implies that companies prioritise their long-term interests over short-term profits, with the further implication that causing negative environmental or social impacts will eventually cause them economic pain as well. However, that further implication only holds true if regulation is appropriately designed to ensure that they are held responsible for those impacts.

Historically, mining companies have often been able to operate in a silo, prioritising shareholder returns to the detriment of the outside world. However, policy-makers increasingly recognise the cost of such self-interest to the rest of society and, particularly, their broader electorate. Much new regulation is therefore intended to 'internalise those externalities' and ensure that companies feel the cost of their activities on the rest of society. Only when they do, will they be economically incentivised to reduce those costs.

So perhaps ESG and sustainability, like SRI and CSR before them, are just stepping stones to an economy that is regulated to ensure companies bear the full external costs of their activities. In a scenario where emissions are properly taxed at their cost to the planet, where environmental damage is required to be compensated and social impacts are required to be directly or indirectly borne by the companies that cause them, those terms may become redundant. They could just be treated like any other aspect of the economics of the business. We have a long way to go, and we may never quite get there, but arguably that is the direction of travel.

Whatever the terminology we use, ESG considerations are an intrinsic and critical element of the mining and minerals business, and will become increasingly so. As these matters become more tightly regulated, enforced and litigated, the quality of a company's ESG strategy and its implementation will be a key factor in its business success. It is for that reason that this book explores the ESG challenges faced by the mining and minerals industry and recent developments and trends in ESG risks and regulation, as well as emerging opportunities. Changes in this area are coming thick and fast, but with this wide-ranging assessment of ESG in mining and minerals, we hope to support participants in the industry to anticipate and prepare for those changes, and to promote their sustainable, responsible success for the benefit of all their stakeholders and the planet we inhabit.

Appendix

Figure 2. ESG norms for mining and minerals

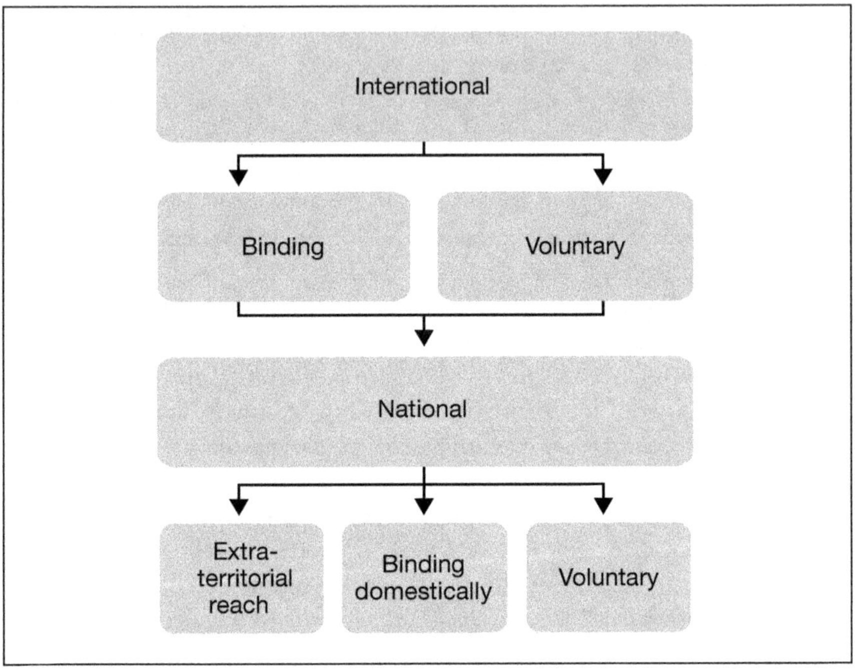

Table 1. National legislation

National

Binding extra-territorially	Binding domestically	Voluntary
Supply Chain Act (Germany)	Critical Raw Materials Act (EU)	ADIIS Leading Practice Handbook: Mine Closure (Australia)
Conflict Minerals Regulations *(tin, tantalum, tungsten and gold)* (EU)	Mining Code of the Democratic Republic of Congo	Mineral Council of Australia's Enduring Value Framework
Modern Slavery Act 2015 (UK)	*Batteries Regulation (EU)*	MAC Towards Sustainable Mining: TSM 101: A Primer (Canada)
Bribery Act 2010 (UK)	Regulation on Ecodesign for Sustainable Products (EU)	US National Action Plan on Responsible Business Conduct
Corporate Sustainability Due Diligence Directive (EU)	Waste Framework Directive (EU)	MAC Towards Sustainable Mining, Biodiversity Conservation Management Protocol (Canada)
Foreign Corrupt Practices Act 1977 (US)	Clean Air Act 1970 (US)	Southern African Development Community Guidelines for Mainstreaming Biodiversity and Ecosystem Services in Extractive Industry
Loi Sapin II (France)	Environmental Impact Assessment Regulations (UK)	JORC (Australia)
	Forestry Code (Brazil)	PERC Standard for Reporting of Exploration Results, Mineral Resources and Mineral Reserves (EU)
	National System of Protected Areas Law (Brazil)	South African Code for the Reporting of Exploration Results, Mineral Resources and Mineral Reserves
	Seabed Mineral Act (Norway)	
	Constitution Act 1982 (Canada)	
	UN Declaration on the Rights of Indigenous Peoples Act (Canada)	
	DRC law on the Protection and Promotion of the Rights of Indigenous Pygmy Peoples	
	Human Rights Act 1998 (UK)	
	Regulation prohibiting products made with forced labour law on the Union market (EU)	
	Corporate Sustainability Reporting Directive (EU)	
	Sustainable Finance Disclosure Regulations (EU)	
	National Instrument 43-101, Standards of Disclosure for Mineral Projects (diamonds, coal, base and precious metals) (Canada)	
	S-K1300 Reporting Regulations (US)	
	Transparency Act (Norway)	
	Ordinance on Due Diligence and Transparency in relation to Minerals and Metals from Conflict-Affected Areas and Child Labour (tin, tantalum, tungsten and gold) (Switzerland)	

	General ESG/sustainability
	Environmental
	Social
	Governance
I	*Commodity specific*

Table 2. International legislation

International

Binding	Voluntary (1)	Voluntary (2)
Convention on Biological Diversity	*Aluminium Stewardship Initiative Standards*	BioCarbon Biodiversity Standard
ESPOO Convention on Environmental Impact Assessment in a Transboundary Context	APEC Mine Closure, Checklist for Governments	Greenhouse Gas Protocol
Minamata Convention on Mercury	*Bettercoal Code*	Kunming-Montreal Global Biodiversity Framework
Protocol on Environmental Protection to the Antarctic Treaty	*Copper (Nickel, Zinc and Molybdenum) Mark*	UN Environment Programme and the World Conservation Monitoring Centre's Mitigation Hierarchy
UN Agreement on Biodiversity Beyond National Jurisdiction (High Seas Treaty)	EBRD Environmental & Social Performance Requirements	ISO 14001 (Environmental Management Systems)
UN Basel Convention on the Control of Transboundary Movements of Hazardous Wastes and their Disposal	Equator Principles	ISO 14040 (Life Cycle Assessment)
UN Convention of the Law of the Sea	Global Industry Standard on Tailings Management	UN Declaration on the Rights of Indigenous Peoples
UN Framework Convention on Climate Change	ICMM Integrated Mine Closure, Good Practice Guide, 2nd Edition	UN Declaration on the Rights of Peasants and Other People Working in Rural Areas
Indigenous and Tribal Peoples Convention, 1989 (No. 169)	ICMM Mining Principles	UN Guiding Principles on Business and Human Rights
African Union Convention on Preventing and Combating Corruption	IFC Environmental, Health, and Safety Guidelines – Mining	Voluntary Principles on Security and Human Rights
UN Convention Against Corruption	Initiative for Responsible Mining Assurance Standard	ISO 45001 (Occupational Health and Safety Management Systems)
Council of Europe's Criminal Law Convention on Corruption	International Cyanide Management Code (Gold and silver)	Climate Disclosure Standards Board Framework
Inter-American Convention Against Corruption	OECD Guidelines for Multinational Enterprises	Committee for Mineral Reserves International Reporting Standards (CRIRSCO)
OECD Anti-Bribery Convention	Principles for Responsible Investment	Extractive Industries Transparency Initiative
	Responsible Jewellery Council Code of Practices	ICC Rules on Combating Corruption
	Responsible Steel International Production Standard	IGF Mining Policy Framework: Mining and Sustainable Development
	UN Global Compact	International Financial Reporting Standards Sustainability Disclosure Standards
	World Gold Council Responsible Gold Mining Principles	OECD Due Diligence Guidance for Responsible Business Conduct
	World Bank Environmental and Social Framework	Sustainable Stock Exchange Initiative Model Guidance on Reporting ESG Information to Investors
	World Bank, Mine Closure: A Toolbox for Government	Information to Investors Transparency International's Business Principles for Countering Bribery
		Wolfsberg Principles
		ISO 37001 (Anti-Bribery Management Systems)

	General ESG/sustainability
	Environmental
	Social
	Governance
I	*Commodity specific*

Measuring, minimising and mitigating the carbon footprint of minerals

Dalia Majumder-Russell
CMS Cameron McKenna Nabarro Olswang LLP

The mining industry is not immune from the pressures to meet the climate goals of the Paris Agreement. However, it is also the industry that our net zero ambitions depend on for satisfying the growing demand for minerals such as copper, lithium and nickel to support the energy transition.[1] Any meaningful transition to a 'green' or climate-focused economy will require the mining sector as a central stakeholder.[2]

To achieve this, there must be a clear quantification of the environmental impacts of mining and identification of ways to reduce them without compromising production.[3] Focusing on the use of the carbon footprint as an environmental indicator, this chapter looks at this method of assessing the carbon emissions of the mining sector, together with the ways it can be both minimised and mitigated through various approaches – a combination of technologies and regulation.

1. But what about existing regulations?

It would be remiss to ignore the ways in which the mining industry is already regulated. Because it is universally accepted that mining activities have significant environmental impacts, there is a plethora of international laws and agreements that aim to regulate mining operations and mitigate their environmental footprint. International conventions such as the Basel Convention on the Control of Transboundary Movements of Hazardous Wastes and Their Disposal (1989) focuses on cross-border movement of hazardous

1 Carbon Trust, "Digging Net Zero pathways for mining green tech metals with IFC", www.carbontrust.com/our-work-and-impact/impact-stories/digging-net-zero-pathways-for-mining-green-tech-metals-with-ifc.

2 Sri Sekar, Kyle Lundin, Christopher Tucker, Joe Figueiredo, Silvana Tordo and Javier Aguilar, "Policy Approaches to Climate Change in Mineral Rich Countries", World Bank Group, 2019, p2, https://openknowledge.worldbank.org/server/api/core/bitstreams/d1b2e44d-59dc-5463-92ea-e9e26b45f026/content.

3 Corey Laamanen, Sabrina M Desjardins, Shannon H McLean and John A Scott, "The use of microalgal sourced biodiesel to help underground mines transition to battery electric vehicles", *Journal of Sustainable Mining* (2022) 21(1), https://jsm.gig.eu/cgi/viewcontent.cgi?article=1327&context=journal-of-sustainable-mining.

waste materials. For mining, it specifically applies to disposal of mining waste which can be extremely hazardous. This is backed up by the so-called 'Espoo Convention' (1991), formally known as the Convention on Environmental Impact Assessment in a Transboundary Context. Pursuant to this treaty, parties to it must assess the environmental impact of certain activities, including mining, as part of their planning activities.

There are also laws and protocols that apply to specific types of elements which are considered hazardous. An example of such regulation is the global treaty focusing on protecting human health and the environment from anthropogenic emissions and releases of mercury and mercury compounds – the Minamata Convention on Mercury (2013). Similarly, the voluntary International Cyanide Management Code promotes management of cyanide used in gold mining to minimise harmful impacts on human health and the environment.

Within these rules and regulations, mining is also subject to existing climate change laws which indirectly affect the mining sector. For example, the United Nations Framework Convention on Climate Change (UNFCCC), is the focus of much of the discussion on limiting greenhouse gas (GHG) emissions, including from the mining sector, which now forms part of the environmental, social and governance (ESG) conversation. Furthermore, ESG reporting borrows and builds on earlier reporting initiatives. Relevant to mining, these include the Extractive Industries Transparency Initiative from 2003, which aims to promote the open and accountable management of extractive resources and bolster systems that help with reporting of such information, and the International Council on Mining and Metals' Mining Principles and Assurance and Validation Procedure.

At a domestic level many countries have laws governing mining activities, for example, in terms of land degradation and restoration, biodiversity, air and water quality or waste management. That said, the piecemeal nature of regulations and the uneven enforcement of existing laws means that mining activities can and do cause significant environmental damage that is overlooked or not seen due to remote locations and/or lack of enforcement capabilities.

With this in mind and noting the technical complexities that make understanding environmental impacts extremely challenging, governments, regulators and stakeholders are beginning to ask questions around what they should be measuring to really assess the impact mining is having on the environment.

2. Measuring the carbon footprint of minerals

Mining and processing of minerals play a crucial role, not only because of their significant contributions to global economic development and necessary involvement in a range of technologies, but also due to their substantial environmental footprint. One of the key metrics for assessing environmental impact is carbon footprint, which quantifies the total GHG emissions caused directly and indirectly by an activity. Globally, mining's Scope 1 emissions represented approximately 4%–7% of total GHG emissions in 2020, which increases to around 28% when the industry's Scope 3 emissions are included.[4] While this is significant, the true emissions footprint of mining may not be as clear and depends on the methodologies used to assess the emissions cycle. Although the mining industry is a significant contributor to global emissions, its carbon footprint is relatively small in comparison to its economic contribution, since minerals have a uniquely high value per tonne of carbon dioxide emitted.[5] Given the importance of minerals for the energy transition, it is therefore key to ensure that the metrics used truly assess the full impact of these activities so that stakeholders are able to factor this into the choices they make.

There are a number of commonly used methodologies that are employed to assess GHG emissions. Three of these are given as examples below.

2.1 The Greenhouse Gas Protocol

The Greenhouse Gas Protocol (GHG Protocol) is an initiative that began in 1998 and was initiated as a partnership between the World Resources Institute and the World Business Council for Sustainable Development. The aim was to develop a voluntary protocol that set internationally accepted GHG accounting and reporting standards. As with other accepted protocols, the GHG Protocol establishes comprehensive global standardised frameworks to measure and manage GHG emissions from private and public sector operations, value chains and mitigation actions.[6] The GHG Protocol is the most commonly used methodology worldwide and therefore a useful way of achieving a common understanding of how emissions calculations and reporting are approached. GHG emissions are classified into three 'scopes':[7]

- Scope 1 emissions: emissions from sources that an organisation owns or controls directly;[8]
- Scope 2 emissions: indirect emissions associated with an organisation's purchase of electricity, steam, heat or cooling;[9] and

---

4 Lindsay Delevingne, Will Glazener, Liesbet Grégoir and Kimberley Henderson, "Climate risk and decarbonization: What every mining CEO needs to know", McKinsey & Company, 28 January 2020, www.mckinsey.com/capabilities/sustainability/our-insights/climate-risk-and-decarbonization-what-every-mining-ceo-needs-to-know#/.

5 Benjamin Cox, Sally Innis, Nadja C Kunz and John Steen, "The mining industry as a net beneficiary of a global tax on carbon emissions", *Communications & Earth Environment* (2022) 3(17): 2, www.nature.com/articles/s43247-022-00346-4.

6 Greenhouse Gas Protocol, "About Us", https://ghgprotocol.org/about-us.

7 Greenhouse Gas Protocol, "FAQ", https://ghgprotocol.org/sites/default/files/standards_supporting/FAQ.pdf.

8 National Grid, "What are scope 1, 2 and 3 carbon emissions?", www.nationalgrid.com/stories/energy-explained/what-are-scope-1-2-3-carbon-emissions#.

9 United States Environmental Protection Agency, "Scope 1 and Scope 2 Inventory Guidance", www.epa.gov/climateleadership/scope-1-and-scope-2-inventory-guidance#:~:text=Scope%202%20emissions%20are%20indirect,of%20the%20organization%27s%20energy%20use.

- Scope 3 emissions: all of the emissions associated indirectly with the organisation, spanning its entire value chain, rather than originating directly from its operations.[10]

According to the Responsible Mining Index, most companies monitor their performance on Scope 1 and 2 emissions, with more than half disclosing detailed tracking data against publicly stated targets.[11]

Ultimately the aim is for all three scopes to be monitored and tracked given that full decarbonisation can only be achieved if the full ecosystem within which mining and minerals operate is engaged.

While the GHG Protocol serves as a valuable framework for carbon accounting, it focuses solely on GHG emissions and does not take express account of other environmental considerations such as water and air quality, water usage, energy consumption and other factors that can be encompassed within a Life Cycle Assessment. Consequently, the GHG Protocol is limited in its capacity to measure environmental impacts beyond GHG emissions that are associated with the entire life cycle of a product, including its production, transportation, utilisation and disposal.

2.2 Life cycle assessment

A life cycle assessment (LCA) is widely considered as a comprehensive technique for assessing the impact of producing goods or services (along with their environmental effects) throughout their entire life cycle. In mining and minerals, this would mean assessing processes starting from raw material extraction through to disposal of the final materials at the end of their use.[12]

This methodology pays careful attention to various stages of the production process, including manufacturing, distribution, usage and disposal to measure natural resource consumption, GHG emissions and pollution across air, water and soil, among other environmental impacts. The LCA method is also standardised because it is regulated by the international standards ISO 14040 and ISO 14044. This means that the guidelines that must be followed form part of the corporate environmental management framework and there are consistent detailed procedures for conducting a thorough and dependable LCA.

Excavation, ore and waste rock transportation, blasting, ore processing and tailings treatments are the main activities considered by LCA during the

---

10 Deloitte, "Zero in on ... Scope 1, 2 and 3 emissions", 12 May 2021, www.deloitte.com/uk/en/issues/climate/zero-in-on-scope-1-2-and-3-emissions.html.

11 IEA, *The Role of Critical Minerals in Clean Energy Transitions*, p204, https://iea.blob.core.windows.net/assets/ffd2a83b-8c30-4e9d-980a-52b6d9a86fdc/TheRoleofCriticalMineralsinCleanEnergyTransitions.pdf.

12 Global Climate Initiatives, "A practical guide to calculating a product's carbon footprint using LCA", https://globalclimateinitiatives.com/en/guide-pratique-pour-calculer-lempreinte-carbone-dun-produit-par-lacv/.

exploitation phase.[13] Under these activities, impacts such as particulate matter formation and land destruction will be commonly considered.

Case study: Afema Mine, Ivory Coast

The Afema mine is located in the southeastern region of the Ivory Coast where oxidised copper ore was exploited by way of opencast mining between 1992 and 1998.[14] The mine used LCA to measure its environmental footprint by examining each phase of the mine, namely exploration, construction, operation and rehabilitation. Each mining phase was further subdivided including to review material production and transport, equipment transport and operation, machinery operation, electricity usage and diesel consumption.[15]

For every stage of the process, the necessary materials, energy and equipment were identified. Primary data was gathered through site visits and included details such as the mine plan, area's geology, ore grade, operating periods and machinery used. Where primary data was unavailable, secondary sources were used to estimate values based on comparable mines in Tanzania and Papua New Guinea, along with manufacturer's emissions data for excavators, diesel trucks, drills and other equipment.[16]

The LCA method used to assess the data was the hierarchical approach in ReCiPe v1.13, which evaluates environmental impacts at both midpoint and endpoint levels. The midpoint level includes 18 impact categories such as climate change, ozone depletion and human toxicity, while the endpoint level aggregates these into three damage categories: human health, ecosystem quality and resource depletion. The study aimed to identify the main contributing categories and activities by first analysing endpoint impacts to determine which midpoint categories to focus on for a comprehensive understanding of the mine's environmental impacts.[17]

2.3 Nickel production emissions

Some mining activities have developed methodologies particular to a certain activity, metal or other criteria. As an example of this, the Nickel Institute publishes specific guidance for nickel producers to help them calculate their GHG emissions. This methodology takes into account the particular complexities of the nickel production industry and therefore creates a comparison between activities of just this sector.[18]

---

13 Kouadio Assemien, François Yao, Yao Blaise Koffi, Olivier Belcourt, David Salze, Lasm Théophile *et al*, "Mining impacts assessment using the LCA methodology: case study of Afema gold mine in Ivory Coast", *Integrated Environmental Assessment and Management* (2021) 17(2): 465–479.

14 *Ibid.*

15 *Ibid.*

16 *Ibid.*

17 *Ibid.*

18 Nickel Institute, "How to calculate GHG emissions from nickel production", 4 May 2022, https://nickelinstitute.org/en/blog/2022 /may/how-to-calculate-ghg-emissions-from-nickel-production/.

The guidance examines various aspects of nickel production, including mining (both open pit and underground), ore preparation (for lateritic ores), beneficiation (for sulfidic ores), primary extraction (encompassing both hydro and pyrometallurgical processes for lateritic and sulfidic ores as well as secondary raw materials) and metal refining. It also addresses the transport of raw materials, electricity generation, wastewater treatment and waste processing. Additionally, it includes the production of fuels, utilities and auxiliary materials essential for the refined nickel production process. By-products generated during production are also considered.[19]

The guidance provides that carbon footprint data for refined nickel must be updated at least every five years or whenever there are significant changes in the production process or other factors affecting emission intensity. This mirrors the frequency required under the European Commission's Product Environmental Footprint requirements[20] which set out precise rules for conducting LCAs in alignment with the EU Green Deal and Taxonomy.[21]

2.4 Mineral recycling

Many minerals and metals can be recycled and reused, thereby keeping them in use longer and reducing the necessity for further mining.

Recycling levels are generally measured using two metrics: end-of-life (EoL) recycling rates, which track the proportion of waste material that gets recycled, and recycling input rates, which evaluate the percentage of total supply derived from secondary sources.[22] Base metals like copper, nickel and aluminium boast high EoL recycling rates, while precious metals such as platinum, palladium, and gold also enjoy high recycling rates, driven by their global market value. However, lithium has almost no recycling infrastructure globally, due to both limited collection efforts and technical difficulties related to its reactive properties.[23]

Monitoring the recycling rates of minerals offers valuable insight into their carbon footprint. By promoting recycling and circular economy practices, it becomes possible to mitigate the carbon emissions associated with mineral extraction and processing.

---

19 Nickel Institute, *How to determine GHG emissions from nickel metal Class 1 production: A guide to calculate nickel's carbon footprint*, https://nickelinstitute.org/media/8da2dba6e789edd/202204-lme-passport-guidance-nickel-institute.pdf.

20 *Ibid.*

21 Ecochain, "Product Environmental Footprint (PEF) – A Complete Overview", https://ecochain.com/blog/product-environmental-footprint/.

22 IEA, *The Role of Critical Minerals in Clean Energy Transitions*, p35, https://iea.blob.core.windows.net/assets/ffd2a83b-8c30-4e9d-980a-52b6d9a86fdc/TheRoleofCriticalMineralsinCleanEnergyTransitions.pdf.

23 *Ibid.*

3. Challenges in measuring carbon footprint

Measuring GHG emissions and the carbon footprint is not without its challenges, including the difficulty of navigating sometimes inconsistent Reporting Frameworks. Despite the growing expectation for companies to disclose GHG emissions, a lack of consistent and coherent reporting on a global scale hinders data comparability and true assessment of the GHG emissions from mining (and other sectors). This comes up in the context of determining the scope and extent of GHG emissions for which a company is responsible – these so-called 'emissions boundaries' are key for understanding, managing and reporting a company's environmental impact, and matter in the context of assessing a company's Scope 1, 2 and 3 emissions. However, this is also why accurately defining and managing emissions boundaries can be complex, especially where activities are outside the direct control of the company. For example, because companies have the flexibility to choose which values to report, the boundaries of emissions categories, and the relevant categories themselves, the data collected cannot be easily compared for all categories as some companies may have chosen not to report on a given metric.[24] Companies may also establish different emissions boundaries and decide whether to use a spend-based method (ie, estimate their Scope 3 emissions based on the amount spent on given goods and services), average data or supplier-specific estimates, which adds to the difficulties in having truly comparable results.[25]

Although reporting obligations are becoming more stringent, especially in Europe, the true picture on GHG emissions may be obscured by companies' choices in the reporting of some emissions. Typically, companies have tended to report only their total emissions, omitting explanations of their calculation methods, use of averaged values and exclusions of emissions categories. This lack of transparency and standardisation means there is no simple way to understand why companies report their emissions as they do. As a result, it is often impossible to determine if companies in the same industry are making similar choices or reporting their emissions similarly. This is changing, however, as reporting requirements get stricter and the consequences of 'greenwashing' more punitive.

Finally, for optimal tracking, full supply chain emissions should be accounted for. Indirect emissions produced by suppliers and industrial customers of mining products have been reported to account for as much as 95% of a mining company's total emissions, highlighting the carbon-intensive reach of the industry.[26] However, obtaining such high-quality data for use in

---

24 *Ibid*, p206.

25 World Economic Forum, *Emissions Measurement in Supply Chains: Business Realities and Challenges*, November 2023, p7, www3.weforum.org/docs/WEF_Emissions_Measurement_in_Supply_Chains_2023.pdf.

26 ICMM, *Scope 3 Emissions Accounting and Reporting Guidance*, p5, www.icmm.com/website/publications/pdfs/environmental-stewardship/2023/guidance_scope-3-reporting.pdf?cb=69120.

methodologies such as calculating Scope 3 emissions under the GHG Protocol is often a difficult and costly endeavour, with the quality, accuracy and availability of data being major obstacles. Environmental information may also be withheld due to concerns regarding privacy or the potential exposure of sensitive business details.[27]

4. Initiatives to improve measuring and reporting

Several initiatives have been proposed to improve the measuring and reporting of GHG emissions in mining and minerals, but the majority of these are currently voluntary. For example, the International Council on Mining and Metals (ICMM) *Scope 3 Emissions Accounting and Reporting Guidance* published in September 2023 provides mining and metals companies with a standardised method to calculate and report their value chain emissions. It builds on the GHG Protocol Scope 3 Standard and adapts it to the needs of the mining and metals industry.[28]

The ICMM's guidance initially encourages organisations to identify and prioritise their most significant emission sources through a materiality assessment. This ensures that resources are focused on areas with the greatest potential for reducing the carbon footprint. Companies then need to establish reporting boundaries for each Scope 3 category. For upstream categories, this includes key supplier emissions from Scope 1, 2 and 3. The minimum boundary is 'cradle-to-gate', covering extraction, production and transportation of goods and services. For downstream categories, a boundary is set at a product stage where the end use is unknown. Mining companies are encouraged to focus on the 'first finished product' following a high-emissions stage and include emissions from the next consumer's 'first-finished downstream product' when material.[29]

Another initiative focuses on the supply chain. The Coalition on Materials Emissions Transparency (COMET) aims to create a harmonised GHG calculation framework applicable to all mineral and industrial supply chains. The initiative was launched at the Davos World Economic Forum Summit in January 2020.[30] The proposals aim to facilitate independent verification of emissions from companies, industries and their supply chains.[31] The COMET framework will be based on the following tenets:

- *Commodity-specific reporting requirements:* What data is required for

---

27 World Economic Forum, *Emissions Measurement in Supply Chains: Business Realities and Challenges*, November 2023, p7, www3.weforum.org/docs/WEF_Emissions_Measurement_in_Supply_Chains_2023.pdf.

28 ICMM, "ICMM publishes guidance to improve the mining and metals industry's disclosure of Scope 3 emissions", 7 September 2023, www.icmm.com/en-gb/news/2023/disclosure-scope-3-emissions.

29 ICMM, *Scope 3 Emissions Accounting and Reporting Guidance*, www.icmm.com/website/publications/pdfs/environmental-stewardship/2023/guidance_scope-3-reporting.pdf?cb=69120.

30 Columbia Center on Sustainable Development, "The Coalition on Materials Emissions Transparency (COMET)", https://ccsi.columbia.edu/content/coalition-materials-emissions-transparency-comet.

31 Colorado School of Mines, *Addressing the Need for Accurate and Comparable Greenhouse Gas Data: The Comet Framework*, p2, https://repository.mines.edu/bitstream/handle/11124/16711/COMET_GHG_Data_White_Paper.pdf?sequence=1&isAllowed=y.

accurate emissions accounting of different commodities? This research can be enhanced by life-cycle assessments, academic research, emissions modelling tools, sustainability reports and net zero pathways.

- *Standardised data requirements:* To analyse the data requirements specified in the commodity-specific reporting requirements to understand the variability in emissions measurements, industrial processes and global supply chains. For regions with diverse production techniques, global supply chains and environmental concerns, COMET will formulate specific data requirements based on these differences. If similar products produced through identical processes have different emissions intensities across supply chains, COMET will create detailed reporting instructions for those variations. For example, if one company reports significantly higher emissions for a certain process compared to another, COMET will investigate the discrepancy and incorporate findings into their guidelines. Companies will be asked to disclose their measurement methods, prioritise the use of primary data and work towards more accurate emissions accounting.
- *Fixed reporting boundaries and corporate data:* Many companies do not handle their entire production process themselves, nor do they exclusively produce a single product. COMET will assist companies in transforming their corporate-level emissions data into product-level data to ensure accurate accounting and allocation of emissions across all products they manufacture.
- *Harmonised carbon disclosure tools:* Various carbon disclosure tools have been created to provide stakeholders with the data necessary to evaluate their environmental performance. The COMET framework does not aim to replace these existing carbon accounting tools but to enhance and support their usage by companies.

Table 1: A select overview of emission standards and reporting policies and measures

Policies and measures	Example
Emission standards	The US Clean Air Act 1970 applies to mining operations regulating dust emissions that accompany operations or tailings disposal in impoundments, exhaust emissions from heavy equipment, and sulphur dioxide and nitrogen oxide emissions from processing facilities, such as smelters.[32]

continued on next page

Policies and measures	Example
Reporting	The National Greenhouse and Energy Reporting Scheme in Australia requires mining companies to report their Scope 1 and Scope 2 GHG emissions, energy production and energy consumption.[33]
Transparency	Mexico's Pollutant Release and Transfer Register (RETC) collects data on the emissions and transfers of pollutants from industrial facilities, including mining operations.[34] The RETC database is publicly accessible, allowing users to search for information on pollutants emitted and transferred by specific facilities.[35]
Regulatory compliance and enforcement	The US Environmental Protection Agency conducts inspections and can impose fines for non-compliance with emissions standards in the mining sector.[36]
International agreements and standards	The Global Reporting Initiative (GRI) provides standards for sustainability reporting, including emissions disclosure specific to the mining sector.[37] The GRI standards are considered the most used and accepted sustainability reporting standards today across the mining industry.[38]

32 American Geosciences Institute, "What are environmental regulations on mining activities?", www.americangeosciences.org/critical-issues/faq/what-are-regulations-mining-activities#:~:text=Clean%20Air%20Act%20(CAA),-The%20CAA%2C%20passed&text=Examples%20of%20mining%2Drelated%20situations,processing%20facilities%2C%20such%20as%20smelters.

33 Australian Government, https://cer.gov.au/schemes/national-greenhouse-and-energy-reporting-scheme/assess-your-obligations#nger-thresholds; www.dcceew.gov.au/climate-change/emissions-reporting/national-greenhouse-energy-reporting-scheme#:~:text=The%20National%20Greenhouse%20and%20Energy,energy%20consumption; https://cer.gov.au/schemes/national-greenhouse-and-energy-reporting-scheme/about-emissions-and-energy-data/emissions-and-energy-types#:~:text=of%20your%20products.-,Reporting%20emissions%20under%20NGER,to%20estimate%20scope%203 %20emissions.

34 Tecma, "Environmental Standards in Mexico Must Be Followed", www.tecma.com/environmental-standards-in-mexico/.

35 Tecma, "Environmental permitting in Mexico at the federal level is an integrated regime", www.tecma.com/environmental-permitting-in-mexico-is-integrated/#:~:text=Semarnat%20records%20this%20information%20in,the%20area%20of%20environmental%20regulation.

36 United States Environmental Protection Agency, "Basic Information on Enforcement", www.epa.gov/enforcement/basic-information-enforcement#:~:text=Criminal%20Actions%20can%20occur%20when,result%20in%20fines%20or%20imprisonment.

5. Minimising the carbon footprint of minerals

As noted above, mining and minerals will remain key to achieving the aims of energy transition to a less fossil fuelled world. With that in mind, and noting the methodologies available to assess existing emissions levels, it is widely believed that there is potential to minimise the carbon footprint across the mineral value chain, from ore extraction, through primary processing and product manufacturing, to use and disposal.[39]

Figure 1: McKinsey's mine decarbonisation model[40]

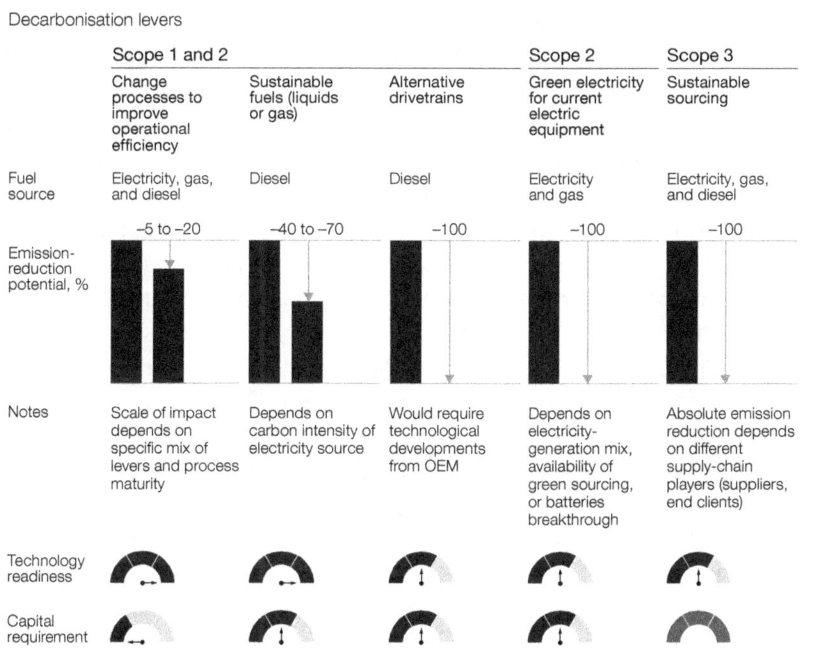

Note: Highly dependent on project. Can be financed 100% off-balance sheet through outside investors.
Source: McKinsey Mine Decarbonisation Model

---

37 Global Reporting Initiative, "Sector Standard for Mining", www.globalreporting.org/standards/standards-development/sector-standard-for-mining/#:~:text=The%20new%20GRI%20Standard%20reflects,metrics%20to%20report%20their%20impacts.&text=The%20Standard%20is%20used%20together,and%20the%20GRI%20Topic%20Standards.

38 Ian Coles, Meaghan Connors and Kevin L Shaw, "Decarbonization: The requirements for – and the role of – mining companies", Mayer Brown, 16 March 2023, www.mayerbrown.com/en/insights/publications/2023/03/decarbonization-the-requirements-forand-role-ofmining-companies.

39 D Giurco and JG Petrie, "Strategies for reducing the carbon footprint of copper: New technologies, more recycling or demand management", *Minerals Engineering* (2007) 20(9): 842–853, www.sciencedirect.com/science/article/abs/pii/S0892687507001148.

40 Figure 1 is from "Creating the zero-carbon mine", McKinsey & Company, June 2021. © 2024 McKinsey & Company. All rights reserved. Reprinted by permission.

Emissions intensity of production can vary considerably across companies and regions depending on their specific operational practices, available power sources and production pathways.[41] Consequentially, decarbonisation efforts must embrace a broad spectrum of available technologies and strategies. In 2021, McKinsey produced a mine decarbonisation model where they benchmarked current zero carbon opportunities against potential readiness of deployment. Their research made clear that we need to be open to using a combination of strategies in the carbon reduction process. This requires consideration of not only the emission reduction potential of these technologies, but also their capital requirements and technology readiness in order to maintain a feasible cost-positive pathway towards the zero-carbon mine.[42]

A key part of reducing GHG emissions is to focus on operational efficiencies. These improvements exist across the mineral value chain, with developments including in mining process optimisation (mine to mill, high intensity sleeve blasting, coarse ore flotation, ore sorting) to the introduction of mining automation, such as in the Boliden Aitik mine in Sweden. The use of a 4G/5G network to automate and remotely control mining equipment at the Boliden Aitik mine not only significantly lowered costs, but also saved 10% in fuel consumption, corresponding to a reduction of 9,400 metric tons of carbon dioxide emissions.[43]

One area worth focusing on for efficiency improvements is comminution, which includes the crushing and grinding processes. This is one of the largest single energy consumers in mining.[44] A 5% incremental improvement in energy efficiency across comminution has the potential to result in a reduction of 30 million tonnes of carbon dioxide equivalent.[45] As noted in Weir Group's study in energy efficiency technologies in comminution, replacing conventional technology with innovative new solutions can cut energy use by 40% while also avoiding 50% of carbon dioxide equivalent emissions in copper ore processing.[46]

---

41 IEA, "The Role of Critical Minerals in Clean Energy Transitions: Sustainable and responsible development of minerals", www.iea.org/reports/the-role-of-critical-minerals-in-clean-energy-transitions/sustainable-and-responsible-development-of-minerals.

42 Henry Legge, Clemens Müller-Falcke, Tomas Nauclér and Erik Östgren, "Creating the zero-carbon mine", McKinsey & Company, 29 June 2021, www.mckinsey.com/industries/metals-and-mining/our-insights/creating-the-zero-carbon-mine.

43 Ericsson, "Mining automation and the reduction of carbon emissions", www.ericsson.com/en/cases/2019/mining-automation-and-the-reduction-of-carbon-emissions.

44 Weir Group, "New study by Weir highlights big energy saving opportunity in mining", 4 December 2023, www.global.weir/newsroom/global-news/new-study-by-weir-highlights-big-energy-saving-opportunity-in-mining/#:~:text=In%20the%20optimal%20combination%2C%20the,to%2050%25%20of%20CO2e%20emissions.

45 Weir Group, "New report identifies major carbon reduction opportunities in global mining", p5, 10 May 2021, www.global.weir/newsroom/global-news/new-report-identifies-major-carbon-reduction-opportunities-in-global-mining/.

46 Weir Group, "New study by Weir highlights big energy saving opportunity in mining", 4 December 2023, www.global.weir/newsroom/global-news/new-study-by-weir-highlights-big-energy-saving-opportunity-in-mining/#:~:text=In%20the%20optimal%20combination%2C%20the,to%2050%25%20of%20CO2e%20emissions.

Case study: Minera Los Pelambres AMSA (MLP AMSA)
Through the fusion of real-time data analysis, advanced process control algorithms and digital twin modelling, the mine was able to utilise optimisation technologies to bolster the throughput of their SAG Mill circuit – the first stage of the grinding circuit in mining processing. Not only successfully bolstering production rates and optimising resource allocation, they also substantially reduced carbon dioxide emissions by 0.26 tons per hour while realising a 3.3% increase in throughput.[47]

While a reduction in the energy intensity of mining can reduce its carbon footprint to an extent, using renewable energy in the generation mix is critical to reducing GHG emissions.[48] The vast majority of energy flows in mining extraction processes are centred around diesel-powered processes, combusted directly to drive mobile equipment, with a significant minority of consumed energy attributed to diesel-powered electricity generation.[49] Clearly, the replacement of diesel or methane gas-powered mobile and station equipment with zero emissions energy sources would make an immediate difference to GHG emissions. Globally, there is a clear push towards integrating renewables into mining operations; in 2015, there were 600MW of renewable energy projects sited on or serving mine sites, by 2019, this had increased to 5GW installed or planned.[50]

This is where the combination of renewable generation coupled with batteries, hydrogen fuel cells, energy storage solutions and autonomous mining machinery – driven by an emphasis within the mining sector on the switch to an 'all electric' mine[51] – can make a real difference. For example, the Onaping Depth, Canada study showed an energy saving of 40% in ventilation and 30% in cooling due to the electrification of transportation.[52]

---

47 Mining.com, "Reducing CO2 Emissions and Enhancing Efficiency in Mining: The ANDRITZ Metris ACE Optimization Technologies – 'Minera los Pelambres' AMSA Case Study", 27 September 2023, www.mining.com/sponsored-content/reducing-co2-emissions-and-enhancing-efficiency-in-mining-the-andritz-metris-ace-optimization-technologies-minera-los-pelambres-amsa-case-study/.

48 T Igogo, K Awuah-Offei, A Newman, T Lowder and J Engel-Cox, "Integrating renewable energy into mining operations: opportunities, challenges, and enabling approaches", *Applied Energy* (2021) 300: 3, https://doi.org/10.1016/j.apenergy.2021.117375.

49 Weir Group, "New report identifies major carbon reduction opportunities in global mining", 10 May 2021, www.global.weir/newsroom/global-news/new-report-identifies-major-carbon-reduction-opportunities-in-global-mining/.

50 T Igogo, K Awuah-Offei, A Newman, T Lowder and J Engel-Cox, "Integrating renewable energy into mining operations: opportunities, challenges, and enabling approaches", *Applied Energy* (2021) 300, https://doi.org/10.1016/j.apenergy.2021.117375, 1.

51 Haiming Bao, Peter Knights, Mehmet Kizil and Micah Nehring, "Electrification Alternatives for Open Pit Mine Haulage", *Mining* (2023) 3(1): 1–25, www.mdpi.com/2673-6489/3/1/1.

52 Nesimi Ertugrul *et al*, "Status of Mine Electrification and Future Potentials", *2020 International Conference on Smart Grids and Energy Systems*, Intro p1, https://ieeexplore.ieee.org/abstract/document/9364565.

Case study: All-electric Borden mine, Chapleau Ontario, Canada

Goldcorp has transitioned Borden mine into being fully electric, using an all-electric mobile equipment fleet, including battery-powered underground vehicles, drilling and blasting equipment, and electric roof bolters and personnel carriers.[53] The company states that this is expected to eliminate all greenhouse gases associated with the movement of ore and waste rock – equal to around 50% of the total GHG emissions on site.[54] Through the impact on other process efficiencies, this transition is expected to reduce the annual GHG emissions by more than 70% in comparison to a baseline mine.[55]

Case study: Diavik Wind Farm, Yellow Knife, Canada

Diavik Diamond Mine, both open pit and underground, located in an extremely remote region in the Arctic, is a joint venture between the subsidiaries of Rio Tinto and Dominion Diamond Corporation.[56] In 2012, they installed four 2.3MW wind turbines (9.3 MW total). Previously, energy demands at this remote mine were met by diesel fuel, post-installation, the turbines were capable of producing 52% of the mine's energy needs, substantially reducing total mine carbon dioxide emissions.[57] Over its first year in 2013, the wind farm resulted in a diesel reduction of 3.8 million litres and an estimated 6% reduction in GHG emissions.[58]

The use of battery electric vehicles particularly in combination with a renewable electricity load can result in improved maintenance and lower underground emissions in comparison to their traditional diesel counterparts.[59] However, current technologies require further development to allow for large-scale implementation in the mining sector. This combines with other concerns, including proper disposal of depleted batteries and fire hazards from damaged batteries reacting with moisture or thermal runaway.[60]

---

53 University of Adelaide, "Mine electrification", p3, www.adelaide.edu.au/iser/system/files/media/documents/2020-07/Mine%20Electrification%20and%20Future%20Directions.pdf.

54 Cecilia Jemasmie, "Canada's Goldcorp to make Borden an all-electric mine", Mining.com, 18 November 2016, www.mining.com/canadas-goldcorp-to-make-borden-an-all-electric-mine/.

55 Daniel Gleeson, "Goldcorp's Borden all-electric underground mine moves towards production", 25 October 2018, https://im-mining.com/2018/10/25/goldcorps-borden-electric-gold-mine-moves-towards-production/.

56 Arctic Council Working Group, "Diavik Wind Farm, Yellow Knife, Canada", https://arctic-council.org/about/working-groups/acap/home/projects/arctic-black-carbon-case-studies-platform/diavik-wind-farm-yellow-knife-canada/.

57 Jack Jeswiet and Alex Szekeres, "Energy Consumption in Mining Comminution" *Procedia CIRP* (2016) 48: 144.

58 Arctic Council Working Group, "Diavik Wind Farm, Yellow Knife, Canada", https://arctic-council.org/about/working-groups/acap/home/projects/arctic-black-carbon-case-studies-platform/diavik-wind-farm-yellow-knife-canada/.

59 Corey Laamanen, Sabrina M Desjardins, Shannon H McLean and John A Scott, "The use of microalgal sourced biodiesel to help underground mines transition to battery electric vehicles", *Journal of Sustainable Mining* (2022) 21(1): 3, https://jsm.gig.eu/cgi/viewcontent.cgi?article=1327&context=journal-of-sustainable-mining.

60 *Ibid.*

Where electrification is not a suitable solution, the industry has begun to rely on low emission forms of hydrogen, particularly in uses such as generating heat, power, as feedstock or fuel for transportation and mining processes and for energy storage. In particular, hydrogen fuel cell vehicles – which may include haulage trucks, drill rigs and excavators for mining purposes – could not only reduce carbon emissions in comparison to diesel-powered vehicles, but also avoid reliance on the volume of critical minerals required for lithium battery-powered vehicles.[61]

As is often the case, a significant barrier to electrification or adoption of hydrogen powered solution are the capital costs and the rate of return in light of the mine life cycle.[62] While presently these capital expenditures often outweigh other cost pressures on mining operators, studies such as that done by McKinsey estimate that by 2030 the total cost of ownership for an electrical or hydrogen fuel cell haulage truck will be approximately 20% and 10% respectively lower than existing diesel trucks due to a reduction in maintenance and fuel costs. Such a move would require significant investment in the design of existing mines, making it more suitable for new and greenfield sites where the opportunity for substantial reductions in both carbon emissions and cost will be at its highest.[63]

6. Mitigating the carbon footprint of minerals

The mining sector is increasingly seeking technologies and strategies to mitigate its carbon footprint. This tends to focus on carbon capture and carbon removals as well as carbon offsetting.

6.1 Carbon capture and storage

Carbon capture and storage (CCS) is stated to have the potential to capture up to 90% of carbon dioxide emissions efficiently and cost effectively.[64] CCS involves capturing carbon dioxide at emission sources using pre-combustion capture, post-combustion capture or oxy-fuel combustion, transporting the captured carbon dioxide and storing it in a suitable location,[65] typically using geological storage where carbon dioxide is injected into sedimentary rocks, or

61 Sibylle Weiler, Amy Donlevey and Clive Hopewell, "Green Hydrogen in Mining", Bird & Bird, 29 June 2023, www.twobirds.com/en/insights/2023/global/gmr-green-hydrogen-in-mining.

62 NS Energy, "How mining companies can embrace sustainable fuels to cut emissions", 21 February 2024, www.nsenergybusiness.com/analysis/how-mining-companies-can-embrace-sustainable-fuels-to-cut-emissions/.

63 Henry Legge, Clemens Müller-Falcke, Tomas Nauclér and Erik Östgren, "Creating the zero-carbon mine", McKinsey & Company, 29 June 2021, www.mckinsey.com/industries/metals-and-mining/our-insights/creating-the-zero-carbon-mine.

64 Souvik Sen *et al*, "Chapter Fourteen – Geoscientific approach for carbon sequestration evaluation: A pragmatic perspective", *Developments in Structural Geology and Tectonics*, Vol 6, 2023, pp417–444, www.sciencedirect.com/science/article/abs/pii/B9780323995931000100.

65 British Geological Survey, "Understanding carbon capture and storage", www.bgs.ac.uk/discovering-geology/climate-change/carbon-capture-and-storage/.

mineral carbonation where carbon dioxide is reacted with naturally occurring iron, magnesium and calcium minerals to form stable carbonates.[66]

CCS technology can be integrated with mining operations by retrofitting post-combustion capture into existing infrastructure or designing new facilities with CCS technology. However, the availability of incentives or regulatory frameworks can influence CCS adoption. Governments and quasi-governmental organisations play a crucial role by providing (depending on their remit) subsidies, tax incentives or mandating carbon reduction targets that encourage the use of CCS.

More advanced CCS technology involves not only reducing and removing carbon dioxide from ongoing activities but also seeking to remove carbon dioxide also from the air (ie, accounting for earlier polluting activities). Direct air capture, a process that uses chemical reactions to extract carbon dioxide directly from the atmosphere,[67] employs one of two main approaches:

- *Solid DAC:* This is based on solid adsorbents operating at ambient to low pressure and medium temperature between 80°C and 120°C.[68]
- *Liquid DAC:* This relies on an aqueous basic solution which releases the captured carbon dioxide through a series of units operating at high temperature between 300°C and 900°C.[69]

Once extracted from the air, the carbon dioxide can then be stored or utilised. To date, 27 DAC plants have been commissioned in Europe, North America, Japan and the Middle East, capturing almost 0.01 million tonnes of carbon dioxide per year.[70] However, whether DAC deployment in mining operations makes sense will depend on the mine location, as it relies on the availability of low-carbon energy sources and carbon storage.[71] As a result, so far this is not a technology that has seen much uptake from the mining companies.

Another removal method that can apply to the mining sector is enhanced rock weathering. This plays on the naturally occurring processes whereby it takes between 100 and 200 million years for carbon to move through the weathering cycle.[72] Enhanced weathering quickens this process. It involves grinding silicate rocks such as basalt to form a powder (EW Powder) to bypass the slow weathering. The EW Powder is spread on large areas of land where plant roots and microbes in the soil accelerate the chemical reactions.[73] As

66 *Ibid.*
67 IEA, "Direct Air Capture", www.iea.org/energy-system/carbon-capture-utilisation-and-storage/direct-air-capture.
68 *Ibid.*
69 *Ibid.*
70 *Ibid.*
71 *Ibid.*
72 Met Office, "Carbon cycle", www.metoffice.gov.uk/weather/climate/climate-explained/carbon-cycle.
73 CarbonBrief, "Guest post: How 'enhanced weathering' could slow climate change and boost crop yields", 19 February 2018, www.carbonbrief.org/guest-post-how-enhanced-weathering-could-slow-climate-change-and-boost-crop-yields/.

natural rock weathering absorbs approximately 0.3% of global fossil fuel emissions, enhanced weathering can help to sequester further carbon dioxide from the atmosphere.[74]

Mining companies can help offset the carbon footprint of mining activities by using enhanced weathering:

- to rehabilitate land disturbed by mining activities to help sequester carbon and restore ecosystems;
- by collaborating with farmers or agricultural communities to spread EW Powder on agricultural land;
- to spread EW Powder in forestry and reforestation areas to support tree growth and carbon sequestration; and
- through designated carbon offset programmes.

Finally, mining companies can offset their GHG emissions by using one of the carbon trading/offsetting mechanisms operating globally. There are 75 carbon pricing instruments in operation globally as of 1 April 2024. Cumulatively, the carbon pricing instruments in place covered almost 13 gigatons of carbon dioxide equivalent, which translates to around 24% of global GHG emissions.[75] While pricing carbon is a low-cost, efficient way to achieve emission mitigation targets, it must be paired with complementary energy and climate policies to utilise the potential of carbon pricing.[76]

The aim of carbon offsets is to add the cost of pollution to the polluters' bills.[77] The resultant price signal can then shift consumption and investment patterns away from high-emission, fossil fuel-based technology towards cleaner technology, making economic development compatible with climate protection.[78] There are two main types of carbon trading and pricing mechanisms:

- *Emission trading system (ETS):* Under an ETS, specified entities must submit carbon allowances to cover their emissions each year, within an overall cap for regulated sectors. They can then purchase and sell credits from, and to, each other.[79] The price of carbon will depend on the balance between demand (the total emissions) and supply (the emission

74 *Ibid.*

75 World Bank Group, *State and Trends of Carbon Pricing 2024*, https://openknowledge.worldbank.org/server/api/core/bitstreams/253e6cdd-9631-4db2-8cc5-1d013956de15/content.

76 United Nations Climate Change, "About Carbon Pricing", https://unfccc.int/about-us/regional-collaboration-centres/the-ciaca/about-carbon-pricing#:~:text=While%20putting%20a%20price%20on,potential%20that%20carbon%20pricing%20promises.

77 World Bank Group, "What is Carbon Pricing?", www.worldbank.org/en/programs/pricing-carbon#:~:text=A%20carbon%20tax%20directly%20sets,carbon%20content%20of%20fossil%20fuels.

78 United Nations Climate Change, "About Carbon Pricing", https://unfccc.int/about-us/regional-collaboration-centres/the-ciaca/about-carbon-pricing#:~:text=While%20putting%20a%20price%20on,potential%20that%20carbon%20pricing%20promises.

79 CarbonBrief, "In-depth Q&A: Can 'carbon offsets' help to tackle climate change", 25 September 2023, https://interactive.carbonbrief.org/carbon-offsets-2023/.

units allocated and available).[80] The UK ETS, the EU ETS, the California Cap-and-Trade Program, the China National ETS are examples.[81]

- *A carbon tax* directly sets the price of carbon by implementing a tax rate on GHG emissions or the carbon content of fossil fuels, thereby incentivising a shift away from carbon-intensive methods.[82] This results in a total reduction of emissions. Unlike an ETS, a carbon tax does not predetermine a minimum level of GHG reductions, but instead provides price certainty.[83]

Case study: Teck Resources, British Columbia

- *Policy:* British Columbia enacted the Carbon Tax Act 2008, that applies to various industries, including mining and minerals. Currently, British Columbia's carbon tax rate is CA $80 per tonne of carbon dioxide equivalent.[84]
- *Impact:* Teck Resources has reduced its GHG emissions by 414,000 tonnes since 2011,[85] acknowledging the carbon tax's key role in driving these changes by increasing the cost of carbon-intensive fuels and operations, thereby incentivising more sustainable practices. In 2023, Teck Resources' British Columbia-based operations incurred CA $114.8 million in carbon tax.[86]

In practice the carbon price signals have meant the development of an active carbon trading market as companies (including in the mining sector) look to offset their GHG emissions by buying credits from projects and producers with eligible activities. There are three types of carbon markets that trade carbon credits:

- *The regulated carbon market (RCM):* These markets are regulated by mandatory national or regional carbon reduction regimes. Mechanisms include trading carbon credits under an ETS and buying carbon offsets. Carbon offsets enable specified entities to purchase approved offsets from external emission-cutting projects to stay within their limits.[87]

---

80 United Nations Climate Change, "About Carbon Pricing", https://unfccc.int/about-us/regional-collaboration-centres/the-ciaca/about-carbon-pricing#:~:text=While%20putting%20a%20price%20on,potential%20that%20carbon%20pricing%20promises.

81 Carbon Credits, "A Guide to Compliance Carbon Credit Markets", https://carboncredits.com/a-guide-to-compliance-carbon-credit-markets/.

82 World Bank Group, "What is Carbon Pricing?", www.worldbank.org/en/programs/pricing-carbon#:~:text=A%20carbon%20tax%20directly%20sets,carbon%20content%20of%20fossil%20fuels.

83 United Nations Climate Change, "About Carbon Pricing", https://unfccc.int/about-us/regional-collaboration-centres/the-ciaca/about-carbon-pricing#:~:text=While%20putting%20a%20price%20on,potential%20that%20carbon%20pricing%20promises.

84 British Columbia, "British Columbia's Carbon Tax", www2.gov.bc.ca/gov/content/environment/climate-change/clean-economy/carbon-tax.

85 Teck, *Climate Change Outlook 2021: Teck's TCFD-Aligned Report*, www.teck.com/media/Teck_Climate_Change_Outlook_2021.pdf.

86 Teck, "Climate Change", www.teck.com/media/Sustainability-Report-Climate-Change.pdf.

87 CarbonBrief, "In-depth Q&A: Can 'carbon offsets' help to tackle climate change", 25 September 2023, https://interactive.carbonbrief.org/carbon-offsets-2023/.

- *The unregulated voluntary carbon market (VCM):* This is not mandated by law and enables individuals, companies and organisations to purchase credits from emission-cutting projects towards their voluntary climate commitments.[88]
- *Article 6.2 of the Paris Agreement:* Enables countries to trade internationally transferred mitigation outcomes to meet their NDCs.[89]

The value of traded carbon dioxide permits reached a record €881 billion globally in 2023, marking a 2% increase from 2022 and representing around 12.5 billion metric tonnes of carbon.[90]

Case study: Hecla, Idaho
Companies such as Idaho-based Hecla Mining Company (Hecla) combine their own sustainability measures with purchasing carbon offsets. Hecla uses 100% renewable hydropower to supply utility power to its Casa Berardi mine and 96% hydropower at its Greens Creek operations, in combination with purchasing carbon offsets. With these cumulative efforts, Hecla has already achieved net zero on its Scope 1 and Scope 2 emissions.[91]

7. Conclusion

Mining and the extraction of minerals are heavily regulated in a number of aspects. Therefore, in many ways the legal obligations already on the developers and operators go some way to addressing issues around environmental impacts which now form part of the newer lexicon that is ESG.

That said, the integration of ESG principles in the mining and minerals sector is not just a regulatory obligation but a strategic imperative for ensuring long-term sustainability and profitability. The industry's traditional image as a significant contributor to environmental degradation and social disruption is being reshaped by proactive measures aimed at measuring, minimising and mitigating its carbon footprint. The accurate measurement of the carbon footprint is foundational to any ESG strategy. Advances in technology and data analytics have enabled more precise tracking of GHG emissions across the mining life cycle, from exploration to extraction, processing and transportation. This data-driven approach not only aids compliance with international standards and reporting frameworks but also provides a benchmark for

---

88 Helen Hooker and Jonathan Wentworth, "Carbon offsetting", UK Parliament Post, 24 January 2024, https://researchbriefings.files.parliament.uk/documents/POST-PN-0713/POST-PN-0713.pdf.

89 *Ibid.*

90 "Global carbon markets value hit record $949 billion in 2023", *The Economic Times*, 13 February 2024, https://economictimes.indiatimes.com/markets/commodities/news/global-carbon-markets-value-hit-record-949-billion-in-2023/articleshow/107642155.cms?from=mdr.

91 Lexology, "Decarbonization: The requirements for – and role of – mining companies", Mayer Brown, 16 March 2023, www.lexology.com/library/detail.aspx?g=42f0720e-9dda-4629-8c38-5f07b6f6faf1.

continuous improvement – only with such effective and accurate measuring will genuine progress be made in minimising and mitigating GHG emissions.

Minimising the carbon footprint requires a multifaceted approach that incorporates operational efficiency, technological innovation and renewable energy integration. Implementing energy-efficient practices, optimising resource usage and adopting cleaner technologies can significantly reduce emissions.

Efforts to mitigate GHG emissions produced by the mining and minerals processing sectors could also consider carbon capture and carbon removal techniques and technologies and carbon offset mechanisms. The effectiveness of such technologies will depend on the availability of regulatory frameworks for measuring Scope 1, Scope 2 and Scope 3 emissions and setting emission standards, regimes supporting reporting, transparency and compliance with such frameworks, government support such as subsidies and tax incentives and research and development.

In essence, the mining and minerals industry stands at a pivotal juncture. By embracing ESG principles and committing to measurable, actionable strategies for reducing their carbon footprint, companies can drive meaningful change. This transition not only safeguards the environment but also enhances corporate reputation, secures investment and ultimately ensures the sector's viability in a carbon-constrained world. As stakeholders increasingly demand responsible practices, the future of mining lies in its ability to innovate sustainably and act as stewards of both the earth's resources and its communities.

The author would like to thank Cameron Finlay-Hylton, Niamh Neville and Honey Kelly-Evans for their contribution to the drafting of this chapter.

Protecting ecosystems and biodiversity in the mining industry

María Cristina Alva
CMS Grau
Daniela Vergel-Riascos
CMS Rodríguez-Azuero

1. What biodiversity means

Biological diversity – or biodiversity – refers to the variety of life on Earth from bacteria, plants, animals and humans to ecosystems such as coral reefs or forests. Biodiversity creates the conditions needed to provide the food, water, stable climate, medicine and the economic growth that we need as human beings. As humans we depend on it to survive, thus, the loss or deterioration of any type of biodiversity (genetic, species or ecosystem diversity) affects directly the balance of life on Earth.

Considering the above, it is very important to understand the different factors that affect biodiversity and the causes and effects of its deterioration. These concerns have generated global awareness, and as we will explain below, there are several initiatives to address this crisis with the objective of finding different solutions to protect and secure the biodiversity of our planet.

According to the United Nations, the main cause of biodiversity loss is humans' use of land – primarily for food production. But also, climate change is increasing its role in the decline of biodiversity, because it "has altered marine, terrestrial, and freshwater ecosystems around the world. It has caused the loss of local species, increased diseases, and driven mass mortality of plants and animals, resulting in the first climate-driven extinctions".[1]

The Living Planet Index 2022[2] has been monitoring global trends in the abundance of mammals, reptiles, birds and amphibians for more than four decades. This indicator shows that between 1970 and 2018 there was an average decrease of 69% in the populations of wild animals that were analysed. In Latin America, this situation is even worse, since the decrease in average population

1 United Nations, "Biodiversity – our strongest natural defense against climate change", www.un.org/en/climatechange/science/climate-issues/biodiversity.

2 REA Almond, M Grooten, D Juffe Bignoli and T Petersen, *Informe Planeta Vivo 2022: Hacia una sociedad con la naturaleza en positivo*, WWF 2020, wwflpr.awsassets.panda.org/downloads/descarga_informe_planeta_vivo_2022_1_1.pdf.

abundance was around 94%. In short, the quantity and diversity of animals worldwide is being strongly impacted by different economic activities and phenomena, among which we can list agriculture, mining, urban development, deforestation, pollution, introduction of invasive species and climate change.

In that sense, and to be able to imagine a sustainable future, we must think about different and diverse solutions.

A global plan executed locally, with a defined deadline, objectives and indicators, is the right answer to make the change that is needed to address this problem. Without prejudice to this, and as we travel this complex path, we believe that there are some interesting alternatives that can be part of that global solution. There is no silver bullet.

It is important to understand that since the adoption of Resolution 48/13 by the UN Human Rights Council in October 2022, the right to a clean, healthy and sustainable environment is now a human right. Therefore, the biodiversity crisis is also considered to be a human rights crisis and we need to take several actions today to mitigate the impact that this crisis will have on future generations.

2. Biodiversity and the mining industry

We all recognise that activities of the minerals and metals industry may pose significant threats to biodiversity, and it does contribute to its loss worldwide. However, this industry has come a long way in understanding its impacts on biodiversity and how to prevent, mitigate and/or compensate for them, to the point that nowadays governments and companies have adopted measures and programmes to prevent and mitigate such impacts globally.

However, the mining sector does not have the highest potential negative impact on biodiversity. According to the pilot analysis of the Finance for Biodiversity Foundation published in April 2023 "the food, beverage and tobacco sector has the highest potential impact on biodiversity of all identified sectors".[3] In fact, a 2021 Chatham House report supported by the UN Environment Programme (UNEP) and Compassion in World Farming found that "our global food system is the primary driver of biodiversity loss, with agriculture alone being the identified threat to 24,000 of the 28,000 (86%) species at risk of extinction".[4]

Nevertheless, the materials sector in which the minerals and metals industry is located is in second place, so its biodiversity mitigation strategies and actions are very important and the consequences too drastic not to incorporate biodiversity management as an integral part of every mining project. Direct

---

3 Finance for Biodiversity Foundation, Briefing paper, "Top 10 biodiversity-impact ranking of company industries", www.financeforbiodiversity.org/wp-content/uploads/Top10_biodiversity-impact_ranking.pdf.

4 T Benton, C Bieg, H Harwatt, R Pudasaini and L Wellesley, Research paper, *Food system impacts on biodiversity loss: Three levers for food system transformation in support of nature*, Chatham House 2021, www.chathamhouse.org/sites/default/files/2021-02/2021-02-03-food-system-biodiversity-loss-benton-et-al_0.pdf.

impacts on biodiversity are classified as either 'sink impacts', which occur when materials from mining operations are added to the ecosystem, or 'source impacts', which arise from the extraction of materials.

However, it is important to note that biodiversity loss does not only occur at the mine site. In fact, mining activities create indirect impacts, which are not usually acknowledged and reported in the industry, such as the acceleration of landscape alteration and biodiversity loss through infrastructure development and expansion of settlements for migrant workers in mining areas.[5] These indirect impacts are often overlooked and therefore usually not assessed.

Mining is a sector that greatly contributes to the creation of employment opportunities, economic development and government revenues. However, mineral resources are often found in sensitive ecosystems with high biodiversity importance and local communities may depend on those ecosystems for other economic activities, including hunting, fishing, agriculture and eco-tourism. Thus, if well managed, mining can be a significant contributor to the achievement of the UN Sustainable Development Goals (SDGs). In that effort, mining projects should collaborate closely with local communities and authorities to obtain their social licence to operate, which should include biodiversity and environmental considerations.

That is why the industry has developed voluntary standards of good practice in the mining sector, which seek to promote the SDGs. For instance, the International Council on Mining and Metals (ICMM) adopted the *Good Practice Guidance for Mining and Biodiversity*[6] to help the mining industry to identify and evaluate biodiversity, understand the connections between mining activities and biodiversity, assess and mitigate potential negative impacts on biodiversity, develop rehabilitation strategies and contribute to conservation.

Also, the Southern African Development Community (SADC) issued in November 2015 its *Guidelines for Mainstreaming Biodiversity and Ecosystem Services in Extractive Industry*[7] to support sustainable development by minimising impacts on biodiversity and ecosystem services and maximising social and environmental opportunities through gathering the information needed to develop strategies and aid decision making throughout the project life cycle.

Towards Sustainable Mining (TSM), an industry self-regulatory standard launched in 2004 by the Mining Association of Canada sets forth a Biodiversity Conservation Management Protocol to be applied by companies through all stages of a mine's life cycle and "seeks to confirm that mining facilities have

---

5 Hamidu Ami Seki, *Environmental impacts of mining on biodiversity and ecosystem services*, University of York, September 2022, https://etheses.whiterose.ac.uk/32791/1/Seki_205037423_Thesis_2022.pdf.

6 ICMM, *Good Practice Guidance for Mining and Biodiversity*, 1 December 2006, www.icmm.com/en-gb/guidance/environmental-stewardship/2006/mining-and-biodiversity.

7 A Bennun *et al*, *Guidelines for Mainstreaming Biodiversity and Ecosystem Services in Extractive Industry*, SADC 2015, https://biopama.org/wp-content/uploads/2021/02/SADC-Extractive-Industry-and-Biodiversity-Guidelines-EN-1.pdf.

made formal commitments to manage biodiversity at their sites ... that the action plans for significant biodiversity aspects are implemented, and that biodiversity conservation reporting systems are in place to inform decision making and to communicate their performance publicly".[8]

Such efforts are essential to improve responsible and more sustainable mining activities, by understanding the pressure made on biodiversity directly and indirectly, adopting proactive measures and innovating on new strategies to achieve, at least, a net zero biodiversity loss. This is one of the great challenges that humanity currently faces, and an international multilateral legal framework has been created to do so.

Also, it is important to take into consideration that mining operations are often located in remote sites, which are directly affected by climate change. Although, according to McKinsey,[9] "mining is currently responsible for 4 to 7 percent of greenhouse-gas (GHG) emissions globally", the industry can also play an important role in addressing the problem through its control of large tracks of land.

Heavy precipitation, extreme heat and other weather conditions will exacerbate the challenges of mining in these remote locations, but preserving or restoring native vegetation, for example, can go some way to mitigating those climate impacts. In that sense, designing policies, programmes and measures to prevent, mitigate or compensate such impacts is fundamental for the sustainability of the mining business.

3. Multilateral legal framework

As already mentioned, two of the biggest international crises that humanity currently faces are climate change and biodiversity loss, which must be addressed together. That is the commitment of signatory states under two different international agreements both established in 1992 at the Rio Earth Summit – the UN Framework Convention on Climate Change (UNFCCC) and the UN Convention on Biological Diversity (CBD).

Under the CBD, in December 2022 during the UN Biodiversity Conference (COP 15) the parties adopted the Kunming-Montreal Global Biodiversity Framework (GBF) to work in synergy with the Paris Agreement on climate change and other agreements to protect forests and oceans and prevent desertification. The GBF sets out the pathway to reach a world living in harmony with nature through the accomplishment of four goals by 2050 and 23 targets by 2030. All 196 signing parties committed to set national goals to

---

8 The Mining Association of Canada, "Biodiversity Conservation Management", 2020, https://mining.ca/towarfds-sustainable-mining/protocols-guides/biodiversity-conservation-management/.

9 Lindsay Delevingne, Will Glazener, Liesbet Grégoir and Kimberley Henderson, "Climate risk and decarbonization: What every mining CEO needs to know", McKinsey Sustainability, 28 January 2020, www.mckinsey.com/capabilities/sustainability/our-insights/climate-risk-and-decarbonization-what-every-mining-ceo-needs-to-know.

implement these targets. GBF is a critical step in addressing the biodiversity crisis by establishing global commitments and objectives to achieve significant progress in the conservation of biodiversity by 2030.

The UN biodiversity negotiations concluded with delegates reaching an agreement to restore 30% of the world's degraded ecosystems by 2030, eliminate or phase out $500 billion of harmful environmental subsidies, and mobilise $200 billion annually by 2030 for biodiversity action, including $30 billion from wealthy countries to developing countries.[10]

Nevertheless, from our perspective, the monitoring and follow-up of progress towards these commitments has remained somewhat in limbo.[11] Although several indicators have been established, it is not clear whether the parties will achieve the agreed commitments and targets by 2030.

Governments need to get involved to determine policies that will address the problem and find different ways to build a solution. But they are not the only ones: because the biodiversity crisis is considered a human rights crisis, private and public organisations also need to participate in the solution.

Biodiversity has become relevant to business, for four main reasons:

> *1. regulatory requirements; 2. external pressures or market access that influence operational practices; 3. access to capital related to a strengthening of lending requirements; and 4. reputational risks that arise from the way a company conducts business and thereby affects the environment and people.*[12]

Unfortunately, there is not a single solution that can fix the problem. It requires a lot of coordination, a joint strategy and prioritisation of key issues. The first step is to create an appropriate regulatory context that allows and encourages companies to adapt. One strategy in that regard is the consolidation of a biodiversity market.

4. Biodiversity market

According to the Nature Conservancy (in partnership with the Paulson Institute and the Cornell Atkinson Center for Sustainability), during 2019 spending on biodiversity conservation was between $124 billion and $143 billion per year, against a total estimated biodiversity protection need of between $722 billion and $967 billion per year. That leaves a biodiversity funding gap of between $598 billion and $824 billion per year.[13] Governments have been the principal

---

10 UN Environment Programme, "COP15 ends with landmark biodiversity agreement", 30 October 2024, https://www.unep.org/news-and-stories/story/cop15-ends-landmark-biodiversity-agreement.

11 Radhika Rao, Esther Sekyoung Choi and Roman Paul Czebiniak, "Can 'Biodiversity Credits' Boost Conservation?", World Resources Institute, 12 March 2024, www.wri.org/insights/biodiversity-credits-explained.

12 N Doswald *et al*, *Biodiversity offsets: voluntary and compliance regimes. A review of existing schemes, initiatives and guidance for financial institutions*, UNEP 2012, https://files.ctctcdn.com/b3b328ed001/7b1aaa64-234c-4918-abb8-27a30c51ac03.pdf.

13 *Financing Nature: Closing the global biodiversity financing gap*, The Paulson Institute 2020, www.paulsoninstitute.org/conservation/financing-nature-report/.

contributor to biodiversity funding, at 83%.[14] According to UNEP State of Finance for Nature, "US$9.5 trillion is needed cumulatively from 2022 to 2050 to keep climate change below 2°C, stabilise biodiversity levels and achieve land degradation neutrality".

Economic instruments such as fees and charges, taxes, environmental subsidies and tradeable permits are rapidly increasing globally. The OECD Policy Instruments for the Environment Database (PINE Database) reported that by 2021 more than 120 countries had approximately 3,680 instruments in force.[15]

Government initiatives are important but will not be enough to close the financial gap and meet the targets set forth by GBF of COP15 if civil society, policymakers and business do not play a bigger role. The private sector could address this matter as an opportunity for sustainable growth, capitalise on change and create value and wealth. The private sector is more agile and innovative and can be a pioneer in defining key commitments and strategies for biodiversity conservation and human rights protection. Nowadays, companies are pressured to address, propose and report their actions to prevent, protect and restore biodiversity loss resulting from their operations. This is an important aspect of ESG reports and part of all the international standards that include a protocol on biodiversity.

The challenge is huge, but there are some strategies that are being implemented by governments and the private sector to reach the targets set forth by the COP 15, particularly Target 19 of GBF, to "Mobilize $200 billion per year for biodiversity from all sources, including $30 billion through international finance"[16] by 2030.

In this chapter, we briefly address two of those strategies: biodiversity offsets and biodiversity credits.

4.1 Biodiversity offsets

Biodiversity offsets are defined as the conservation activities intended to compensate the unavoidable impacts that some activities can have on genetics, species and ecosystems, that remain even after other mitigation measures have been taken. These offsets are often intended to ensure no net loss, or even a net gain on biodiversity.

Offsets are essential for large-scale development projects like mining, by

---

14 Radhika Rao, Esther Sekyoung Choi and Roman Paul Czebiniak, "Can 'Biodiversity Credits' Boost Conservation?", World Resources Institute, 12 March 2024, www.wri.org/insights/biodiversity-credits-explained.

15 OECD, *Tracking Economic Instruments and Finance for Biodiversity*, 2021. See https://issuu.com/oecd.publishing/docs/tracking-economic-instruments-and-f_0a75a6b51b5838#:~:text=on%20biodiversity%20finance.&text=Key%20highlights%20%2D%202021%20The%20number,PINE%20database%2C%20spanning%2062%20countries.

16 Convention on Biological Diversity, "The Biodiversity Plan for Life On Earth: 2030 Targets (with Guidance Notes): Target 19: Mobilize $200 Billion per Year for Biodiversity From all Sources, Including $30 Billion Through International Finance", www.cbd.int/gbf/targets.

allowing impacts on biodiversity to be balanced or outweighed by promoting or preserving nature elsewhere.

The UN Environment Programme – the global authority for the environment for sustainable development – and the World Conservation Monitoring Centre have developed the concept of 'mitigation hierarchy', a set of four principles to respond to negative impacts on biodiversity and to ensure no net loss. Biodiversity offsets are the last measure when avoidance, mitigation, restoration and, finally, rehabilitation have taken place and yet negative impacts still remain, as set out in Figure 1.[17]

Figure 1. Mitigation hierarchy

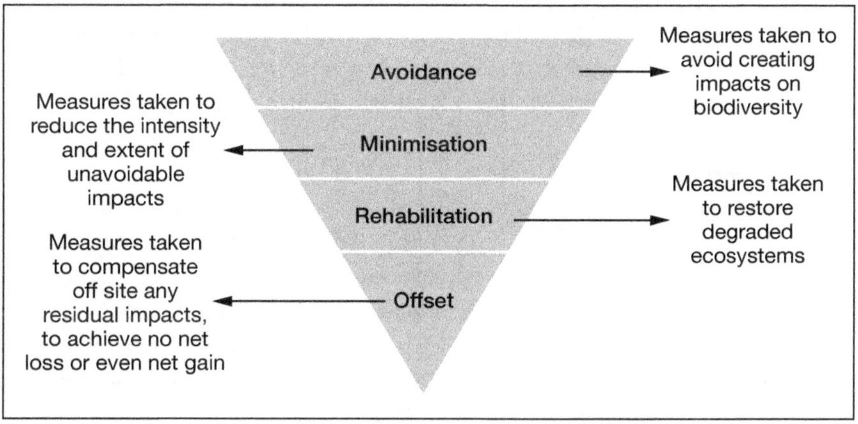

A mandatory offset market has been developed through the adoption of legislation and regulation by governments, driven by their commitments made internationally as parties to CBD and other treaties. The compliance regimes consist of three main legislative frameworks:

(a) Species and habitat legislation

Initially developed in the United States in 1972 through the Clean Water Act and then, in the 1990s, through the introduction of so-called 'habitat banks' (HBs) where mitigation and conservation actions are placed for endangered species. This "involves the purchase (and conservation/restoration/creation) by a third party organization of land or habitat, which is then converted into credits that can be purchased by developers needing to offset a development".[18] This nature conservation tool has been very successful and has attracted the

17 N Doswald *et al*, *Biodiversity offsets: voluntary and compliance regimes. A review of existing schemes, initiatives and guidance for financial institutions*, UNEP 2012, https://files.ctctcdn.com/b3b328ed001/7b1aaa64-234c-4918-abb8-27a30c51ac03.pdf.

18 *Ibid.*

interest of other countries including in Europe, Latin America, the Caribbean and Australia.

Habitat banks can be beneficial for governments around the world to prevent or reduce and manage biodiversity loss in their country, not only through enforcement of environmental legislation, but also providing positive incentives for the private sector. Governments should consider developing their own national, regional or even a global HB market.

(b) Environmental Impact Assessment (EIA) regulations

Through this regulatory mechanism, environmental authorities require offset compensation measures to obtain an environmental licence for the development of projects. Although this mechanism has been widely adopted in Latin America, the details of requirements, tools and outcomes differ significantly between countries. EIAs constitute a valuable tool to enforce mandatory offsets and, therefore, to promote a market for them.

(c) Compensation regulations

In some countries, offset or compensation regulations have been adopted independently. For instance, since the early 1990s in the Netherlands, the National Ecological Network demanded the increase of nature areas from 460,000 hectares in 1991 to 730,000 hectares by 2018, so any proposal to encroach on those areas requires the application of the mitigation hierarchy to obtain 'no net loss of biodiversity'. In Brazil, offset compensations are required by the Forestry Code and the Protected Areas Law.[19]

Some examples of the countries that have developed these three framework strategies can be seen in Table 1.

Table 1. Examples of offsets regulation

Species I Habitat Legislation	EIA Regulation	Offset I Compensation
United States; Canada; European Union; Germany; Switzerland; Australia	Mexico; Chile; South Africa; China; Pakistan; Colombia; India; Japan; Malaysia; Mongolia; Russia; South Korea; Thailand; Costa Rica	United States; Mexico; Netherlands; Colombia; Paraguay; Australia; Brazil; Gabon; China; the Philippines; Saipan, Vietnam

19 *Ibid.*

According to the OECD PINE Database:

At least 37 countries have laws requiring biodiversity offsets as a prerequisite for certain developments. Close to 13,000 offset projects have been identified across these countries (Bull and Strange, 2018). Finance mobilised by biodiversity offsets has been estimated at USD 6–9 billion per year (Deutz et al. 2020). OECD's questionnaire found that one scheme alone in the U.S. (NRCS Wetland Mitigation Banking) channeled USD 3.3 million per year towards the restoration, creation or enhancement of wetlands from 2017–2019.[20]

However, not all the biodiversity offset schemes are mandatory. Throughout the last decade, the voluntary offset market has been evolving and growing globally. Many economic sectors have used biodiversity offsets as a voluntary measure to achieve a long-term sustainable development, where the motivation is "demonstrating leadership, gaining an ability to influence the regulatory process, reducing operational risk exposure, and taking advantage of new business development opportunities".[21]

Voluntary biodiversity offsets are usually undertaken jointly between companies and conservation organisations or consulting firms, especially in extractives industries and for water and urban development projects. These initiatives are incentivised by the Equator Principles (EPs), "a voluntary set of standards for determining, assessing and managing social and environmental risk in project financing with capital costs exceeding USD 10 million, [which] apply the mitigation hierarchy".[22] Nowadays, the IFC Performance Standards have explicitly included biodiversity offsets, so now all financial institutions that comply with the EPs have to apply the mitigation hierarchy in project finance. This means that when biodiversity offsets are proposed by a project, in order to be financed by a financial institution, the client must demonstrate that the project's residual impacts will be adequately mitigated.

Other multilateral financial institutions have also adopted the mitigation hierarchy approach to ensure that projects comply with the minimum ESG criteria to access finance, including the Asian Development Bank, European Bank for Reconstruction and Development, European Investment Bank and Inter-American Development Bank.

By way of example, under the TSM Biodiversity Protocol, the mining industry collaborated with government, academic and environmental groups in

20 OECD, *Tracking Economic Instruments and Finance for Biodiversity*, 2021. See https://issuu.com/oecd.publishing/docs/tracking-economic-instruments-and-f_0a75a6b51b5838#:~:text=on%20biodiversity%20finance.&text=Key%20highlights%20%2D%202021%20The%20number,PINE%20database%2C%20spanning%2062%20countries.

21 N Doswald *et al*, *Biodiversity offsets: voluntary and compliance regimes. A review of existing schemes, initiatives and guidance for financial institutions*, UNEP 2012, https://files.ctctcdn.com/b3b328ed001/7b1aaa64-234c-4918-abb8-27a30c51ac03.pdf.

22 *Ibid.*

Alberta, Canada, to develop a biodiversity offset programme to prevent the irreversible decline of species and biodiversity in Alberta's Boreal Forest.[23]

Certainly, the biodiversity offset market faces challenges. One of the concerns is that voluntary offset programmes will be insufficient to protect biodiversity due to the lack of economic, legal or regulatory requirements to ensure credible commitments to manage offsets over long periods of time.

Another concern is that offsets could become 'a licence to trash'. That is why it is so important for industries to keep developing and implementing protocols with strong assessment methodologies to ensure the mitigation hierarchy has been properly run, as well as the principles developed in the CBD.

Another question that arises is how to measure or value biodiversity. Many regulatory schemes use a proxy measure based on an area of land. However, a more sophisticated option would consider the equivalence between the offset site to the developed site. In any case, "it is agreed that offsets should be on a 'like-for-like' (or 'in-kind') basis whereby the biodiversity values being conserved are equal to the values being lost"[24] or even 'like-for-like-or-better' as has been recently promoted.

In the end, it is essential that governments, academia, civil society and businesses play an active role in the protection, conservation and restoration of biodiversity, at every level. Biodiversity offset science is still new and its design needs much more development, for example, establishing better metrics, defining the threshold between the mitigation and offsetting of impacts, and the management of uncertainty regarding projects in the future, among other issues. Another challenge concerns the high costs and timing of the offsets over long periods of time to guarantee the perpetuity of the measures adopted. It is especially important to properly manage and mitigate reputational risks associated with poor outcomes, which is a sensitive challenge for the developers of specific projects, but also for the credibility of the biodiversity offset market as a whole.

However, biodiversity offset markets, both voluntary and mandatory, are here to stay and we expect their use to keep growing around the world in the mining and minerals sector, as in many others.

4.2 Biodiversity credits

Biodiversity credits "are a verifiable, quantifiable and tradeable financial instrument that rewards positive nature and biodiversity outcome (eg, species ecosystems and natural habitats) through the creation and sale of either land or

---

23 S Dyer, J Grant, T Lesack and M Weber, *Catching up: Conservation and Biodiversity Offsets in Alberta's Boreal Forest*, Canadian Boreal Initiative 2008, www.pembina.org/reports/CatchingUp-Offsets.pdf.

24 N Doswald *et al*, *Biodiversity offsets: voluntary and compliance regimes. A review of existing schemes, initiatives and guidance for financial institutions*, UNEP 2012, https://files.ctctcdn.com/b3b328ed001/ 7b1aaa64-234c-4918-abb8-27a30c51ac03.pdf.

ocean-based biodiversity units over a fixed period"[25] and can be offered by public and private organisations and governments.

These credits represent an alternative for compensating the loss of species and the degradation of habitats in highly affected ecosystems. Biodiversity credits are under development and so is the market they trade in.

The biodiversity crisis represents a concern, but also an opportunity to create value over time and address the issue in a more proactive way. Expert consensus emphasises that to stop further biodiversity deterioration and achieve GBF targets, private and public sectors need to be engaged and incentivised to prevent and reverse nature loss. It is very clear that this problem is not restricted to a single industry but represents a big opportunity for the mining industry and its value chain.

As we have said, the biodiversity credit market is under construction and it is fundamental that it builds on scientific, verifiable and quantifiable data: if not, it will start to crumble.

The biodiversity credits market has also been part of the World Economic Forum's (WEF's) Nature Action Agenda, which seeks to expand financing for nature-positive outcomes. In 2022 the WEF launched the Biodiversity Credits Initiative[26] to explore the potential of a biodiversity credit market in which organisations can benefit from nature positive impacts resulting from the actions they make to avoid and/or reduce negative environmental impacts. Biodiversity credit markets can be:

- *Mandatory market* regulated by governments, which create a demand for biodiversity by setting a limit on the negative impacts on habitats and/or species for their jurisdiction. These limits allow public and/or private entities to offer certain mechanisms to comply with the limits that have been set. This then creates a market that needs to have certain standards to obtain the positive impact that is expected; or
- *Voluntary market* developed by private and/or public organisations interested in biodiversity benefits to advance corporate social responsibility policies or reputational objectives, among other reasons. This is an important opportunity to create more projects to achieve the goals that were set by GBF, in terms of biodiversity loss. It is also an important funding source that can help to close the current biodiversity financing gap of between $598 billion and $824 billion per year.

There are several aspects that need to be taken into consideration in developing conservation biodiversity credits (BDC). The BioCarbon Biodiversity

25 World Economic Forum, Biodiversity Credits Initiative "Financing for Nature", https://initiatives.weforum.org/financing-for-nature/home.
26 Science Based Targets Network, https://sciencebasedtargetsnetwork.org/companies/.

Standard – BBS, based in the United States, provides tools for the management and administration of biodiversity, encouraging the participation of private and public actors, helping to articulate conservation actions, quantify net profits and participate in environmental credit markets through verification and compliance with the following requirements:[27]

- *Dates.* The project shall specifically determine the date on which the measurable net biodiversity gains begin, as well as the first measurement date for net biodiversity gain, and subsequent monitoring periods;
- *Geographical delimitation.* The developer must define, using UTM (Universal Transverse Mercator) coordinates, or any other coordinate system, the area in which the project will take place. It also must verify the area's ecosystemic characteristics and divide the project into Minimum Spatial Units of one hectare;
- *Baseline.* This is a fundamental aspect of the project because it has a direct impact on quantification of net biodiversity gain. As we have already stated, ecosystems are not the same, and that is one of the most important challenges of this market. In that sense, a comprehensive analysis to establish the biodiversity baseline must be conducted, and it shall include the state of ecosystems within the established geographical boundaries, to identify conservation strategies, and assure biodiversity net gain;
- *Identification of biodiversity transformation and loss.* Biodiversity conservation initiatives must be designed based on transparent and accurate data related to the activities (all of them) that have an impact over the ecosystems and biodiversity of a certain project. Causes and sources must be identified;
- *Objectives.* Goals must be determined to understand, measure and demonstrate the impact of a particular project. These objectives are directly related to the baseline, the identification of the causes of biodiversity and transformation loss and the identified risks;
- *Additionality.* The party responsible for an initiative must demonstrate, both qualitatively and quantitatively, how it contributes to conservation efforts beyond what would have occurred if the initiative had not been implemented;
- *Results.* Every project needs to showcase its results. They shall be verifiable and quantifiable and shall consider all the above-mentioned aspects;
- *Stakeholders.* Another relevant aspect of the design of these projects is the need to make them sustainable. This is not a one-year activity. On the

27 ProClima International, Standard for the Certification and Registration of Biodiversity Conservation Initiatives, 2021, https://biocarbonstandard.com/en/biodiversity-standard/.

contrary, these are long-term projects that need to consider and involve any third party that is directly or indirectly affected by the area of the project. These initiatives must be socially sustainable to be successful; and

- *Legislation.* As we have already said, this is a developing market. Governments are just starting to regulate and because of this these initiatives must be prepared to comply with new regulations and adapt to rules that will be progressively established by each government. Considering that these are locally executed mechanisms to address global concerns, they also need to be aligned with the SDGs adopted by all UN member states in 2015, as part of the 2030 Agenda for Sustainable Development.

Certification bodies are responsible for conducting an audit to assess compliance with the requirements, evaluating the methodology used. If all requirements have been satisfied, the certification body will submit an attestation or certificate of compliance.[28] Once this certification is obtained, BioCarbon performs a final revision of the information and then issues a formal written 'biodiversity credits issuance statement' to be registered in the public registry platform where the BDCs are each assigned a unique serial number, which is also connected to a blockchain system that guarantees the security, traceability and transparency of the BDC.

As a market in development, it is important to address some emerging challenges. For instance, it is difficult to compare and standardise this market. Ecosystems have different dynamics and it is fundamental to understand that they are not equivalent, and that each one regenerates differently, and over different periods of time. Because each initiative is different, standardisation of the market is complex.

It is also a big challenge to create effective and transparent mechanisms to measure the impacts of a particular initiative over time. Effective monitoring and reporting mechanisms will be fundamental to preserve and secure the legitimacy of this market.

Finally, considering that these projects are implemented over large land areas, a comprehensive socio-ecological approach must be adopted. The connection with individuals and communities and their interrelationship with the territory is crucial to ensure the long-term success of these projects.

28 BioCarbon Standard, *Biocarbon Biodiversity Standard (BBS): Nature-based solutions for quantifying net gains*, 2024, https://biocarbonstandard.com/wp-content/uploads/BCR_Biodiversity-Standard.pdf.

5. Conclusion

As we have shown, the biodiversity crisis must be prioritised by all sectors – governments, civil society, multilateral organisations and companies at a global level – because the subsistence of humanity ultimately depends on it. To achieve this, there is no single solution and all sectors must contribute to make biodiversity conservation a reality. Biodiversity offsets and credits are a couple of the tools available to create a market that promotes good corporate behaviour in preserving our environment.

Many challenges exist to the maturing of these markets, but the foundations are there and the commitment of interested parties has also been growing. In fact, in June 2024, the International Finance Corporation and BBVA Colombia bank issued the first biodiversity bond in the world of $50 million, intended to finance projects focused on reforestation, regeneration of natural forests in deserted land, conservation and rehabilitation of mangroves, habitat restoration, among others.

Also, the permanent collaboration between governments, international financial institutions and the private sector is not new, especially in the mining and metals sector. For instance, to protect forests and prevent deforestation, a forest bond was developed by the International Finance Corporation (IFC), Conservation International and mining company BHP Billiton. Under this initiative, the Forest Bond that supports the Kasigau Corridor REDD+ Project in East Kenya raised $152 million from institutional investors and is listed on the London Stock Exchange. The Forest Bond "provides a choice for investors to receive coupons in the form of carbon credits generated from avoided deforestation and issued under the Verified Carbon Standard, instead of cash coupons".[29] BHP Billiton provides a price support mechanism of $12 million to guarantee that the project sells a predetermined minimum quantity of carbon credits every year until the maturity of the bond.

Another example is Rio Tinto's biodiversity strategy, which recognises that "we work in remote locations and sensitive environments, our activities have the potential to cause harm through pollution or land disturbance, and we have a significant carbon footprint".[30] As a result, it has developed a set of actions and strategies to mitigate those impacts, through collaborative relationships with communities, to assess and minimise their impacts on the environment and biodiversity. "For example, every year, at the Diavik Diamond Mine, in Canada's Northwest Territories, we bring together biologists and members from the local Indigenous communities to sample the water and assess the fish. And in Australia, at our Weipa operations in Far North Queensland, we are working

---

29 BHP Billiton, "BHP Billiton and IFC collaborate on new Forests Bond", 31 October 2016, www.bhp.com/news/media-centre/releases/2016/10/bhp-billiton-and-ifc-collaborate-on-new-forests-bond.

30 Rio Tinto, "Environment: Caring for the planet", www.riotinto.com/en/sustainability/environment.

with Traditional Owners and Local Aboriginal People to rehabilitate land using ancient seeds to make sure the right plants are grown in the right areas. These plants will be used for medicine, food and ceremonies."[31]

Another practice of the mining industry is to engage with global organisations to protect biodiversity. An example is the Proteus Partnership, a strategy created in collaboration with the United Nations Environment Programme's World Conservation Monitoring Center that supports companies to contribute to 'nature-positive'. Current Proteus Partners include AngloAmerican, BHP, RioTinto, ArcelorMittal, Fortescue, BP, Chevron, Engie, Eni, Equinor, Hydro, Newmont, Repsol, Shell, Teck and TotalEnergies, among others.

The Science Based Targets Network[32] is another organisation responsible for developing science-based targets for nature, through the science-based targets (SBTs) initiative. The SBTs are "measurable, actionable, and time-bound objectives, based on the best available science, that allow actors to align with Earth's limits and societal sustainability goals".[33] This allows organisations to set objectives and actions that will help and reverse the crisis of biodiversity loss and climate change in a more accurate and coordinated way. As we said – it is important to develop a global plan and execute it locally.

The adoption of these mechanisms in voluntary codes of conduct by the mining industry demonstrate a commitment to improvement and, when they are effective, will allow for the development of conservation strategies that are more flexible and less regulated.

The mining industry and all the businesses directly or indirectly related to the sector must play an important and active role in the establishment of policies, programmes and environmental and social commitments to help reverse the dual crises of climate change and biodiversity loss.

---

31 *Ibid.*

32 Science Based Targets Network, "Who we are", https://sciencebasedtargetsnetwork.org/about/: "A civil-society and science-led initiative founded in 2019 by a group of global NGOs who have come together to help collectively define what is necessary for companies and cities to do, to stay within Earth's limits and meet society's needs".

33 Science Based Targets Network, "What are SBTs?", https://sciencebasedtargetsnetwork.org/about/what-are-sbts/.

ESG litigation trends: emerging risks for international mining companies

Sarah Grenfell
CMS Cameron McKenna Nabarro Olswang LLP

1. Introduction

Mining plays a crucial role in the global economy; it serves as the basis for producing the majority of consumer goods used in our daily lives and is a significant driver of socio-economic development in many countries.

Nevertheless, it is a fact that mining has been and remains a risky activity. Over time, awareness has increased of the environmental and social implications of mining operations, leading to a growing need to evaluate their potential impacts. The result has been twofold: legislation regarding the regulation of mining activity has become more stringent and mining companies have sought to improve their operational processes in order to minimise the potential impacts of their activities while working towards meeting sustainability and environmental, social and governance (ESG) goals.[1]

Mining therefore has the potential to give rise to a broad range of environmental actions or claims,[2] ranging from revocation of mining licences/permits and/or fines by regulatory bodies where statutory obligations have been breached and/or conditions of licences/permits contravened through to private law claims against the mine owner/operator. The latter category of claim is usually founded upon common law nuisance and/or negligence or the equivalent in other jurisdictions. In addition, in recent years climate change activism has been increasingly played out in the courts, with claims being

1 Actions include modernisation of equipment, increased monitoring of processing activities, prudent use of water and natural resources during exploration and mining, proper management of waste and tailings with input reuse, control and treatment of emissions and noise, monitoring of potentially impacted areas (vegetation, fauna and natural resources) and adoption of safety and emergency response protocols.

2 The specific regulatory and legal obligations that a mining company will be subject to, and consequences of any breach, will depend upon a variety of factors including the country in which the mining project is located, the location of any individuals impacted by the acts or omissions of the mine owner/operator and/or the country in which the environmental harm occurred and/or the country in which the mine owner/operator (and any other party against which proceedings are commenced) is domiciled. For a country-by-country analysis, the reader is referred to *Mining and Minerals: A Practical Guide to the Life Cycle of a Mining Project* (Globe Law and Business, 2018).

advanced against public authorities under human rights legislation (eg, the UK Human Rights Act 1998) and against company directors, in an effort to influence corporate behaviour (through shareholder derivative claims). In the ESG space in particular, companies are now coming under increased scrutiny by regulators regarding their sustainability credentials and potential claimants are seeking to rely upon published ESG commitments to establish or evidence their claims.

This chapter explores recent developments in private law claims in the English courts, together with two aspects that are key to any claim: the party or parties against whom claims are advanced and jurisdictional challenges.

2. The defendant(s) – pursuing the parent company

When an act or incident occurs at a mine that gives rise to a claim, one might conclude that the most logical course of action is for the claimant(s) to pursue the company which is directly responsible for the incident. That will, most often, be the locally incorporated company which owns and operates the mine. However, where the locally incorporated company is a subsidiary of a multinational corporation, a claimant may see merit in (also) bringing proceedings against the ultimate parent company of the relevant subsidiary. One of the reasons for doing so relates to enforcement: if the local company is a subsidiary of a multinational, the parent company will usually have 'deeper pockets' against which to enforce a judgment. Proceedings brought against the parent company also have the potential to attract greater media attention, which may exert commercial pressure on the defendant mining company to settle the claims out of court.

However, under English law, a parent company and subsidiary are treated as separate legal entities; the mere fact that they are related does not make the parent company liable for the acts of its subsidiary.[3] Nevertheless, some jurisdictions (such as England) have recognised that in certain circumstances a parent company may owe a duty of care in relation to the acts or omissions of its subsidiaries, so as to enable a claim to be brought against the parent company in common law negligence. As set out in further detail below, in recent years, claimants have repeatedly adopted this 'model' of litigation.

3. Jurisdiction in which proceedings are commenced

Before turning to the grounds upon which private environmental claims are most often founded, it is necessary to say something about jurisdiction. In order for a court to determine a dispute between parties, it must have jurisdiction to do so. Often there will be more than one country in which proceedings may be commenced (ie, more than one court that may have jurisdiction); it is not

---

3 *Saloman v Saloman & Co Ltd* [1897] AC 22 HL.

uncommon in these circumstances for claimants to commence proceedings in more than one jurisdiction, or in the jurisdiction they consider most favourable to them. To the extent the defendant(s) dispute the court's jurisdiction, it will fall to the court to rule on such issue.

As regards the position at English law, prior to 2005, defendants who disputed jurisdiction would often do so on the basis that the English court was not the 'proper forum' for the dispute to be heard. This is commonly referred to as the *forum non conveniens* defence. However, in 2005, the European Court of Justice made clear that a claimant was permitted to bring a claim against a defendant domiciled in the United Kingdom under the Recast Brussels Regulation.[4] The defendant could not, in such circumstances, dispute jurisdiction on the basis that the English court was not the 'proper forum', and this defence fell out of use.

However, as of 31 December 2020 (the end of the Brexit transition period), the Recast Brussels Regulation ceased to apply to the United Kingdom. Although the United Kingdom applied to join the 2007 Lugano Convention in April 2020 (which is similarly worded to the Recast Brussels Regulations and would therefore have similarly precluded reliance on the *forum non conveniens* defence), membership was opposed by the European Commission; it remains unclear whether membership will be permitted in due course (and if so, when). The present position is therefore similar to the pre-2005 position, such that a defendant domiciled in the United Kingdom may again seek to rely upon the *forum non conveniens* argument to seek to persuade the English courts that they should not assume jurisdiction over a UK-domiciled company. As a consequence, a model of litigation that has previously been adopted in the English courts whereby the claimant(s) pursue an 'anchor' defendant that is domiciled in the United Kingdom (against which jurisdiction is established via the Recast Brussels Regulations) and a foreign defendant (located in the jurisdiction in which the incident occurred),[5] will no longer be available to claimant parties (although this may change if the United Kingdom becomes a member of the Lugano Convention 2007). Claimants may now find it more

---

4 The Recast Brussels Regulation (Regulation (EU) No 1215/2012) is a legal framework which aims to improve and simplify cross-border litigation within the European Union. It addresses jurisdiction, recognition and enforcement of judgments in civil and commercial matters between EU member states.

5 In order for a claim to be brought against the 'foreign' defendant in such circumstances, it was necessary to meet the requirements of the 'necessary or proper party gateway', which is now enshrined in the Civil Procedure Rules. In order to utilise such gateway, the claimant must demonstrate the following:

(i) that the claims against the anchor defendant involve a real issue to be tried;
(ii) if so, that it is reasonable for the court to try that issue;
(iii) that the foreign defendant is a necessary or proper party to the claims against the anchor defendant;
(iv) that the claims against the foreign defendant have a real prospect of success; and
(v) that either England is the proper place in which to bring the combined claims or that there is a real risk that the claimants will not obtain substantial justice in the alternative foreign jurisdiction, even if it would otherwise have been the proper place, or the convenient or natural forum.

difficult to pursue claims before the English courts in respect of incidents that occurred in a foreign jurisdiction.[6]

The *forum non conveniens* ground was recently considered by the Court of Appeal in the matter of *Município de Mariana v BHP Group Plc (formerly BHP Billiton Plc)*[7] and, given the increased likelihood that defendants will rely upon this defence going forward, is worth considering.

The *Mariana* claim was brought in relation to the collapse of a tailings dam in Brazil in 2015, which caused the release of around 40 million cubic metres of tailings from an iron ore mine. The collapse and flood killed 19 people and destroyed entire villages; it has been described as Brazil's worst environmental disaster, with costs of remediation and compensation estimated to be around US$25 billion.

The dam was owned and operated by Samarco Mineração SA (Samarco), a Brazilian company jointly owned in equal shares by two other Brazilian companies, Vale SA (Vale) and BHP Billiton Brasil Ltda (BHP Brazil). BHP Brazil is a subsidiary within the BHP group. The defendants in the *Mariana* claim, BHP England and BHP Australia, sit at the head of the BHP group. The *forum non conveniens* argument was only advanced by BHP Australia (as BHP England is incorporated in the United Kingdom so that the Recast Brussels Regulation applied).

As explained by the court in the *Mariana* judgment, in order to succeed with a *forum non conveniens* defence, a defendant would need to satisfy a two-stage test:[8] first, to show that there is another available forum of competent jurisdiction which is clearly and distinctly more appropriate as the forum, in which the case may be tried more suitably for the interests of all the parties and the ends of justice. Second, even if the defendant satisfies that burden, the court will nevertheless refuse a stay (and therefore hear the matter) if the claimant satisfies it that there are circumstances by reason of which justice requires such refusal, including in particular if it is established by cogent evidence that there is a real risk that the claimant will not obtain justice in the foreign forum. BHP's application succeeded in the first instance but was overturned by the Court of Appeal.

Notably, in the *Vedanta* matter (the details of which are set out in further detail below), notwithstanding that the Supreme Court concluded that Zambia was the proper place in which the case should be tried, the court determined that there was a real risk that substantial justice would not be obtainable in that foreign jurisdiction (ie, stage 2 was satisfied by the claimant such that the *forum non conveniens* argument was defeated). The key reasons which led to this decision

---

6 Matters recently decided by the Supreme Court (*Okpabi* and *Vedanta*) and Court of Appeal (*Mariana*) concerned issues of jurisdiction; however, in each of these cases, the Recast Brussels Regulations still applied.

7 [2022] EWCA Civ 951.

8 See [2022] EWCA Civ 951 at paragraphs 316 to 327.

included the absence of funding in Zambia (legal aid was not available and claims could not be funded by a conditional fee agreement, which is unlawful in Zambia) and the court's finding that the Zambian legal profession lacked the resources and experience with which to conduct such litigation successfully.[9]

Of course, it is not only for reasons of justice that claims may be commenced in an alternative jurisdiction; it may therefore be helpful for the reader to have an awareness of other reasons why the English courts may be preferred over another jurisdiction (noting that what may be helpful to the claimant may not be helpful to the defendant). These factors include publicity (claims brought in the English courts against large mining or energy companies are likely to attract media interest which can have the effect of applying pressure on the defendant company to settle the matter out of court), the independence of the English judiciary,[10] the experience that the English courts have in relation to large-scale, complex claims and/or group litigation/class actions and, last but not least, the breadth and depth of English jurisprudence (should it apply).[11]

4. Negligence

Noting that the grounds on which private law claims are frequently advanced are nuisance and/or negligence, recent cases suggest that the latter area is expanding, potentially as a consequence of changing attitudes to the environment and ESG obligations.[12]

The requirements of a claim for negligence under English law are: (i) that the claimant has suffered a type of harm (loss, injury or damage) which can be the subject matter of a claim in negligence; (ii) the existence in law of a duty of care; (iii) a breach of that duty of care; (iv) a causal connection between the defendant's careless conduct and the damage that has occurred; and (v) that the particular kind of damage to the particular claimant is not so unforeseeable as to be too remote.[13]

The English common law confines a duty of care since to do otherwise

---

9 See paragraphs 177 to 198 of the judgment of Justice Coulson ([2016] EWHC 975 (TCC)). See also paragraph 89 of the judgment of the Supreme Court ([2019] UKSC 20).

10 In *Vedanta*, referring to litigation that had come before the Zambian courts, Justice Coulson (the judge at first instance) stated that "I cannot discount the findings of [the Zambian judge] that [the defendant] was shielded from prosecution by political connections and financial influence". See [2016] EWHC 975 (TCC) at paragraph 197.

11 English law is the foundation for many legal systems around the world; it is also the case that many foreign courts are permitted to take into account the position at English law, particularly where judicial authority in the foreign jurisdiction is limited.

12 This chapter focuses on the position under English law. However, there is an increase in ESG-related litigation worldwide shaping and developing the legal landscape. Notably, in a 2021 landmark ruling, the District Court of The Hague ruled that Shell was required to reduce its greenhouse gas emissions globally by 45% by 2030, on the basis that it had a duty of care to take steps to mitigate climate change (*Milieudefensie et al v Royal Dutch Shell*). This encouraged similar cases to be brought by environmental groups in other jurisdictions. In November 2024, however, The Hague Court of Appeal allowed Shell's appeal in the aforementioned case, ruling that Shell is not required to reduce emissions by a specified percentage when deciding how to achieve climate targets. The law in this area, and the approach of courts in various jurisdictions in ESG-related cases, is expected to continue to evolve.

13 *Clerk & Lindsell on Torts*, 24th edition, Chapter 7, Section 1, paragraph 7-04.

would risk opening the litigation floodgates. However, the list of situations that give rise to a duty of care is not fixed; rather, the English courts have expressly recognised that this concept may develop and adapt to social conditions and standards and the "changing circumstances of life".[14] It is therefore unsurprising that in an era when standards in relation to environmental obligations are developing and changing apace, claimant parties might pursue claims that seek to stretch established boundaries of duty and liability.

The cases referred to below are cases that have recently come before the English courts. In addition to providing guidance as to how future matters may be decided in the same forum, where the claim is advanced under English law, these cases may also provide guidance as to how courts in other common law jurisdictions may approach negligence claims.

4.1 *Vedanta*

The *Vedanta* matter relates to alleged toxic emissions from the Nchanga Copper Mine in the Chingola District of Zambia. The claimants, numbering 1,826 Zambian citizens living in the Chingola district, alleged that their health and farming activities had been damaged by repeated discharges of toxic matter from the mine from 2005 onwards. The defendants to the proceedings were the mine owner, Konkola Copper Mines plc (KCM), a significant public company incorporated in Zambia and Vedanta Resources plc (Vedanta), KCM's ultimate parent company; it is also the parent of a multinational group and is listed on the London Stock Exchange.[15]

The claimants brought claims in the English High Court,[16] alleging common law negligence and breach of statutory duty. The claims were advanced against KCM on the basis that it was the operator of the mine; as against Vedanta, a duty of care was said to have been assumed as a result of Vedanta's assumption of responsibility "for ensuring that [KCM's] mining operations do not cause harm to the environment or local communities".[17] This was said to be evidenced by the "very high level of control and direction that [Vedanta] exercised at all material times over the mining operations of [KCM] and its compliance with applicable health, safety and environmental standards".[18] The claimants relied on (among other things) material published by Vedanta in which it asserted its responsibility

---

14 In the seminal case of *Donoghue v Stevenson* [1932] AC 562 Lord Macmillan stated (at 619): "The grounds of action may be as various and manifold as human errancy; and the conception of legal responsibility may develop in adaptation to altering social conditions and standards. The criterion of judgment must adjust and adapt itself to the changing circumstances of life. The categories of negligence are never closed."

15 KCM is not a 100% subsidiary of Vedanta, as the Zambian government holds a significant minority stake, but the court noted that materials published by Vedanta state that its ultimate control of KCM is not thereby to be regarded as any less than it would be if wholly owned.

16 [2016] EWHC 975 (TCC).

17 *Ibid.* at paragraph 31.

18 *Ibid.*

for the establishment of appropriate group-wide environmental control and sustainability standards, for their implementation throughout the group by training and for their monitoring and enforcement.[19]

The jurisdiction of the English courts was unsuccessfully disputed by Vedanta and KCM (both in the first instance[20] and on appeal to the Court of Appeal[21] and Supreme Court[22]). The Supreme Court decision, handed down in April 2019, determined that the English courts did have jurisdiction to hear the claims on the basis that there was a real risk that substantial justice would not be obtainable if the claims were to be heard in the foreign jurisdiction (Zambia).

The Supreme Court also considered whether there was a real issue to be tried against Vedanta. On this issue, the critical question identified by the Supreme Court was whether Vedanta sufficiently intervened in the management of the mine to have incurred a common law duty of care to the claimants.[23] In short, the Supreme Court rejected the notion that the liability of parent companies in relation to activities of their subsidiaries was a distinct category of liability in common law negligence. The Supreme Court clarified that direct or indirect ownership by one company of all or a majority of the shares of another company may enable the parent to take control of the management of the operations of the business or of land owned by a subsidiary (but did not impose a duty to do so), which may give rise to a duty of care to third parties. Whereas the Supreme Court considered that cases where a duty of care might arise included: (i) where a parent had in substance taken over the management of the relevant activity of the subsidiary in place of or jointly with the subsidiary's own management; and (ii) where the parent has given relevant advice to the subsidiary about how it should manage a particular risk,[24] the Supreme Court was reluctant to seek to shoehorn all cases into these categories, stating that there is no limit to the models of management and control which may be put in place within a multinational group of companies.[25]

As to whether or not the laying down of group-wide policies and guidelines by the parent company in expectation that each subsidiary comply with them would cause the parent company to incur a duty of care, the Supreme Court did not rule out that such acts could have such a consequence. The Supreme Court also considered that where a parent company took active steps, by training, supervision and enforcement, to see that the policies were implemented, or

---

19 See [2016] EWHC 975 (TCC) at paragraph 119 and [2019] UKSC 20 at paragraph 55.

20 [2016] EWHC 975 (TCC) at paragraph 31.

21 [2017] EWCA Civ 1528.

22 [2019] UKSC 20.

23 Although this was a matter of Zambian law, the English courts decided the issue by reference to English law on the basis that it was arguable that the Zambian courts would identify the relevant principles of Zambian common law in accordance with those established in England – see [2019] UKSC 20 at paragraph 56.

24 These were categories identified by Sales LJ in *AAA v Unilever plc* [2018] EWCA Civ 1532 at paragraph 37.

25 [2019] UKSC 20 at paragraph 51.

where a parent company held itself out as exercising that degree of supervision and control of its subsidiaries (even if it did not in fact do so) that this may give rise to a duty of care to third parties.

Notably, the High Court, Court of Appeal and Supreme Court each formed the view that the materials relied upon by the claimants were indicative of at least an arguable case that Vedanta owed a duty of care (although their views differed somewhat as to the material by which they were persuaded).

This is a potentially important decision for mining companies; apart from confirming that a parent company may have a duty of care to third parties by reason of the activities of their subsidiaries, such duty may be shown to exist by reason of the assumption of responsibility by the parent company for maintenance of proper standards of environmental control over the activities of its subsidiaries. In an era where multinational companies commonly publish (and often report against) group-wide ESG commitments, it seems that in doing so, the seeds may be planted for third parties to argue (and evidence) that a duty of care has been incurred.

4.2 *Okpabi*

Not long after deciding the *Vedanta* case, the Supreme Court decided the matter of *Okpabi and others* (Okpabi) *v Royal Dutch Shell plc* (RDS).[26] This matter concerned over 40,000 Nigerians from two communities in Rivers State, Nigeria, who claimed that numerous oil spills had occurred from oil pipelines and associated infrastructure in the vicinity of the claimants' communities which had caused widespread environmental damage, including serious water and ground contamination. As a consequence of these spills, it was alleged that the communities' water sources were not safe for drinking, fishing, agriculture, washing or recreational purposes.[27] The oil spills were said to have been caused by the negligence of the pipeline operator, Shell Petroleum Development Company of Nigeria Ltd (SPDC), a Nigerian registered company. Okpabi also brought proceedings against RDS, of which SPDC was a subsidiary. Okpabi claimed that RDS owed a common law duty of care because it exercised significant control over material aspects of SPDC's operations and/or assumed responsibility for SPDC's operations, including by the promulgation and imposition of mandatory health, safety and environmental policies, standards and manuals which allegedly failed to protect Okpabi against the risk of foreseeable harm arising from SPDC's operations.

The case advanced by Okpabi was that the duty of care owed by RDS arose through four routes which were described as the 'Vedanta' routes. These were as follows:

---

26 *Okpabi and others (Appellants) v Royal Dutch Shell Plc and another (Respondents)* [2021] UKSC 3.
27 *Ibid* at paragraphs 3 and 4.

- RDS taking over the management or joint management of the relevant activity of SPDC;
- RDS providing defective advice and/or promulgating defective group-wide safety/environmental policies which were implemented as matter of course by SPDC;
- RDS promulgating group-wide safety/environmental policies and taking active steps to ensure their implementation by SPDC; and
- RDS holding out that it exercises a particular degree of supervision and control of SPDC.

Okpabi asserted that these 'routes' were evidenced by (among other things) RDS having established a global Health, Security, Safety and Environment (HSSE) policy, RDS monitoring compliance with this standard, RDS's CEO and executive committee having overall responsibility for implementing HSSE standards and social performance for its subsidiaries and the establishment of a corporate and social responsibility committee (which reported to RDS's board of directors).[28] The court noted that all of these allegations were particularised, many with references to published documents such as RDS's sustainability reports.

Okpabi also relied upon an 'RDS control framework' which set out the control framework that applied to all Shell companies and the RDS HSSE control framework. These were said to demonstrate that the Shell Group is organised along business and functional lines rather than simply according to corporate status,[29] such that organisational authority would first be provided at RDS level (ie, parent company level) before formal approval was provided by a particular legal entity such as SPDC (ie, the subsidiary). In summary, Okpabi alleged that RDS had deliberately structured the Shell Group in a way that enabled RDS to direct, control and intervene in the management of its subsidiaries' operations.

On this issue, the Supreme Court provided further clarification as to what may give rise to a duty of care as follows:

---

28 Other grounds relied upon included: RDS's responsibility for monitoring compliance by its subsidiaries with its business principles and standards, with the heads of businesses and functions reporting on this to the CEO at the end of each year; the laying out of standards by RDS for all its subsidiaries' assets, facilities and infrastructure and its assumption of responsibility for ensuring that best practice was observed and that unplanned releases of hydrocarbons were prevented; the fact that RDS's executive remuneration scheme depended to a significant degree on the sustainable development performance of SPDC, which had dragged overall Shell Group performance standards down; the fact that SPDC reported key performance indicators to RDS on a monthly basis, including asset maintenance, safety and the environment, and detailed business plans and budgets annually; the specific provisions made and the specific standards set by RDS for dealing with and responding to oil spills; RDS's control over its global oil spill response procedure; RDS's control over specific areas of SPDC's business and operations of particular relevance to the claim, including SPDC's security apparatus and pipeline replacement and divestment; and the fact that a number of individuals working for RDS played key roles in managing SPDC's business and operations.

29 *Okpabi and others (Appellants) v Royal Dutch Shell Plc and another (Respondents)* [2021] UKSC 3 at paragraphs 156 and 157.

- The promulgation by a parent company of group-wide policies or standards could give rise to a duty of care.[30]
- As to whether proof of the exercise of control by the parent company was critical to establishing a duty of care, the Supreme Court considered that control was "just the starting point".[31] For example, a parent might incur the relevant responsibility simply by holding out in published materials that it exercised the relevant degree of supervision and control of subsidiaries, even if it did not in fact do so.
- That it would be wrong to approach the issue of whether or not a duty of care was owed by reference to any generalised assumption or presumption (eg, the Supreme Court did not agree that, generally speaking, the establishment of a corporate structure of overseas subsidiaries with their own management structures gave rise to the presumption that no duty of care existed).[32]

On the question of whether or not there was a real issue to be tried, the Supreme Court considered that the pleaded case (which was fortified by the framework documents relied upon by Okpabi) supported there being a real issue to be tried under *Vedanta* routes 1 and 3.[33]

It is appropriate to emphasise that these decisions only determined issues of jurisdiction and did not finally determine the substantive issues. Nevertheless, given the court's decisions and given also that it is commonplace in the mining sector for a parent company to create health, safety and environmental standards and to seek to implement those standards on a group-wide basis, these decisions do appear to create a risk to parent-companies for acts or omissions of a subsidiary.

4.3 *Begum v Maran*

Another notable case that was recently decided by the English courts is that of *Hamada Begum v Maran (UK) Ltd.*[34] The case involved a claim brought on behalf of Mr Khalil Mollah who fell to his death while working on the demolition of a vessel in a shipyard in Bangladesh. Claims were advanced under English law

---

30 In response to a finding by the Court of Appeal to the contrary, the Supreme Court stated: "To the extent that the Court of Appeal indicated that the promulgation by a parent company of group wide policies or standards can never in itself give rise to a duty of care, that is inconsistent with Vedanta." See *Okpabi and others (Appellants) v Royal Dutch Shell Plc and another (Respondents)* [2021] UKSC 3 at paragraph 143.

31 *Okpabi and others (Appellants) v Royal Dutch Shell Plc and another (Respondents)* [2021] UKSC 3 at paragraph 147.

32 *Ibid* at paragraph 150.

33 Given the Supreme Court considered that it had been established that there was a real issue to be tried under these routes, the Supreme Court did not consider it necessary to make any ruling regarding routes 2 and 4 – see *Okpabi and others (Appellants) v Royal Dutch Shell Plc and another (Respondents)* [2021] UKSC 3 at paragraph 153.

34 [2020] EWHC 1846 (QB); [2021] EWCA Civ 326.

and, in the alternative, under Bangladeshi law. In response, the defendant sought summary judgment[35] for the claims to be struck out.

The application required the High Court to determine whether there were viable claims in English law in (among other claims) the tort of negligence. In particular, the claimant alleged that Maran was factually and legally responsible for the vessel ending up in Bangladesh, where working conditions were known to be highly dangerous.[36] That allegation was made in the context of there being a number of parties to which ownership of the vessel was transferred after Maran disposed of the vessel, that were not related to Maran. Nevertheless, the claimant invited the court to infer that Maran knew that the vessel would be broken up in Bangladesh.[37] The High Court was then asked to determine (among other things) whether the defendant owed a duty of care to the deceased.[38]

Following analysis of the defendant's arguments and relevant jurisprudence, the High Court found that the facts of the case did not fit neatly into any of the recognised exceptions to the basic principle that there can be no liability by one party for the conduct of a third party. The High Court went on to state that:

> *... the endeavour is not to strive to find a remedy in order to punish allegedly unscrupulous shipowners and their agents seeking to shuffle off their responsibilities for these vessels. The correct approach must be to seek to ascertain whether, recognising the general rule that liability cannot attach in the absence of a relationship of proximity between the parties, it can fairly and properly be said that the defendant created a danger to which the deceased was exposed, thereby creating the requisite legal nexus.*[39]

The High Court referred to this as the "creation of danger" principle.[40]

The High Court recognised that there were:

---

35 Summary judgment may only be ordered if the court considers that the claimant has no real prospect of succeeding on its claim. Such a decision is to be reached without conducting a mini-trial or anticipating what disclosure may provide. See, for example, paragraph 5 of the court's judgment ([2020] EWHC 1846 (QB)).

36 For the purpose of the application, the defendant accepted that the method by which the vessel was demolished, referred to as the "beaching" method, and which method had been carried out in India, Pakistan and Bangladesh since 1960 was an inherently dangerous working practice (EWHC 1846 (QB) at paragraph 13).

37 The key parts of the claimant's pleaded case were as follows:

> *88. At all material times, the Defendant owed the Deceased a common law duty of care. The duty of care required the Defendant to take all reasonable steps to ensure that its negotiated and agreed end of life sale and the consequent disposal of the Vessel for demolition would not and did not endanger human health, damage the environment and/or breach international regulations for the protection of human health and the environment.*
>
> *89. The Claimant contends that the duty of care falls within well recognised categories of the tort of negligence. In particular, it concerns the duty owed by a party who was fully aware, by virtue of their position within the international shipping industry that their act/omissions would directly expose highly vulnerable third parties to the risk of death and very serious injury. Alternatively, the Claimant avers that it would be just and reasonable to impose a duty of care.*

38 Since the judgment was made in response to an application for summary judgment, as the court acknowledged, at a minimum it was necessary to determine whether the claimant had a real prospect of establishing the existence of such a duty on the facts (EWHC 1846 (QB) at paragraph 20).

39 [2020] EWHC 1846 (QB) at paragraph 53.

40 [2020] EWHC 1846 (QB) at paragraph 53.

> *... arguments which cut both ways as to whether considerations of fairness, justice and reasonableness, the safeguarding of the environment and exploited workers in the developing world, and commercial practice, should operate in a case such as this to guide the court in placing it either within or without the creation of danger principle, in so doing possibly slightly stretching the boundaries of established norms.*[41]

However, the High Court considered that the basis upon which a duty of care might be founded (whether by reference to the court's preferred analysis, the creation of danger principle or the claimant's alternative case, that the court should extend the law on an incremental basis in line with what was fair, just and reasonable) was an area of law which was "uncertain across the board and may be developing";[42] as such, it was not appropriate for summary judgment.

The Court of Appeal had some sympathy with the defendant's submission that the ramifications of finding a duty of care in this context might be "extremely far-reaching".[43] Nonetheless, it recognised the 'creation of danger' exception,[44] and agreed with the High Court that the alleged duty of care was at least arguable such that it should not be struck out or decided at an interim stage by way of summary judgment.[45] It is possible that claimant parties will seek to expand this developing area in future mining claims against the relevant parent company.

5. Shareholder derivative claims

Another potential avenue for litigants seeking to impact corporate behaviour in respect of ESG commitments is for shareholders of a company to bring a claim, on behalf of the company, against directors of the company for breach of directors' duties owed to the company. Referred to as a 'shareholder derivative claim', the claimant shareholder(s) must first obtain the permission of the High Court[46] to bring such a claim.

In 2023, ClientEarth, a non-profit environmental law organisation made such application, alleging that directors of Royal Dutch Shell plc (Shell) had breached their directors' duties. The claims were said to arise out of acts or omissions relating to Shell's climate change risk management strategy. Breaches

---

41 [2020] EWHC 1846 (QB) at paragraph 63.
42 [2020] EWHC 1846 (QB) at paragraph 64.
43 [2021] EWCA Civ 326 at paragraph 66.
44 [2021] EWCA Civ 326 at paragraphs 52–65.
45 [2021] EWCA Civ 326 at paragraphs 66 and 72.
46 The derivative claim is addressed at length in chapter 6 of Robin Hollington, *Hollington on Shareholders' Rights*, 10th edition, 2023. Briefly, the proper claimant where a company has been wronged is through its proper constitutional organs. However, given that a director who has breached his or her director's duties is unlikely to initiate proceedings in respect of such wrongdoing, derivative claims exist as the exception to the rule, permitting shareholders (acting on behalf of the company) to seek redress in respect of such breaches. This is a statutory remedy, which may be advanced under Part 11 (Sections 260 to 269) of the Corporations Act 2006. It only applies to a company incorporated under this act such that it does not permit claims to be advanced against foreign companies.

relating to an order of The Hague District Court in relation to Shell were also alleged.[47]

The directors' duties relied upon by ClientEarth included the duty to promote the success of Shell (Section 172 of the Companies Act 2006) and the duty to exercise reasonable care, skill and diligence (Section 172 of the Companies Act 2006). ClientEarth pleaded that duties that were incidental to these statutory duties included: (i) a duty to make judgments regarding climate risk based upon a reasonable consensus of scientific opinion; (ii) a duty to accord appropriate weight to climate risk; (iii) a duty to implement reasonable measures to mitigate the risks to the long-term financial profitability and resilience of Shell in the transition to a global energy system and economy aligned with the global temperature objective of 1.5°C under the Paris Agreement on Climate Change 2015; (iv) a duty to adopt strategies which are reasonably likely to meet Shell's targets to mitigate climate risk; (v) a duty to ensure that the strategies adopted to manage climate risk are reasonably in the control of both existing and future directors; and (vi) a duty to ensure that Shell takes reasonable steps to comply with applicable legal obligations.

ClientEarth sought to rely upon the fact that directors had, by adopting an energy transition strategy which set an overall target for Shell to become a net zero energy business by 2050, identified that its climate strategy is a commercial objective which is most likely to promote the success of Shell.[48] It was said that Shell had thereby determined that this target was, among other measures, necessary to protect medium- and long-term shareholder value. Given this is a target adopted by a number of multinational corporations in the mining (and energy) space, a decision in favour of ClientEarth would likely have led to further claims of this type being initiated against mining companies.[49]

However, the application was not successful. What seems to have proved fatal to this claim (and what is likely to prove a difficult hurdle to overcome in claims of this type) is that the specific duties which Shell was said to be in breach of were found to be inconsistent with the well-established principle that it is for directors themselves to determine (acting in good faith) how best to promote the success of a company for the benefit of its members as a whole.[50] For example, in circumstances where Shell did have policies and targets in place to achieve net zero by 2050, ClientEarth had failed to show that 'no reasonable director' could have properly adopted such approach. Here, the court

47 On 26 May 2021, The Hague District Court handed down its judgment in the matter of *Milieudefensie v Royal Dutch Shell plc* ECLI:NL:RBDHA:2021:5339.

48 [2023] EWHC 1897 (Ch) at paragraph 24.

49 Simply by way of example, BHP sets out its GHG emission reduction targets and goals on its webpage; these include a 'target' to "Reduce operational greenhouse gas emissions by at least 30% from FY2020 levels" and a 'goal' to "Achieve net zero operational greenhouse gas emissions" by 2050, www.bhp.com/sustainability/climate-change.

50 [2023] EWHC 1897 (Ch) at paragraph 28.

recognised that the management of a business of the size and complexity of that of Shell will require the directors to take into account a range of competing considerations, the proper balancing of which is a classic management decision with which the court is ill-equipped to (and, therefore, was not inclined to) interfere.

6. Human Rights Act

Another avenue that claimant parties have sought to rely upon to advance climate change related claims is enforcement of human rights obligations, as illustrated by the recent decision in *Verein KlimaSeniorinnen Schweiz and Others v Switzerland*[51] in which the European Court of Human Rights (ECtHR) issued a ruling on climate change. This decision has the potential to impact individuals, corporations and governments involved in mining projects (and beyond).

In summary, the applicants[52] applied to the ECtHR alleging that their human rights were being violated by Switzerland's failure to take sufficient action against climate change.[53] The application accused the Swiss Confederation of failing to enact and implement adequate climate change legislation to, among other things, ensure respect for private and family life (Article 8).

The ECtHR found that there was a violation of the right for respect for private and family life under Article 8. It held that "Article 8 must be seen as encompassing a right for individuals to effective protection by the State authorities from serious adverse effects of climate change on their life, health, well-being and quality of life".[54] As a result, the ECtHR ruled that Switzerland owed positive obligations concerning climate change under Article 8:

> *The State's obligation under Article 8 is to do its part to ensure such protection. In this context, the State's primary duty is to adopt, and to effectively apply in practice, regulations and measures capable of mitigating the existing and potentially irreversible, future effects of climate change. This obligation flows from the causal relationship between climate change and the enjoyment of Convention rights.*[55]

The ECtHR held that Switzerland failed to comply with this newly stated positive obligation, as critical gaps existed in its climate change legislation. Such

---

51 *Verein KlimaSeniorinnen Schweiz and Others v Switzerland*, Application no 53600/20.

52 The applicants comprised the applicant association (Verein KlimaSeniorinnen Schweiz) and four of its members (the individual applicants).

53 The applicants initially requested, on 25 November 2016, that the Federal Council, Federal Department of the Environment, Transport, Energy and Communications, Federal Office for the Environment and the Federal Office for Energy in Switzerland to provide legal remedies regarding omissions by the Swiss Confederation *vis-à-vis* climate protection. The application was dismissed, as were appeals on 25 April 2017, 27 November 2018 and 5 May 2020. The applicants then lodged an application with the ECtHR on 26 November 2020.

54 See the judgment dated 9 April 2024 at paragraph 519.

55 *Ibid* at paragraph 545.

failures included not quantifying a carbon budget or limitations on greenhouse gas (GHG) emissions and failing to meet its own past GHG emission budgets.[56]

The ECtHR's decision garnered mixed reviews and it remains to be seen how the decision will be implemented. For some, this decision has the potential to create a radical change in domestic law that may have a serious and wide-ranging impact on all areas of government (including creating positive obligations to act). For others, the decision represents a clear elaboration and application of ECtHR principles, which is unlikely to lead to any significant changes in state policy.

However, given that potential repercussions of the decision include the implementation of more rigorous legislation to regulate GHG emissions, along with stricter enforcement mechanisms to ensure compliance (and given also that mining is currently responsible for 4% to 7% of GHG emissions globally),[57] the mining industry may come under increasing pressure to be part of the decarbonisation solution.

7. Conclusion

As illustrated above, the categories of claims which continue to be brought against mining companies, the jurisdictions in which such claims are pursued (ie, including outside of the jurisdiction of the project) and the 'model' of litigation adopted (pursuing the parent company and relevant subsidiary) are not novel. What does appear to have changed in recent years is an increased focus on ESG obligations and climate change risk (by governments and companies alike) and reliance upon those ESG obligations/commitments by claimant parties, either to establish a duty of care and/or evidence a claim. In an age where companies are under increasing pressure to prepare and publish their own (satisfactory) ESG obligations, to operate in compliance with those obligations and report against them, corporate accountability (including at the parent company level) is likely to be an area of continued and increasing scrutiny and litigation risk for companies operating in the mining sector.

The author would like to thank Leontine Mathew, senior associate at CMS Cameron McKenna Nabarro Olswang LLP, for her assistance with this chapter.

---

56 *Ibid* at paragraphs 558 to 574.

57 McKinsey reported in a 2020 climate risk and decarbonisation article on the mining sector as follows: "Scope 1 and Scope 2 CO2 emissions from the sector (those incurred through mining operations and power consumption, respectively) amount to 1 percent, and fugitive-methane emissions from coal mining are estimated at 3 to 6 percent. A significant share of global emissions – 28 percent – would be considered Scope 3 (indirect) emissions, including the combustion of coal." See www.mckinsey.com/capabilities/sustainability/our-insights/climate-risk-and-decarbonization-what-every-mining-ceo-needs-to-know.

Mine closure, land reclamation and legacy projects

Jeff Parshley
SRK Consulting (US) Inc

1. Introduction

Mine closure encompasses a multifaceted and intricate process and critical phase in the life cycle of a mining operation, involving the mitigation of environmental and public health and safety impacts, reduction of legal and financial liabilities, and compliance with regulatory frameworks. Mine closure – and post-closure – are now recognised as integral parts of the mining life cycle that require early planning and a holistic approach to mitigate some of the impacts of mining and restore the mining area to a safe and productive condition.

Historically, the primary focus of mine closure – environmental protection and public health and safety – was largely driven by laws and regulations. While these objectives are still critical to good mine closure planning, the approach to closure and closure planning has evolved to include collaboration with a broad group of stakeholders, including affected communities, the general public, company shareholders, traditional landowners/users, employees and government entities.

2. Planning and designing for closure

The concept of planning for closure has evolved significantly since the 1990s. Before then, there was limited understanding and acknowledgement of the necessity for closure planning, but by the 1990s the industry recognised the importance of early planning. The period from 2000 to 2004 marked a learning phase where the industry realised the gaps in their knowledge and understanding, leading to numerous changes in regulations, corporate policies and international standards. The post-2004 era has been characterised by increased involvement from capital providers and the influence of social media, emphasising the importance of sustainable development and socio-economic impacts. These developments reflect an increasing recognition of the need for sustainable development practices and the role of stakeholders in the closure process.

Because mining activities can significantly alter a landscape and can profoundly affect the social, cultural and economic fabric of surrounding communities. Depending on the type of mine and the environmental and social context of the affected area, the impacts can be significant and long-lasting. However, a well-designed closure plan developed as part of the initial mine design process can greatly facilitate closure and mitigation of adverse impacts. Some legal jurisdictions require preparation of a mine closure plan as part of the permitting process and many companies have developed internal standards and guidelines to ensure proper closure planning occurs even in jurisdictions where there is no legal requirement.

Although physical mine closure works occur primarily late in the mine life cycle, planning should begin early, preferably in the design phase of a mine. The IFC EHS guidelines for mining indicate mine closure plans should be "an integral part of the project life cycle".[1] By planning for closure early in the life of a mine, designs can incorporate closure considerations and operational plans developed to ensure closure objectives are met, and impacts are mitigated to the degree feasible given the site-specific context of the mine.

A well-structured mine closure plan integrates physical rehabilitation with socio-economic considerations to ensure long-term benefits for affected communities, minimise adverse impacts and maximise socio-economic benefits.[2] Because each mining site is unique, closure plans must consider the site-specific environmental and social context of the area and affected stakeholders.

Mine closure planning begins by acknowledging some changes caused by mining can be reversed or reduced with proper planning, but others will be permanent. With proper design, planning, operation and closure practices, the net impact can be positive. Effective mine planning starts with a clear vision of the end goal. The ICMM defines a closure vision as a "... high level aspirational description of what an operation or company and stakeholders want to achieve through implementation of the closure plan".[3] This vision should be translated into clear objectives and indicators for measuring success.

A common shared vision for the future of the mine site typically includes identification of future land uses, opportunities for repurposing of infrastructure and potential measures to help transition local communities from a mining to a post-mining economy. Future uses of the land and possibly mining infrastructure can be as simple as habitat restoration or as involved as development of alternative commercial or industrial uses, such as green power generation.

---

1 International Finance Corporation (IFC), "Environmental, Health, and Safety Guidelines – Mining", 10 December 2007.

2 *Ibid.*

3 International Council on Mining & Metals (ICMM), *Integrated Mine Closure, Good Practice Guide*, 2nd edition, 7 January 2019, www.icmm.com/website/publications/pdfs/environmental-stewardship/2019/guidance_integrated-mine-closure.pdf?cb=60008.

Once the closure goals have been defined, the closure planning team needs to assess data requirements, identify key risks, possible closure measures, closure scheduling and an estimated cost for closure. One typical outcome of this process is a work plan that identifies critical information gaps, assumptions that will be required in the absence of that information and a schedule for filling the gaps. The closure planning team should include closure specialists, government and community relations staff, environmental experts, mine waste engineers, hydrologists and hydrogeologists, geochemists, financial staff and mine planners – at a minimum. During the planning process, operational staff should be consulted to take advantage of opportunities to integrate closure planning with mine operations.[4]

Effective closure plans are not static, they are living documents that should constantly evolve over the life of the mine to reflect changes in the mine plan and additional information as it becomes available. "A closure plan is a dynamic document that needs to be regularly reviewed and progressively developed and refined over time to ensure that detail in the plan reflects current knowledge relevant to the development and rehabilitation status of the mine."[5] Many jurisdictions require regular updates to closure plans and estimated costs.

3. Future use and repurposing

The ultimate goal of mine closure is to ensure sustainable and beneficial post-mining land uses that protect public health and safety, comply with legal requirements and support community development. Future use viability assessments involve evaluating economically practical, technically achievable and legally compliant options that align with national and regional contexts. Stakeholder engagement and managing expectations are crucial in this process. Typical post-closure land use options include agriculture, forestry, nature conservation, clean energy generation and transmission, education and culture, tourism and recreation, aquaculture, and small and medium commercial or industrial enterprises.

Challenges to repurposing mining lands and infrastructure include legal requirements, technical constraints, local capacity and availability of financial resources for redevelopment. Addressing these challenges requires a clear understanding of the site's physical and socio-economic conditions and long-term community engagement. Long-term engagement with local communities and stakeholders is crucial to ensure the sustainability of repurposed land uses.

---

4 CD Grant and PR Botha, "Integrated closure planning: case studies on changing operational strategies to reduce closure liabilities" in AB Fourie, M Tibbett, L Sawatsky and D van Zyl (eds), *Mine Closure 2015*, InfoMine Inc, 2015.

5 World Bank Group, *Mine Closure: A Toolbox for Governments*, 23 April 2021, http://documents.worldbank.org/curated/en/278831617774355047/Mine-Closure-A-Toolbox-for-Governments.

4. Bio-physical closure

The objective of bio-physical mine closure requires careful planning and execution to ensure the site remains physically and chemically stable, safe for future use and capable of supporting biodiversity. The technical aspects of mine closure involve addressing several key components, including physical and chemical stability, biodiversity restoration and the mitigation of soil and water contamination.[6]

4.1 Physical stability

Mine closure must address the long-term physical stability of the site to prevent hazardous conditions, such as landslides, slope failures and accelerated erosion. The physical closure methods include reshaping and regrading the land to create stable landforms that can withstand natural erosive forces. Waste rock piles, tailings dams and other mine structures must be engineered to ensure they remain stable after closure under various environmental conditions. For instance, tailings dams should be designed to withstand future seismic events (in earthquake zones) and extreme weather events, including heavy rainfall. The purpose of ensuring long-term physical stability after closure is to prevent catastrophic failures that could cause public safety risks and/or lead to the release of contaminants into the environment, causing significant harm to ecosystems and nearby communities.

Slope stabilisation techniques often include the use of geotechnical engineering methods, such as buttressing slopes, installing drainage systems to manage water flow and applying erosion control measures like vegetation cover or synthetic liners. These measures are critical in ensuring the physical structures of the closed mine site do not degrade over time, leading to environmental contamination or safety hazards.

4.2 Chemical stability

Ensuring chemical stability is crucial to prevent the leaching of harmful substances, such as heavy metals and acid rock drainage/metal leaching (ARD/ML), into the surrounding environment. These potentially harmful constituents can be released from pit walls, tailings, waste rock and underground workings. ARD/ML can be a significant risk associated with mine closure, occurring when sulphide minerals in waste rock or tailings react with water and oxygen, producing sulfuric acid. This acid can then dissolve heavy metals from the surrounding rocks, leading to contamination of nearby water sources. Even under alkaline or neutral pH conditions, contaminants can be leached from mine waste facilities. Other sources of potential chemical instability at mine sites include residual processing reagents and laboratory wastes.

---

6 *Ibid.*

The potential for post-closure migration of contaminants from the site should be ascertained during baseline studies to allow for mitigation measures to be incorporated into the design of the mine, particularly the mine waste facilities. By determining the potential risk early, the operator can trial solutions and monitor the results at a field scale during operations.

To prevent contamination of the surrounding environment, various mitigation strategies can be employed. One effective method is the encapsulation of reactive materials in low permeability barriers, which prevent water and oxygen from reaching the contaminant sources. Another approach involves the use of alkaline materials, such as lime, to buffer acid and reduce leaching of deleterious constituents. Mitigation measurements for neutral drainage tend to focus on management of water through diversion or physical barriers (covers) that prevent water from contacting potentially leachable mine waste.

When contaminant sources cannot be sufficiently isolated and water resources are expected to be impacted, passive or active treatment may be required. The construction of wetlands or other passive treatment systems can naturally filter contaminants from water before they are released into the environment, using plants and microorganisms to absorb or break down pollutants. Active treatment of water after closure is generally considered a method of last resort as it is likely to require a long-term or perpetual obligation with significant economic implications.

The importance of maintaining chemical stability cannot be overstated, as the failure to do so can result in long-term environmental degradation, affecting human health, water quality, soil health and the overall ecosystem.

4.3 Biodiversity restoration

Restoring or enhancing biodiversity is a vital component of mine closure, as it helps to rehabilitate ecosystems that have been disturbed by mining activities and in accordance with the closure vision and future uses. The importance of biodiversity restoration lies in its ability to create sustainable habitats that support indigenous wildlife and contribute to the overall health of the ecosystem. The Mining Association of Canada's Biodiversity Conservation Management Protocol states reclamation and closure planning should consider the concept of No Net Loss.[7]

The process begins with soil restoration, as healthy soil is fundamental to supporting plant life. Techniques, such as replacing salvaged topsoil, applying organic amendments and carefully selecting native plant species that are well-suited to the local climate and soil conditions are essential.[8] By re-establishing

---

7 The Mining Association of Canada, *Facts & Figures 2021, The State of Canada's Mining Industry*, 9 March 2022, https://mining.ca/resources/reports/facts-figures-2021/.

8 World Bank Group, *Mine Closure: A Toolbox for Governments*, 23 April 2021, http://documents.worldbank.org/curated/en/278831617774355047/Mine-Closure-A-Toolbox-for-Governments.

self-sustaining native vegetation, mine closure can help to prevent soil erosion, improve water quality and provide food and shelter for animals, encouraging the return of species that may have been displaced by mining activities.

In some cases, mine closure offers opportunities to enhance biodiversity beyond the pre-mining baseline. For example, creating wetlands, ponds or other aquatic habitats can attract a variety of species and increase the ecological value of the site, which can support a greater diversity of species. Establishing or re-establishing conservation areas or wildlife corridors as part of the closure plan can also help connect fragmented habitats, allowing species to migrate and maintain healthy populations. The restoration of biodiversity is not only important for ecological reasons but also for the long-term sustainability of the site, as a diverse ecosystem is more resilient to environmental changes. Monitoring of success and/or desired trajectories of site biodiversity after closure ensures the site will remain stable and self-sustaining.[9]

4.4 Mitigation of soil and water contamination

Addressing soil and water contamination is critical during mine closure to protect human health and the environment. Contaminants, such as heavy metals, arsenic and cyanide, which may be present in mine tailings or waste rock, can leach into surrounding soils and water bodies posing risks to ecosystems and communities. Other potential contaminants associated with mining operations include fuels, lubricants, and process and laboratory chemicals.

To mitigate soil contamination, strategies include the removal of contaminated soils, the use of containment systems, such as liners or covers and *in situ* treatment methods that immobilise contaminants within the soil. For instance, phytoremediation, which involves the use of plants to absorb and concentrate contaminants from the soil, can be an effective and environmentally friendly method. Treatment – passive or active – can be used to treat contaminated water in or discharging from mine waste facilities. Treatment may only be required for a short period post-closure to treat residual process solutions, or long-term to manage post-closure discharges from mine waste facilities.

Passive systems, including constructed wetlands and evaporation, use natural processes to treat contaminated water, offering a low-maintenance, cost-effective solution for long-term water management. Active treatment plants can be used to dispose of remaining process solutions, such as tailings supernatant or to treat contaminants through processes like pH adjustment, filtration,

9 International Council on Mining & Metals (ICMM), *Integrated Mine Closure, Good Practice Guide*, 2nd edition, 7 January 2019, www.icmm.com/website/publications/pdfs/environmental-stewardship/2019/guidance_integrated-mine-closure.pdf?cb=60008.

chemical precipitation, reverse osmosis and ion exchange. Active management of water for the purposes of disposal of process solutions also includes active evaporation systems, such as snow-maker type evaporators.

5. Managing closure risks

Effective post-closure risk management requires a comprehensive approach that integrates technical, environmental and social considerations. This involves conducting detailed risk assessments throughout the mine life cycle to identify potential hazards, developing contingency plans to address unwanted events and involving stakeholders in the planning process to ensure their concerns are addressed. Financial provisions must also be made to ensure funds are available for ongoing maintenance and monitoring after the mine has closed.

6. Socio-economic transitioning

Boom and bust cycles are inherent to mining economies, leading to ghost towns once operations cease. These cycles involve phases of economic growth and decline, impacting employment, economic development and community services. Socio-economic transitioning aims to address these impacts by planning for a positive legacy through the integration of socio-economic aspects into the closure process. This involves proactive planning and recognising local values, needs, priorities and capacity. This transition is essential for mitigating significant socio-economic impacts on dependent communities, including direct and indirect employment, community services, health services and social investment programmes. Proactive planning and integration of socio-economic aspects into the closure process can create a positive legacy.

Socio-economic transitioning is a key component of the post-closure vision, which should be shared by all stakeholders, defined early in the mine life cycle and revised periodically. Benefits of socio-economic transitioning include creating sustainable opportunities, improving social licence, and reducing financial and reputational liabilities. It also ensures post-closure transitions are consistent with the socio-economic context and minimises stakeholder concerns regarding closure impacts.

The socio-economic component of the closure vision should be ambitious yet practical and achievable, based on a comprehensive understanding of the mining zone of influence, stakeholder relationships, government development goals, local capacity and land tenure. The closure plan must define specific, achievable social and economic objectives. These objectives should be informed by pre-closure baseline studies and impact assessments.

Proactive planning and integration of socio-economic aspects into the closure process can create a net positive legacy, facilitating a smoother transition for the affected communities. This requires early engagement and economic development planning during operations. Identifying and developing sustainable parallel economies by the time closure occurs requires that the process begins during operations and that clear division of responsibilities for future economic development are defined among mining companies, governments, NGOs and communities.[10] Mining companies support economic development programmes aimed at socio-economic transitioning, conduct pre-closure social baseline assessments, manage retrenchment and prepare sites and infrastructure for repurposing. Governments develop and implement laws and policies related to social aspects of closure, review closure plans and monitor post-closure activities. Communities provide input to the closure vision, collaborate with economic development programmes and assist in monitoring duties. Joint efforts by mining companies, governments, local communities and NGOs are required for effective stakeholder engagement, development of post-closure visions and implementation of socio-economic transitioning plans. Increasingly, public-private partnerships and other types of collaborative programmes are being considered for supporting socio-economic transitioning at mine closure, though examples of this are currently limited.[11]

The transition from a mining to a post-mining economic context can pose significant challenges. Operating mines usually have substantial positive socio-economic impacts on dependent communities, affecting direct and indirect employment, economic development, community services, health services and social investment programmes. At closure, many of these positive aspects will be eliminated or diminished. For many communities, particularly remote ones, the wealth generated during mining operations is often unsustainable post-closure, necessitating comprehensive assessments of socio-economic impacts prior to operations and as closure approaches. Challenges for socio-economic transitioning include limited government or local capacity, achieving meaningful engagement, managing expectations and defining measurable, achievable success criteria. In many jurisdictions weak legislation regarding socio-economic planning for closure further complicates the process.

As with all aspects of mine closure, monitoring of socio-economic conditions post-closure should be included as part of the process. This should focus on the effectiveness of measures implemented by monitoring, earnings relative to pre-mining conditions, continued operation of existing businesses, social investment programme, new businesses created, changing demographics and migration trends.[12]

---

10 World Bank Group, *Mine Closure: A Toolbox for Governments*, 23 April 2021, http://documents.worldbank.org/curated/en/278831617774355047/Mine-Closure-A-Toolbox-for-Governments.

11 *Ibid.*

12 International Council on Mining & Metals (ICMM), *Integrated Mine Closure, Good Practice Guide*, 2nd edition, 7 January 2019, www.icmm.com/website/publications/pdfs/environmental-stewardship/2019/guidance_integrated-mine-closure.pdf?cb=60008.

7. **Stakeholder engagement for closure**

Stakeholder engagement throughout the closure process is vital, commencing early and continuing through the mine's operational life. Many jurisdictions have enacted legislation that requires stakeholder engagement for mining projects, including as part of the closure planning process. International standards and best practice also require early and regular stakeholder engagement. This engagement for closure helps in setting realistic expectations, balancing stakeholder desires with practical opportunities, and determining funding and execution responsibilities for closure plans. Stakeholder engagement for closure should begin early but should increase as closure approaches and continue after closure is complete.[13]

8. **Financial responsibility for mine closure**

Mine closure can be expensive and should be incorporated into the design and planning throughout the mine life cycle. All the major mine closure guidelines and standards, and most mine closure legislation and corporate policies, acknowledge the financial responsibility of the mine operators for closure. Most mine closure legislation requires the estimation of closure cost as part of the permitting process, and many require operators to post a financial guarantee that covers the cost of closure. Financial reporting standards oblige operators to disclose any material closure obligations to shareholders. Mine operators recognise closure is a significant cost in the overall development of a mine and budget for it from early project development.

Successful mine closure requires comprehensive financial planning to ensure all necessary activities are adequately funded and avoid the risks associated with insufficient resources at the end of the mine's life. It involves estimating the costs of physical rehabilitation, socio-economic transitioning, post-closure monitoring and long-term management of the site. Because of the often-significant cost of closure, mining companies often manage mine closure as a capital project that requires adherence to corporate policies similar to those implemented for project approval. This requires thorough evaluation of requirements and options leading to risk assessment, trade-off studies and detailed design. A robust financial plan must then be developed for the final closure design. Funding mechanisms vary depending on the company, site and cost of the project.

Best practice requires the full cost of closure be estimated before operations begin and periodically reviewed and updated. The methods used in closure cost calculations range from benchmarking to use of average costs to detailed construction cost estimates. The most accurate cost estimates are those based on

---

13 World Bank Group, *Mine Closure: A Toolbox for Governments*, 23 April 2021, http://documents.worldbank.org/curated/en/278831617774355047/Mine-Closure-A-Toolbox-for-Governments.

a detailed closure plan and use accepted construction cost estimating methodologies, such as those approved by AACE International, including provisions for contingencies.

In addition to capital closure costs, post-closure site management costs must also be assessed, particularly for issues such as water treatment that may persist long after operations have ceased. These costs include environmental monitoring, maintenance of physical structures and any necessary remediation efforts to ensure the long-term stability and safety of the site. Estimation of these post-closure costs generally requires an understanding of expected annual operating costs and periodic sustaining capital costs, and the length of time during which these will be incurred. For projects requiring perpetual care, the trust must be funded and managed such that there will always be sufficient funds for estimated costs, accounting for inflation and providing a contingency to cover unanticipated expenses.

8.1 Financial assurance

The purpose of financial assurance in mine closure is to ensure the funds necessary for closure activities are available when needed, regardless of the financial condition of the mining company at the time of closure. Financial assurance mechanisms are designed to protect the public and the environment by providing a financial guarantee to ensure closure and reclamation activities are carried out even if the mining company is unable or unwilling to fulfil its obligations. This assurance is critical in safeguarding against the possibility of orphaned or abandoned mines, where the responsibility for closure and remediation might otherwise fall on the government or local communities.

The amount of financial assurance required varies based on the jurisdiction. A few require 100% of the estimated closure cost to be covered by a financial instrument before operations begin. Others require only a portion of the cost to be guaranteed, and still other jurisdictions will increase the amount of the financial assurance over time.[14]

Financial assurance may be phased to cover only those liabilities that will exist during a defined period, often determined by a permit renewal or review period. This approach protects the government from current and near-term liabilities but does not penalise the operator for future liabilities that have yet to be realised, such as a future tailings impoundment.

Various financial instruments are used for financial assurance depending on the jurisdictions, including surety bonds, letters of credit, trust funds, asset assignment, self-guarantees and insurance policies. Surety bonds and letters of credit are commonly used. Each type of instrument has its advantages and disadvantages, depending on the regulatory environment, the financial health

---

14 *Ibid.*

of the mining company and the specific requirements of the closure plan. For instance, surety bonds and letters of credit are often preferred for their liquidity and ease of access in case of default, while trust funds provide a more long-term, stable source of funding that can be built up over the life of the mine.[15] Trust funds, often established early in the life of a mine, accumulate funds over time to cover closure, and often post-closure costs. Insurance policies may also be used to cover specific risks associated with mine closure.

Long-term trusts are an increasingly common approach to funding post-closure site management. These trusts are established to ensure that sufficient funds are available for long-term management of the site. The use of long-term trusts is particularly important for ensuring the sustainability of closure outcomes, as they provide a dedicated source of funding that is insulated from the financial risks of the mining company. Trust funds are typically managed by an independent third party, ensuring the funds are used solely for their intended purpose.

The release of financial assurance is typically contingent upon the successful completion of closure activities as outlined in the mine closure plan. This process usually involves an inspection or inspections to confirm the site has been rehabilitated in accordance with the plan, environmental and safety standards have been met, and any post-closure monitoring or maintenance programmes are in place and functioning as required. The timing and conditions for the release of financial assurance vary depending on the jurisdiction and the specific terms of the financial instruments used but may occur progressively as closure of portions of the site is completed.

9. Closure timing

Generally, the majority of closure activities occur after mining and/or processing has ceased. In many cases, processing will continue beyond mining activities either by processing stockpiled ore or continuing mineral recovery operations. Typically, closure activities will be scheduled to allow maximum use of existing equipment and human resources, considering the most effective sequence for closure. Some facilities, such as equipment maintenance and fuelling facilities will need to remain until late in the closure period. Tailings impoundments are often closed progressively as they drain and consolidate, which may take years. The timing of post-closure activities is determined by the type and duration of activities required.

Although most closure actions occur after mining and/or processing ceases at a site, closure of facilities or portions of facilities may occur progressively during operations. Progressive or contemporaneous closure occurs when individual facilities or areas of the mine site have been completed and are no

15 *Ibid.*

longer needed for operations. Progressive closure not only reduces future closure liability, but it also provides an opportunity to test the effectiveness of the proposed methods and types of closure activities, such as cover designs, surface water management and revegetation performance at a field scale. Depending on availability of equipment and staff, progressive closure could occur continuously or periodically during operations. If monitoring of the progressive closure indicates alternatives to the currently proposed methods are needed, those approaches could be tested and modifications to the plan made, as required. Examples of areas upon which progressive closure could occur include waste rock dump lifts, tailings embankments and depleted pits.

10. Relinquishment

Relinquishment of responsibility for mine closure occurs when all closure goals are met and sufficient monitoring data have been collected to conclude the site is stable or is on a trend to being stable. The process for formal transfer of ownership and responsibility to another party, often the government, varies by jurisdiction. This is typically a formal process that requires a sign-off by the government and may include consultation with stakeholders.[16]

In some instances, and/or jurisdictions, relinquishment may not be possible or never fully occur. For example, in the United States, the federal government may invoke the Comprehensive Environmental Response, Compensation and Liability Act (CERCLA) to implement remedial measures and recover costs from responsible parties even if the site was previously relinquished under other legislation. In other jurisdictions, governments may be reluctant to assume future liability until there is overwhelming evidence the site is stable and will not pose future environmental or safety risks.

11. Abandoned mine sites

Planned mine closure refers to the orderly shutdown of mining operations according to a pre-established closure plan that addresses all necessary physical, environmental and social considerations. In contrast, abandoned mines are those where mining operations have ceased without proper closure, often leaving behind significant environmental and safety hazards. Abandoned mines may or may not have operated prior to the enactment of mine closure legislation and may pose substantial risks to the environment and nearby communities, because they generally have no responsible party to finance proper closure and remediation. In such cases, responsibility for closure rests with the government. The distinction between planned closure and abandoned mines highlights the importance of early and ongoing closure planning and

16 Australian Government Department of Industry, Innovation and Science, "Leading Practice Handbook: Mine Closure", September 2016.

financial assurance, as well as the need for effective regulatory frameworks to prevent mines from becoming abandoned.

Policy and funding for abandoned mine sites have become increasingly important, particularly in jurisdictions with a legacy of historic mining activities. Governments are often required to step in to manage these sites, with funding typically sourced from public and private funds or through special levies on the mining industry. In some cases, international organisations and development banks may also provide funding and technical assistance for the remediation of abandoned mines, particularly in developing countries where resources are limited. These policies aim to develop abandoned mine inventories and ensure abandoned mines are rehabilitated to a safe and stable condition, minimising their impact on the environment and surrounding communities.[17]

12. Mine closure governance frameworks

A mine closure governance framework consists of legislation (statutory and regulatory), policy and guidance, each serving different purposes with varying degrees of enforceability. Statutory legislation creates high-level obligations, such as requiring the submission of closure plans as part of a mining permit application.[18] Regulatory legislation provides detailed requirements for achieving the objectives set out in the statutory legislation and may define the processes for the collection of fees and enforcement. Policies include qualitative statements about the intent of the legislation and acceptable methods for demonstrating compliance. Guidance documents, produced by the government or referenced third-party documents, provide methodologies for achieving legislative objectives.

Benefits of a closure governance framework include providing a structured approach to managing mine closure, ensuring closure plans are developed and implemented consistently and addressing environmental and socio-economic impacts. Such a framework helps in mitigating long-term risks and liabilities associated with mine closure, promoting sustainable post-closure land use and ensuring closure activities are conducted in a manner that protects public health and safety.

An effective approach to developing a mine closure governance framework is described in *Mine Closure: A Toolbox for Governments* published by the World Bank.[19] The process involves creating a working group of key stakeholders who define the overall purpose, essential aspects of the framework and a process for

---

17 Intergovernmental Forum on Mining, Minerals, Metals and Sustainable Development, "Mining Policy Framework Mining and Sustainable Development", 2023.

18 World Bank Group, *Mine Closure: A Toolbox for Governments*, 23 April 2021, http://documents.worldbank.org/curated/en/278831617774355047/Mine-Closure-A-Toolbox-for-Governments.

19 *Ibid.*

implementation. Once the overall purpose is defined by the government in consultation with key stakeholders, a working group comprising key stakeholders, including representatives from the mining industry, finance, environmental and land use planning bodies, is formed to create a mutually acceptable risk-based framework acceptable to all parties.

Defining the objectives of the new framework is a critical early step, including review of similar in country or international frameworks and international guidelines. After reviewing any existing framework components and a comparison to other sources, the working group should conduct a gap analysis between existing legislation and the defined framework objectives.[20] Where gaps are identified in the current legal system, solutions implemented in other jurisdictions may address those gaps, possibly with modification. A draft framework is prepared with involvement from legal and technical experts. After the draft framework is reviewed and possibly provided to the general public for comment, it would be finalised by the working group. Often a trial or transition period is useful, particularly where no or a minimal framework previously existed, to test the framework. Feedback from the trial period could be used to refine the framework through modification of legislation and/or preparation of policies or guidance.

The time required to create an effective closure governance framework varies based on the legislative process in the country, local experience with mining, and the amount of training and guidance documentation required for mine operators and government regulators. Governments should expect that the framework will not be static and is likely to require modification periodically as the framework is implemented, information is gathered from operations and success of closure projects is monitored.

20 Asia-Pacific Economic Cooperation, *Mine Closure, Checklist for Governments*, February 2018.

Socio-economic impacts of mining and mineral development

Neal Brewster
Elemental Economics

1. Introduction

The socio-economic costs and benefits of mining have long been argued over and discussion as to whether mining represents a 'blessing' or a 'curse' hangs over the industry much more than other sectors. This can be a highly polarised debate, bringing together conflicting views on the relative importance of environmental versus development goals and intergenerational transfers of wealth. That most of the costs of mining are incurred locally, whereas a larger proportion of the benefits are shared nationally or globally, exacerbates tensions at different levels of society and between different parts of the world.

Moral questions enter this debate, such as: Who owns the Earth's resources and who is empowered to license their destruction? Who should benefit from the destruction of irreplaceable natural resources? How should the distribution in the consumption of mineral products be shared? And who has the moral right to deny aspiring poor countries or individuals the supply of the mineral resources required for them to achieve living standards enjoyed by today's rich? To put the scale of such questions and their implications for future minerals output in perspective, to reach its current level of development the United States has consumed over 23 tonnes of steel per capita and 0.5 tonnes of copper. These are 2.5× and 4× the global average respectively. For the world to equalise to the United States' historical total consumption would require current rates of global steel production to be maintained for 50 years, or 100 years in the case of copper.[1]

Over the last 20 years mining companies, governments and multinational bodies like the OECD have made great strides to better monitor the environmental, social and governance (ESG) impacts of mining activity and to improve industry standards and processes. Organisations such as the International Council on Mining and Metals (ICMM) have been established to coordinate such activity. Laws like the Dodd-Frank Act and the EU Conflict

1 Calculations based on data from the United States Geological Survey, the International Iron and Steel Institute and the International Copper Study Group.

Minerals Regulations have been passed to ensure that profits from mining are not used to perpetuate violence, that forced or child labour and the abuse of human rights is clamped down on, working conditions are made safer and that corruption and bribery is more properly addressed. In parallel, the industry has embarked on a concerted campaign to mend negative external perceptions about it and to engage more fully with its stakeholders. This is often characterised by the industry in terms of it maintaining its licence to operate. Views, however, differ as to whether the steps taken to date are sufficient to achieve this goal, especially given increasing societal expectations.

The importance of mineral products to society and to the economy, along with greater public awareness of their role, has been given impetus by the emergence of supply chain bottlenecks during and after the COVID-19 pandemic and from increasing global political tensions and concerns over the cost and access to critical raw materials necessary for defence and for the energy transition. Under its 2023 net zero emissions (NZE) scenario the International Energy Agency (IEA) project demand for lithium will rise by 454% between 2022 and 2030, cobalt demand will rise by 115%, neodymium by 103% and copper demand by 40%. Demand then keeps on growing strongly upwards to 2050 and beyond. In all of these cases the overwhelming driver behind increases in consumption is from clean energy technologies.[2] The supply challenge created by this rising demand generates both risks and opportunities for the mining sector, but undoubtedly raises its socio-economic profile.

2. The socio-economic benefits of mining

In many ways mining is an industry just like any other, with profit-seeking firms and individuals seeking to maximise their returns, while governments, state entities and civil society lobby, tax and regulate the sector according to their particular concerns or wants. Beyond such narrow interests though there is also a broader moral case for mining, resting on the proposition that:

- mined products are the 'vitamins' necessary for nearly all other economic activity;
- undiscovered or undeveloped ore deposits are valueless;
- most of the economic benefits of mining go to society; and
- mining can be the catalyst for wider economic development.

That mining is essential to the global economy and maintaining or improving living standards is hard to deny. Prehistoric eras – the stone, bronze and iron ages – were, after all, named after breakthroughs in the use of minerals and in mineral processing. Today, perhaps half of all economic activity would

---

2 IEA, "Critical Minerals Market Review 2023", July 2023, www.iea.org/reports/critical-minerals-market-review-2023.

cease if mining activity stopped. Maintaining crop yields relies upon nutrients such as potash and phosphate sourced from mining operations. Sand, gravel and aggregates along with steel are – literally – the foundations for constructing roads, houses, offices, schools and factories. Steel, whose constituents include iron ore, manganese, chrome and various noble alloys, base metals (including copper, aluminium, nickel, zinc and tin) along with a myriad of industrial minerals are used in a vast range of applications: from the generation and distribution of electricity to industrial plant and machinery, consumer durables, chemicals and even pharmaceutical products. Precious metals and diamonds are key to some manufacturing processes, in machine tools and as catalysts used in chemical processing and pollution control.

The energy transition depends on building massive new battery storage, which in turn presently requires significant quantities of battery raw materials including lithium, nickel, cobalt, manganese and graphite as well as copper and aluminium. Rare earths are a key constituent to the strong magnets used in motors and wind turbines. Silicon is a core component of computer chips, solar cells and fibreoptic cables.

It is sometimes argued that recycled materials could take up the slack if mining ceased. But while recycling accounts for a significant part of the supply of many minerals there is simply not enough recoverable secondary material available in nearly all mineral markets to meet current and future levels of demand. In some instances, recycling of minerals is physically limited or not possible and quality issues can limit the use of recycled material. In markets where mined materials are used as processing aids (as in plastics), in dissipative uses such as paints or gasoline additives, coatings, or as fillers and extenders for more valuable raw materials (as in the paper industry), they are not recyclable.

Where minerals are more easily recoverable, while enhanced policy measures, such as regulation, leaner processing and improvements in recycling technology, can partly close the gap not all obsolete material can be practically or economically recovered and the ratio of historical consumption to current levels globally is usually such that the pool of recyclable supply is insufficient to meet current levels of demand. While it is true that nearly all steel production in the United States is from recycled material, that is not the case globally. Despite rising efforts and incentives to improve recycling rates, the proportion of copper globally supplied by recycled material has remained at around one-quarter of total usage for the last quarter of a century.

Given this, and the natural tendency for mine production to decline as existing orebodies deplete, heavy thrifting or rationing of demand would be required to close the gap between supply and demand without new investment in mining. Absent this, mineral prices would rise to levels unlikely to be acceptable to society. While in time manufacturers would respond to such price hikes and shortages by adjusting their use of materials, as we have seen in the composition of battery metals over the last decade, such switching would simply replace use of one mined product for another.

While the full economic value of mineral products arguably goes well beyond their price, the direct economic importance of mining is only a small part of the global economy. The industry is heavily weighted towards use of capital rather than labour and the formal mining sector accounts for around 21 million employees or 0.6% of global employment. It represents around 1%–2% of global GDP and 4% of global merchandise trade.[3] Even more starkly, in terms of market capitalisation, the value of shares in Apple Inc of approximately $3 billion is significantly greater than that of all globally listed mining companies, and 25 times that of the largest individual listed mining company, BHP.[4]

A particular focus of governments in terms of measuring the economic importance of different parts of the economy is taxation. The top 40 mining companies paid $40 billion in corporation taxes in 2023.[5] This is a huge amount on its own, but previous studies have shown that corporate taxes represent just 40% of the total tax contribution of the industry after including royalties, mining taxes, employer social security, property taxes, payroll taxes, VAT and withholding taxes.[6] Across the whole of the mining sector its total direct tax contribution globally is therefore likely to be in the hundreds of billions of dollars. Mining companies also make significant payments directly to communities, in the order of $570 million for the gold sector alone in 2022.[7] Data for the overall social and economic contributions of the gold sector, compiled by the World Gold Council for 2022, are summarised in Figure 1.

Mining's direct share of global GDP of 1%–2% excludes the value of payments to suppliers and of economic activity induced by the distribution and spending of wages and profits from mining, or its multiplier effects across the broader economy. The level of this additional activity, and its location, depends on factors such as the proportion of inputs procured locally, domestic business capacities, the strength of supplier networks and their absorption capacities as the location and type of downstream mineral processing and end use markets. The World Gold Council estimates that for every direct mining job six jobs are indirectly supported and four additional jobs are induced.[8]

While the direct economic benefits of mining are a small part of the global

---

3 Calculations based on data from the International Labour Organization and the World Bank.

4 Yahoo finance, 26 February 2024, https://uk.finance.yahoo.com.

5 PwC, *Mine 2024*, 21st edition, Preparing for Impact, June 2024, www.pwc.com/gx/en/mining/assets/pwc-global-mine-2024.pdf.

6 PwC, *Total Tax Contribution: Understanding the economic contribution that large companies make to UK public finances*, March 2011, www.pwc.co.uk/assets/pdf/total-tax-contribution-hundred-group-report-final.pdf.

7 World Gold Council, *The social and economic contribution of gold mining – 2023 data update*, www.gold.org/esg/the-social-and-economic-contribution-of-gold-mining-2023-data-update.

8 World Gold Council, *The Social and Economic Contribution of Gold Mining*, 2021, www.gold.org/esg/the-social-and-economic-contribution-of-gold-mining#:~:text=This%20report%20provides%20quantitative%20insights,national%20and%20local%20community%20level.

Figure 1. Social and economic contribution of gold mining in 2022

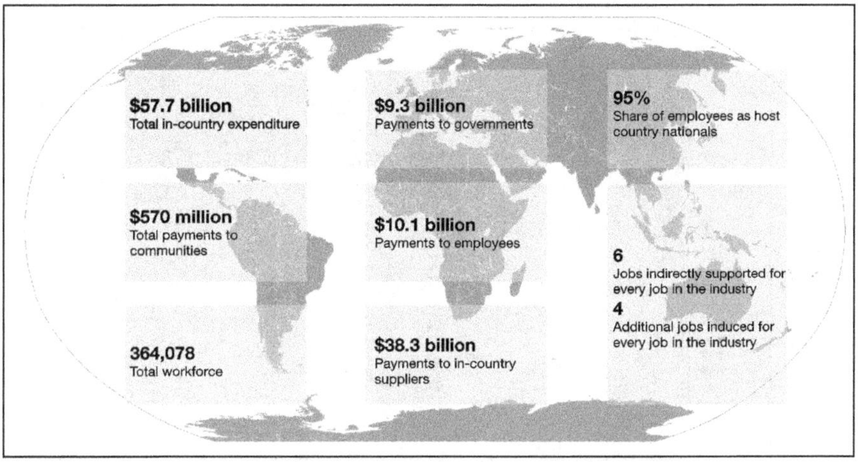

Source: Elemental Economics using data from World Gold Council.

economy some countries on their own are much more reliant on the mining sector. In Chile, for example, direct taxes from copper production averaged around 11.7% of total fiscal revenues between 2006 and 2024.[9] For countries such as the Democratic Republic of Congo (DRC), Botswana and Mongolia up to one-quarter of their economy is directly related to mining and there are a number of other countries in Africa and Latin America, such as Namibia, Chile and Bolivia, where it accounts for 10%–20%. For Australia the mining sector (excluding oil and gas) directly accounts for 10% of the economy. Around 8% of the South African economy is from mining and for Canada it represents around 5%.[10]

For major economies like those in Europe, the United States, China and India mining is a much smaller share of GDP; it is around 1.5% in the case of both the United States and China. But in absolute terms these countries still have globally significant mining industries. Figure 2 on the next page shows exports of ore and metals in dollar terms, as a share of GDP and as a share of merchandise exports in 2022.

3. The socio-economic costs of mining

Despite its economic benefits, concerns over the exploitative nature of mining and its sustainability credentials permeate societal views of the industry. Some specific factors which drive a negative public profile of the mining industry include:

- its use of land and depletion of resources, viewed as a 'one-off' activity;
- large cash margins seen to be generated by mining operations after

9 Cochilco, 2024, see www.cendachile.cl/series-cenda/mineria/precios-del-cobre#h.p_5gOc0x5dqgG6.
10 World Bank DataBank, https://databank.worldbank.org/home.

Figure 2. Global exports of ores and metals by country in 2022

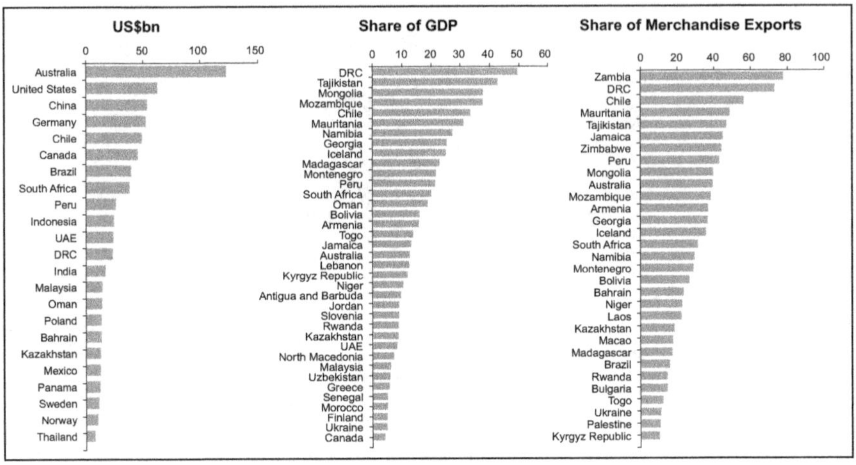

Source: Elemental Economics using data from UN Statistics.

capital has been invested and mines are in production, viewed as indicating excessive profits;

- mining's environmental footprint and carbon emissions driven by mining, refining and mineral processing and from the consumption of mine products;
- the export of unprocessed mine products and the concentration of downstream processing and employment in foreign countries;
- relatively low direct employment and the use of foreign nationals, especially in more senior positions;
- social and environmental costs of mining incurred locally whereas the benefits are spread globally;
- role of multilaterals and foreign ownership;
- legacy/historical issues (eg, colonialism and Indigenous land rights); and
- ongoing mining disasters (eg, tailings dam failures).

A particularly vexing philosophical issue for potential investors in mining is a question of its sustainability – mining is essentially a depleting activity as once an orebody has been exploited it cannot be used again. The Brutland Commission[11] defined sustainability as "development which meets the needs of the present without compromising the ability of future generations to meet their own needs". In its strictest reading mining cannot be sustainable based on this definition, but if the life cycle of mined products, including recycling, is

11 United Nations, *Report of the World Commission on Environment and Development: Our Common Future*, 1987, www.un-documents.net/our-common-future.pdf.

taken into account and if the benefits and revenues from mining are invested and used to generate sustainable growth in other parts of the economy it can perhaps come close to meeting a broader understanding of sustainability. Furthermore, while an individual orebody is finite there is always the potential to expand the reserve and resource base through drilling and exploration activity and improvements in mining and processing or market conditions which change the economic viability of exploiting a mineral deposit. Despite ongoing mineral extraction, the world's remaining reserves and resources have been continually rising over time for nearly all minerals, even if the grade and the complexity of the remaining orebodies in the ground have been declining.

The issue of mineral exploitation is often bound up in questions of ownership, especially where resources or mining assets are in foreign and/or multinational hands, along with a belief that the owners of such mining assets make excess profits. Where there is limited domestic downstream processing of mined production, or where the final consumption of mineral products is in other countries to those where the mining takes place, can create a perception of unfairness. It is the case that, once they are in operation, large-scale mining assets typically generate significant free cash flows. Global resource rents from mining calculated by the World Bank typically represent around 0.5% of global GDP, or over $500 billion based on the size of today's global economy.[12]

Figure 3. Mineral rents as a share of world GDP

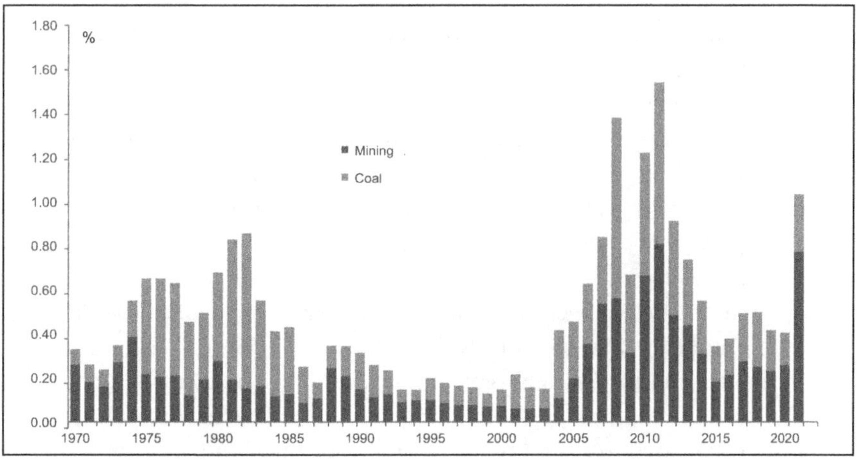

Source: Elemental Economics using data from World Bank for gold, silver, copper, lead, nickel, tin, zinc, bauxite, iron and phosphate only.

12 World Bank, https://data.worldbank.org/indicator/NY.GDP.MINR.RT.ZS. Note: The World Bank calculates resources rents as "the difference between the price of a commodity and the average cost of producing it. This is done by estimating the price of units of specific commodities and subtracting estimates of average unit costs of extraction or harvesting costs. These unit rents are then multiplied by the physical quantities countries extract or harvest to determine the rents for each commodity".

For some countries though, rents from mining exceed 10% of GDP. In the particular case of Mongolia, the DRC and Zambia they have been estimated by the World Bank to be over one-quarter of the size of the whole economy.

Figure 4. Mineral rents as a share of country GDP, 2021

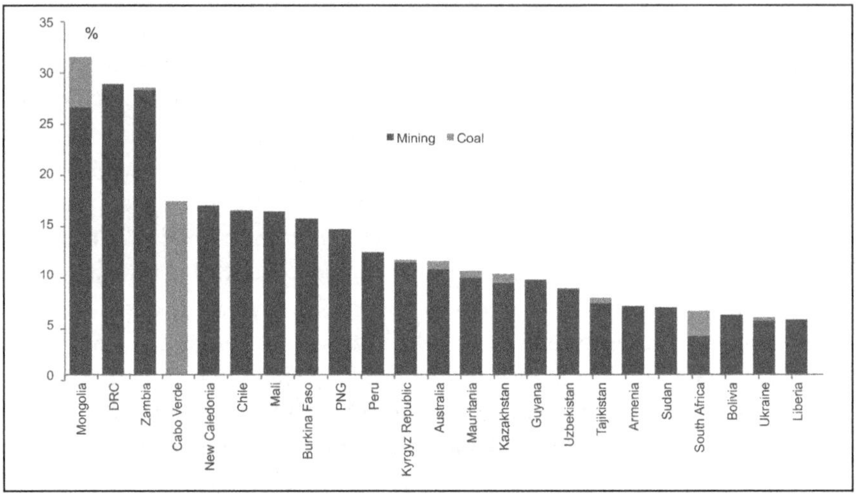

Source: Elemental Economics using data from World Bank for gold, silver, copper, lead, nickel, tin, zinc, bauxite, iron and phosphate only.

The size of such rents significantly impacts on views of the mining sector. However, the World Bank calculations exclude the initial cost of building mining operations, which can run into the tens of billions of dollars for the largest mines. Such projects also have long development lead times and can be financially very risky as they are exposed to significant operating, political and market risks. In fact, while profitability across the mining industry has improved in recent years, over the longer run the sector has, in aggregate, struggled to cover its cost of capital. Indeed, it can plausibly be argued that low profitability has been a major contributory factor behind the difficulty which the industry has historically had in meeting its socio-economic challenges. Perhaps, unsurprisingly, given the level of risks incurred and its historical financial performance, investor confidence in the mining industry is currently low, constraining the industry's ability to invest in the new minerals supply necessary for the energy transition.

In terms of mining's environmental footprint, it is very hard to turn a hole in the ground into something which is nature-positive and the physical volumes moved by the mining industry are enormous. Global ore production (including sand, gravel and aggregates) is in the order of 80 billion tonnes a year. Including waste as well as ore, total movement is likely to be more than

120 billion tonnes. These quantities of rock would be enough to bury the island of Manhattan to a depth of 30–50 km.[13]

But despite these massive physical volumes, the actual area of land used by mining of 57,000 square kilometres accounts for just 0.04% of the world's land area.[14] Compared to agriculture, which accounts for somewhere around half of the planetary footprint, it is a very small user of land. Mining though often happens in areas where nature is very sensitive to change and there is sometimes a sacral or quasi-sacral element to mining's use of land. Despite being in an area with a long history of mining and high local unemployment the underground Resolution Copper project in the United States has been beset by delays linked to concerns over its impact on the adjacent Apache Leap escarpment and on camping grounds in the neighbourhood. The true level of risk around any impacts are probably extremely small but, although the mine could supply 25% of the United States' annual copper requirements, the project remains many years from development.

Other environmental impacts of mining operations are their effects on noise, air, water and biodiversity. At a very local level, neighbours can be annoyed by dust blown from exposed mine sites and congestion. Of more global significance, a 2022 UN report[15] highlighted how the 50 billion tonnes of sand mined or dredged each year negatively impacts countries as diverse as Cambodia, China and the United States through its impact on erosion, fishing and agriculture. The industry is also a major consumer of water for mining, dust suppression and processing. Each tonne of copper produced in Chile is estimated to require 350 cubic metres of water.[16] Access to water in what are sometimes water-stressed regions in which mining competes with agriculture, along with the depletion of aquifers, are major issues for the mining industry. It is not just the volume of water used which is of concern. Pollution of water as a result of acid mine drainage (from ground water coming into contact with sulphide rich materials) and the pollution of waterbodies with mining effluents or the riverine or dumping-at-sea of tailings are further issues at some mining operations, for example at Freeport-McMoran's Grasberg operation in Indonesia, one of the largest copper and gold mines in the world.

Opening up a new area for debate concerning water, several mining companies are now looking at the potential for the mining of deep-sea nodules containing scarce metals like nickel, copper manganese, cobalt and precious

---

13 Estimates by Elemental Economics based on USGS minerals production data, www.usgs.gov/science/science-explorer/minerals/mineral-commodities.

14 V Maus, S Giljum, J Gutschlhofer *et al*, "A global-scale data set of mining areas" (2020) 7 *Scientific Data* 289.

15 UN Environment Programme, *Sand and Sustainability: 10 strategic recommendations to avert a crisis*, 26 April 2022, www.unep.org/resources/report/sand-and-sustainability-10-strategic-recommendations-avert-crisis.

16 BGR, "Copper Sustainability Information", 20 July 2020, www.bgr.bund.de/EN/Gemeinsames/Produkte/Downloads/Informationen_Nachhaltigkeit/kupfer_en.html.

metals. The economics of such dredging or hydraulic extraction operations and their impact on ocean-floor environments are not yet fully understood. While it is hard to conceive that the environmental cost of deep-sea mining could be greater than that of much of the mining on land which such activity might displace, environmentalists would rather focus on reducing demand than developing such an alternative source of supply. This debate is a transnational issue and the UN International Seabed Authority has set 2025 as a goal by when to issue rules governing seafloor minerals extraction.

A different and especially sensitive environmental issue in the light of two recent high-profile incidents in Brazil are risks when storing fine mining residues or tailings, the by-products from mining after separating ore from gangue. These are usually stored in earth-filled embankment dams but the liquid or slurry form in which they are deposited is often toxic and unstable. A tailings dam burst at Samarco's iron ore joint venture in 2015 in the south-east of Brazil caused a giant mudslide that killed 19 people and severely polluted the Rio Doce River. Even more tragically, when the Brumadinho tailings dam failed at Vale's Minas Gerais iron ore operation in 2019 the mudflow advanced through the mine's offices, and neighbouring houses, farms and roads downstream, leading to 270 deaths and the destruction of swathes of agricultural areas and livestock. Both incidents led to multi-billion dollar fines, along with major costs from repairing the environmental damage and paying reparations to the communities affected.[17, 18]

Even before such tragic incidents occur the potential for environmental and reputational damage can impact the viability of the mining industry. This was highlighted in 2023 by the closure of First Quantum Minerals' Cobre Panamá copper mine in Panama – despite it generating 5% of the county's GDP and employing more than 2% of the country's workforce. This closure followed a high court ruling after campaigners brought forward a case that the operation's use of water and the alleged contamination of water was hurting local ecosystems in a biodiverse jungle area.

At the more macro level are concerns over the impact of mining and the production of mineral products on the planet's climate. Despite its huge physical size direct greenhouse gas emissions directly related to mining (Scope 1 & 2 emissions) represent only 0.7% of the global total. However, including methane-bed emissions (predominantly from coal mining) this rises to 4%–7% and including Scope 3 emissions (incurred in downstream processing, including the burning of coal and the production of steel) this jumps to 28%.[19] Even if

17 https://en.wikipedia.org/wiki/Mariana_dam_disaster.

18 https://en.wikipedia.org/wiki/Brumadinho_dam_disaster.

19 Lindsay Delevingne, Will Glazener, Liesbet Grégoir and Kimberly Henderson, "Climate risk and decarbonization: What every mining CEO needs to know", McKinsey, 28 January 2020, www.mckinsey.com/capabilities/sustainability/our-insights/climate-risk-and-decarbonization-what-every-mining-ceo-needs-to-know.

coal is excluded, Scope 1–3 emissions from mining would still account for around 7% of the global total.

Over half of the world's major mining companies are committed to eliminating their Scope 1 & 2 emissions. The fourth largest iron ore producer Fortescue Metals Group has, for example, allocated $6.2 billion to achieve its plan of eliminating approximately 90% of the CO_2 equivalent emissions associated with its Australian iron operations by 2030. Projects to achieve that outcome include electrification of its mining, processing and rail infrastructure and switching to the use of renewable-based ammonia fuels, backed up by investment in wind and solar projects.[20] Such green investments will, inevitably, come at a cost of less capital being available to build new mine supply.

Elimination of downstream (Scope 3) emissions is beyond the direct control of mining companies and will be more challenging to achieve. It will require innovation in processing technologies, carbon capture and switching to the use of green hydrogen or other renewable fuels. Mining companies can, however, assist in this process and the effects of carbon pricing are already changing the relative value of different mine products and the way in which mining companies prioritise their investments. The world's second largest mining company, Rio Tinto, recently approved the development of its vast Simandou iron ore project in Guinea, which will shift the balance in its future iron ore production away from low grade ores in Australia to high grade output in West Africa with lower associated downstream processing emissions.

The impact of mining on communities is the next socio-economic area of concern. On the positive side, apart from agricultural work (and sometimes tourism) there are often few other job opportunities in remote mining areas and mining operations can contribute positively to local communities through developing improved local infrastructure, providing training opportunities or making direct financial payments to local institutions. When planning projects, mining companies typically carry out socio-economic impact assessments and environmental impact assessments alongside the financial, geological, engineering and other project studies. These, along with a programme of mitigating actions, will often also be required by governments prior to obtaining project approvals and aim to ensure that local groups benefit fairly from the investment, are compensated adequately or protected from any harm, and that risks to them are minimised.

Mining, though, has a troubled history of community relations. This stretches back to colonial or even ancient times when native populations were sometimes deprived of land and other resources and used as cheap, or indentured and abused, labour to operate mines. Tensions between local communities and mining can, though, exist even in independent sovereign and

20 Fortescue Metals Group, https://fortescue.com/sustainability/climate-change.

democratic countries under domestic or state-owned and managed mining enterprises. The relatively low level of employment in the mining industry but high relative wages can exacerbate inequality and particular social issues arise where mining brings outsiders into contact with local communities. As well as the number of jobs created for local people, a point of tension can be where local groups feel they are not benefitting sufficiently from taxes and other revenues received by central or federal governments and mine owners from a mine, while they are subject to the bulk of environmental and other costs. When Rio Tinto destroyed 46,000-year-old sacred rock shelters in Western Australia in 2020 in the process of expanding an iron ore mine without consulting local Indigenous groups the public outcry enlivened public debate about deep structural inequalities in Australian society and the company's CEO and two other senior executives were forced to leave the company.[21]

At the extreme such unrest can trip into physical conflict. Community tensions around CRA's Panguna copper mine – at the time the world's largest open-pit copper and gold mine – contributed to an uprising by sections of the local Bougainvillian population in 1988 as they sought to secede from Papua New Guinea. The resulting armed conflict led to around 20,000 deaths. The mine closed in 1989 and has never reopened. Such tensions are not unique to developing countries, but particular areas of concern have risen in recent years with the arrival Chinese traders in parts of Africa, buying minerals like tantalum and niobium, and the Russian Wagner mercenary group (now the Africa Corps), which offers 'security services' in exchange for control of mining rights and other economic interests.

4. The particular issues of artisanal mining

A particular socio-economic issue for the mining sector is that of artisanal and small mining (ASM). This is the mining industry's equivalent of subsistence agriculture and employs perhaps 44 million people worldwide – over twice the workforce in the formal part of the industry.[22] While ASM is often thought of as an African issue the largest ASM workforces are in India and China, and there is significant ASM activity in Latin America.

ASM operations are mostly concentrated in high unit value product markets, such as gold and gemstones and tin and tantalum. Perhaps 80% of sapphires, 26% of tantalum, 25% of tin, 20% of gold, 20% of diamonds and over 6% of tungsten is from artisanal mines. Elsewhere the share is under 5%.[23] Overall, ASM mines likely account for 8%–10% of the world's non-fuel mineral production.

---

21 https://en.wikipedia.org/wiki/Juukan_Gorge and www.riotinto.com/en/news/trending-topics/juukan-gorge.

22 EITI database (2023), https://eiti.org.

23 International Institute for Sustainable Development, *Global Trends in Artisanal and Small-Scale Mining (ASM): A review of key numbers and issues*, January 2018, www.iisd.org/publications/report/global-trends-artisanal-and-small-scale-mining-asm-review-key-numbers-and.

ASM often operates on the fringes of the law and is generally pursued as a route out of poverty or as an activity to complement insufficient other income, especially in communities where alternative employment is limited. The ASM sector is diverse though and its challenges vary from region to region (and often from site to site). It ranges from subsistence farmers – many families turn to ASM to supplement their farming earnings and use the money earnt to invest in farming and farm inputs – to skilled workers who have migrated from urban areas in search of work. Women and children are routinely employed in the ASM sector, often on a family basis. According to Extractive Industries Transparency Initiative (EITI), 30% of ASM employees are female. The International Labour Organization has estimated that over a million children work in mines and quarries. This is associated most closely with the mining of gold and cobalt and the problem is particularly acute in the DRC.[24]

ASM mines are labour rather than capital intensive often making do with extremely primitive equipment. Health and safety conditions in the sector are typically rudimentary to non-existent. As well as concerns over human rights the unregulated nature of the ASM sector means its impact on the environment, including through the use of mercury and other pollutants, can be highly adverse. ASM mines may scavenge ore that has been left behind by larger-scale mining companies – as in some of the older Bolivian mines – but elsewhere by mining only high-grade areas of mineral deposits it sterilises the value of lower grade parts of the orebody so it can be highly economically inefficient.

Many governments are ambivalent about small-scale mining, and their mining codes and tax systems are often inappropriate. Simply clamping down on ASM activity and moving people straight out of mining into other sectors is not a realistic strategy. Even if achievable there are typically few other employment opportunities and ASM provides a critical source of income for many people. Initiatives now instead emphasise the formalisation of ASM sites to ensure that higher standards are upheld rather than simply trying to outlaw it. Positive results have been achieved from programmes aiming to encourage more income-generating activities along the ASM supply chain (such as gemstone cutting and polishing) and from seeing agriculture and ASM as complementary, as opposed to two activities that are fundamentally at odds.

Ethical certification schemes and standards along with 'chain of custody' initiatives have also been used in recent years to support moves towards formalisation and to improve social and environmental practices in the ASM sector. Industry initiatives include the Fair Cobalt Alliance and Fairtrade Gold set up by the Alliance for Responsible Mining (ARM) and the Responsible Minerals Initiative. Access to capital is increasingly linked to such certification

24 International Labour Organization, "Child Labour in Mining and Global Supply Chains", 2019, www.ilo.org/publications/child-labour-mining-and-global-supply-chains.

programmes and the World Bank Communities and Small-Scale Mining (CASM) networking group has introduced a small grants scheme to increase sustainable development in ASM. Evidence on the success of certification schemes though is, as yet, unclear. Purchasers of mined products usually have a low willingness to pay higher prices for 'more ESG friendly' production in practice and most markets for minerals are simply too competitive and fragmented by geography and by end use or, unlike agricultural products, too distant from final consumer demand for them to be effective in excluding 'low ESG' production from the market.

5. Evidence and recent trends

Mining is a potential source of wealth and a route to economic prosperity and higher welfare. But whether that potential is realised depends on a range of factors. Australia and Chile are 'poster children' for how mining can be an engine for broader national economic development. Mongolia and Indonesia may be role models for this in the future (albeit at significant environmental cost in the case of Indonesia). But parts of Africa and elsewhere contain cases where mining has instead destabilised economic and political systems. Whether the environmental and social costs of mining are greater than the economic gains is an ongoing area of conjecture.

In 1993 the British academic Richard Auty published a book highlighting the "Paradoxical situation in which a country underperforms economically, despite being home to valuable natural resources", or what became known as the 'resource curse'.[25] Symptoms of this included observations that: overall living standards in oil and mineral dependent states were exceptionally low – lower than they should be given their per capita incomes; higher levels of mineral dependence were strongly correlated with higher poverty rates; oil and mineral dependent states tended to suffer from exceptionally high rates of child mortality; mineral dependence was strongly correlated with income inequality; and both oil and mineral dependent states were exceptionally vulnerable to economic shocks.

Factors which might cause a negative relationship between dependence on mining and economic welfare divide between external market forces and politics. On the first of these, economic stresses and strains from mining revenues can result in distortions elsewhere in the economy. Short-term volatility in commodity prices and 'lumpy' income flows, make economies difficult to manage. Volatile commodity prices often lead to procyclical public spending, which undermines the effectiveness of government expenditure in promoting economic growth. This volatility can also lead to underinvestment in other sectors, making the rest of the economy more vulnerable. A particular example of a country's economy becoming highly dependent on natural

---

25 Richard Auty, *Sustaining Development in Mineral Economies: The Resource Curse Thesis* (Routledge, 1993).

resources, failing to diversify and then contracting sharply when resources were depleted as the rest of the economy had been hollowed-out is associated with the Netherlands in the 1970s and became popularised as the 'Dutch disease'. On top of this, during the 1980s, 1990s and early 2000s, long-term trends in commodity prices relative to manufactured goods were declining. This negative 'terms of trade' trend meant that mineral-exporting counties needed to export rising volumes of production just to maintain export earnings. This relative declining trend in mineral prices has since reversed (see Figure 5 for data on trade in ores and metals) but whether this change will endure over coming decades is, as yet, unclear.

Figure 5. Global exports of ores and minerals

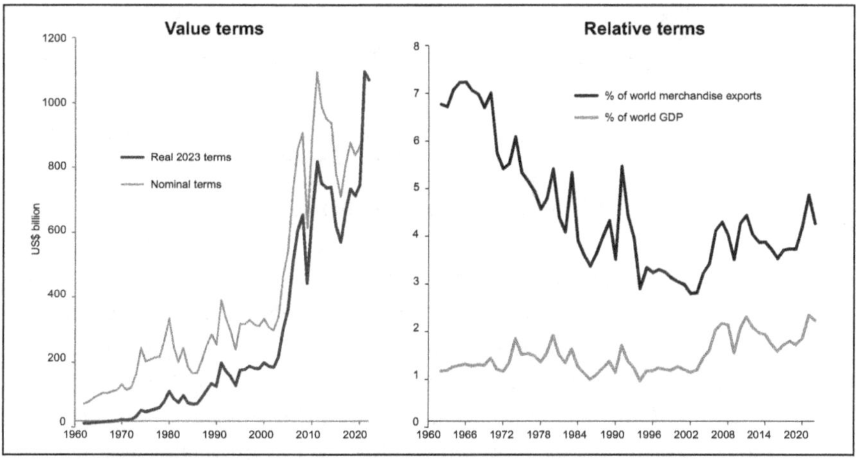

Source: Elemental Economics using data from UN Statistics.

Political explanations for poor economic performance as a result of a dependence on mining are explained by how governments and other societal groups respond to booming or large windfall revenues, by their impact on inequality and the squandering or misuse of mining revenues through poor policies, protectionism and mismanagement. Rent-seeking behaviour and corruption as competing groups seek access to mining revenues can lead to civil strife, conflict and war. It can also weaken institutions.

Proving or disproving the resource curse is difficult as the alternative comparative outcomes which would have materialised if countries had not developed a mining or natural resource sector are not available. More recent data on the relationship between economic growth and dependence on mining since 2000 also suggests a more positive link between mining and economic growth (see Figure 6). But there is a wide range of variation around such relationships suggesting that, unsurprisingly, how the economic benefits of mining are realised, managed and distributed – or the quality of a country's governance – are as important as the size of the mining sector itself.

Figure 6. GDP growth and mineral export share of GDP in the 2000s

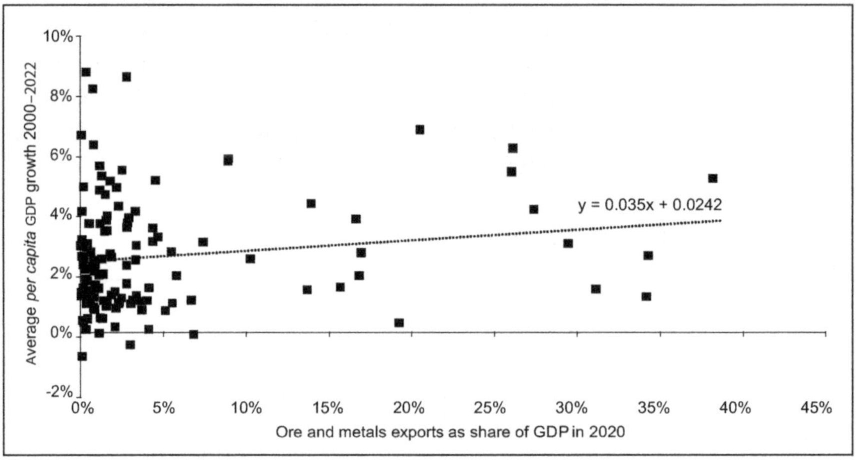

Source: Elemental Economics using data from UN Statistics.

The potential negative external costs of mining, low direct employment relative to revenues, and rent-seeking behaviour have contributed to many governments periodically seeking to impose greater state control over their domestic mining industries. There is a strong ideological component to this which changes over time according to shifting political orthodoxies, but the fixed location of mining makes the sector especially vulnerable to such interventions. The 1960s and 1970s saw significant growth in state control of mining, not only in newly independent ex-colonial countries like Zambia and the DRC (then Zaire) but also in Chile and across Europe.

The result of state ownership or control of mining has been mixed. State-owned mining firms have often suffered from institutional corruption, mispricing and management incentives which have valued employment over efficiency. Along with a lack of long-run investment due to the focus on short-term cash generation to fund current spending and political rather than business priorities, this can spiral into stagnant or falling output. Such factors led to copper production in the DRC falling from over 500,000 tonnes in 1981 to just 26,000 tonnes in 2002.[26]

Recognition of the failures of state control and a broader shift in political ideology towards free markets, combined with pressure on operating margins from falling commodity prices, led to an opening up and privatisation of the

26 ICSG, *World Copper Factbook 2024*, https://icsg.org/copper-factbook/.

mining industry in many jurisdictions in the 1980s and 1990s. After state control was eased and Western and Chinese firms were allowed to come in and invest, copper production in the DRC has grown strongly and now exceeds 2.5 million tonnes a year. Rather than maintaining total control, governments have instead kept minority holdings in mining assets with Western or Chinese private partners, while moving towards taxation and royalty regimes which better balance the wish of governments to raise revenues with investor needs and incentives.

Mining codes – the regulations, laws and rules which govern the ownership and operation of mining assets – have also become more transparent and investor friendly and there is more awareness of the potential macroeconomic costs of mining to the broader economy. Better attempts have been made to manage or mitigate these. For example, although still prone to financing current spending from windfall gains, the Mongolian government has established three wealth funds, the Fiscal Stability Fund, the Future Heritage Fund and the Unified Accumulation Fund to manage revenues from its natural resources boom.

The interest by states in taking a more direct role in mining tends to be cyclical and is subject to broader political changes. This pattern often follows trends in prices and the boom in demand for battery raw materials encouraged the Chilean government to bring its lithium sector under state control in 2023. 'Excess profits' taxes or tiered 'super royalty rates' have also been periodically imposed in a number of jurisdictions, even if the effects of these on investment are not usually properly understood.

There is also pressure in many countries to make mining permits conditional on the domestic processing of ores and concentrates. The economics of mineral processing and downstream manufacturing tend to be very different from mining though and historically such measures have tended to be unsuccessful; the effect has been for mining investors to simply move all of their efforts to other jurisdictions. However, where there are limited alternative options for sourcing raw materials such moves may be more effective. Indonesia imposed a ban on exporting unprocessed nickel ores in 2020 and the country has since signed over $15 billion in deals for domestic nickel smelters and battery materials and electric vehicle production. Such resource nationalism is not just an issue in developing countries. Tax credits for clean energy and electric vehicle production in President Biden's 2022 Inflation Reduction Act in the United States contain threshold provisions for their domestically sourced mineral content.

6. Conclusions

An honest conversation about mining needs to reflect the fact that the need for new mine output is unlikely to end – and indeed is essential if societal needs are to be met and if the energy transition is to be successful. In order to be incentivised to invest in this future the mining industry will need to have a reasonable expectation that it will make an adequate return on capital. But at the same time these investments, by their very physical nature and fixed location, will generate socio-economic tensions. To address these different needs and tensions, mining companies and states will need to work with downstream consumers, financiers, local communities and those NGOs that want to participate positively to better manage mining's social and environmental costs within improved legal and fiscal frameworks, and with a fair compensation and sharing of the broader economic benefits generated by the industry.

Progressing beyond a social licence to operate

Kevin PCJ D'Souza
KD Consulting

1. Defining the 'S' in ESG

The 'E' of ESG – environment – has tended to get the lion's share of attention in the mining sector. This has probably been warranted by the increasingly prescriptive nature of environmental regulations and performance standards, especially concerning issues like mine tailings, water stewardship, mine closure, climate change and, increasingly, biodiversity (natural capital) management. In general, it is also a more tangible construct, easier to study, assess and address. Most modernised mineral codes introduced over the past decade or so, together with new environmental legislation, mean that the risks from the environmental issues associated with mining are largely known; they are legislated, defined, quantifiable and, hence, more manageable.

In the post-pandemic world, we are witnessing growing societal rifts and transformation. Civil society's relationship with business has shifted and narratives and biases shape the increasingly interconnected and image-dominated world. Polarisation and misinformation flourish, deglobalisation and protectionism are increasing, and the sophistication and popularity of anti-mining NGOs, environmental human rights defenders and civil society continues to rise across the globe, most of whom are focused on the social risks and impacts created by the mining industry. The list of mines that have recently faced significant socio-political challenges continues to grow: Cobre in Panama; Barroso in Portugal; Parsa Kente in India; Jadar in Serbia; Escobal in Guatemala; Gibraltar in Canada; Pebble, Thacker Pass and Resolution Copper in the United States; Tia Maria, Las Bambas and Minas Conga in Peru; Kallak in Sweden; Amulsar in Armenia; Kirazli in Turkey; North Mara in Tanzania; and Kumtor in Kyrgyzstan. Going forward, the mining industry will need to have a more human-centric focus with greater effort put towards 'social performance' and managing its operations in ways that contribute to an overall societal net positive for host communities – or risk losing the privilege and ability to function in the countries in which they need to operate.

The International Council of Mining and Metals (ICMM)[1] succinctly defines

1 ICCM, Social Performance, www.icmm.com/en-gb/our-work/social-performance.

social performance as "the outcome of a mining company's engagement, activities and commitments that directly and indirectly impact stakeholders, particularly the local communities that live close to mining operations". Getting such social performance right – the 'S' in ESG – is critical, as mining operations and the communities and regions that host them are inextricably linked. The increased scrutiny has made mining companies more responsive to the growing global imperative to foster sustainable social performance and help create and protect community resilience. If the mining industry is to build and maintain societal respect and trust, the 'S' in ESG is going to need far greater attention. Ultimately, it must be about mining's utility to humanity and putting people first.

Social risks and impacts in mining tend to be an intricate tangle of interrelated intangible positives and negatives. These are typically subjective, and often further complicated by legacy issues, linguistic complexities, intergenerational responsibilities, socio-economic imbalances, cross-cultural barriers and, ultimately, the adaptive capacity of host communities around mines. Success and a 'return on investment' concerning social performance can be difficult to analyse, let alone quantify, and often evolve over the life cycle of a mine, from early exploration to closure. These factors are generally poorly understood by many mining professionals, whose comfort zone is typically data-driven and formulaic. Meanwhile, social performance professionals who understand and have the necessary skills to make a difference have remained outsiders, frequently neither recognised nor valued, and seldom considered a critical part of mining operations. Yet, the reality is that mining companies face a growing – and increasingly public – number of social incidents involving human rights abuse allegations, conflict with artisanal miners, mistreatment of Indigenous Peoples, the destruction of cultural heritage, and issues related to workplace sexism, racism and harassment. Such recent events have demonstrated that a lack of strong board and executive governance relating to social performance, coupled with reactive, transactional or arrogant behaviours, can lead to a multitude of negative outcomes. These include operational disruptions, reputational damage and material financial impacts for miners and investors. And there is no off-the-shelf curative toolkit to help miners facing such incidents to successfully backtrack and retrofit robust social performance.

At the local level, these outcomes can be devastating and can include undermining traditional values, social dynamics and cohesion, and overall community resilience; outrage over negative impacts, failed promises and failure to deliver on shared benefits; increased distrust leading to inter- and intra-community conflict; exacerbation of wealth inequalities and social divisions; deterioration in the quality of life, psycho-social problems, induced poverty and increased social and economic vulnerabilities; uncontrolled influx of migrants resulting in xenophobia, localised inflation and pressure on social infrastructure; and increased exposure to harassment and human rights abuses, including gender-based violence. Broader consequences include significant commercial and reputational downsides for mining companies, governments, local communities and investors alike. In defence of the mining industry, there has been more progress than many may realise. While they are not always given the credit they deserve, explorers and miners have been focused on monitoring negative social impacts and doing 'less harm' for quite some time. On the other hand, for the most part, they have not proactively focused on creating long-term social value and delivering on an equitable 'social contract'.

Political unrest, climate-related disasters, global food shortages, rising inflation and energy costs, supply chain disruptions, and the lingering impacts of COVID are all exacerbating the tensions between mines and local and Indigenous communities where, in some instances, inequalities are growing, and social value is not being created and, in the worst cases, eroded. Mining companies and their investors who fail to take social performance seriously are going to face increasing criticism, backlash and alienation. It can be easy to talk about social performance and 'propose' what to do from afar in the comfort of a corporate office. However, it is an appreciation of the realities of boots-on-the-ground implementation that separates the budding number of ESG theorists from the few seasoned practitioners. As mentioned, today miners face higher stakeholder expectations and growing risks of local community dependency, combined with a lack of public trust. But if they can adopt a more 'human-centric' focus and manage their operations in ways that contribute to an overall societal net positive for host communities, they have a better chance of keeping their 'social licence to operate' while also increasing social value. Authentic social performance – the 'S' in ESG – must be focused on the site level, encompassing a wide range of issues: human rights, grievance resolution, land access and use, involuntary displacement, gender empowerment, social health and welfare, community safety and security, strategic social investment, and labour practices and rights.

2. Historical context

In the distant past, mining was all about shareholder value and not breaking the law. In the 1970s, environmental concerns and associated liabilities were a new and unknown aspect of corporate risk for the industry. By the late 1990s, the mining industry started to co-opt the environmental activist language of responsibility and sustainability. The term 'sustainability' started becoming popularised after a United Nations conference in Stockholm in 1972, but it wasn't until the 1980s that a growing emphasis was placed on the economic needs of people in the global south and less on just environmental impacts. The term 'sustainable development' morphed into something that the 1987 Brundtland Commission defined as "meets the needs of the present without compromising the ability of future generations to meet their own needs".[2] Various mining industry stakeholders then attempted to adopt more jargon including terms like 'shared value', 'triple bottom line', 'people, planet and profit', 'corporate social responsibility', 'net positive impact' and so many other restatements which have generally all been very similar.

Today we have the acronym 'ESG' which, regrettably, has been falsely framed as an ideology, particularly in the United States where these three simple letters have been weaponised and fallen prey to undemocratic and partisan agendas. Interestingly, the first time the term ESG came into being was in the 2004 *Who Cares Wins Report*[3] which was a joint initiative of financial institutions at the invitation of the United Nations who together established a crucial link between ESG actions and financial performance. Contemporary ESG dynamics in the mining sector are wide-ranging, complex and inherently interrelated. When properly aligned, the 'E', 'S' and 'G' mutually reinforce each other, creating more successful outcomes for mining companies, governments, local stakeholders and investors alike.

Focusing on social performance practices, these have steadily progressed in the mining sector, compared to even the recent past, when these had more to do with piecemeal corporate social responsibility (CSR) investments and feel-good public-relations checklists than day-to-day operational practice. CSR tended to manifest with mining companies focusing on maintaining relationships merely to secure permits and then boasting about how much has been 'given' to do projects 'for' the community, rather than having an honest discourse about local impacts and actual stakeholder relationships. Such patronism engendered dependency and indifference to the benefits being received and led over time to resentment from local communities and a rising risk of social conflict. Civil society viewed CSR as an urban-elite narrative based on a phony value system. Ultimately, for many mining companies, CSR was more of an attempt to satisfy an inferred obligation, with the hope of doing the right things rather than doing those things right. It was also seen by some companies as a means to address environmental concerns through economic arguments – creating jobs and business opportunities, paying royalties and taxes and funding social programmes. Thankfully most in the mining industry have moved beyond band-aid CSR approaches and realised that governments may grant permits, but it is local communities that grant permission. However, there is much further to go.

It is irrefutable that mining disrupts communities, yet many miners and

---

2 See *Report of the World Commission on Environment and Development*, https://digitallibrary.un.org/record/139811?v=pdf#files.

3 The Global Compact, *Who Cares Wins: Connecting Financial Markets to a Changing World*, https://documents1.worldbank.org/curated/en/280911488968799581/pdf/113237-WP-WhoCaresWins-2004.pdf.

investors tend to focus on inbound risks to their operations (securing business continuity) from the community rather than risks to the community from their activities and operations. The fact is, social risk is not a new phenomenon. The Panguna mine was once one of the world's largest and most profitable gold-copper mines in the Bougainville autonomous region of Papua New Guinea (PNG). In 1989, amid rising community anger at the environmental and social impacts, including disputes over the sharing of its economic benefits and the impacts of those benefits on predominantly cashless societies, the mine was forced to close. The PNG government sent in heavy-handed troops against its own citizens to restart the foreign-owned mine sparking a bloody, decade-long separatist conflict that eventually engulfed the entire province. The protracted and violent conflict in Bougainville caused the deaths of hundreds of soldiers and rebels and an estimated 10,000 to 15,000 civilians, either from the fighting or from disease and deprivation. A peace settlement was finally brokered in 2001.

Despite claiming to have implemented grievance mechanisms, few miners genuinely try to identify and understand community aspirations, concerns and 'outrage', which is the intuitive (and emotional) reaction to such risks that in turn fuels community perceptions. This parochial one-way approach masks the root causes of company-community distrust and conflict. Such approaches tried patronisingly to dismiss arguments from communities and environmental opponents as 'emotional' while assuming their (self-interest) economic arguments of 'we know what's best' in favour of mine development were naturally 'rational'. Oftentimes local stakeholders feel they will bear a disproportionate share of the environmental, social or safety risks – be it emissions or potential spills – and the mining company will earn a disproportionate share of the economic rewards. It is evident that the inability to fully recognise, respond and provide non-patronising remedies to such community perception and outrage continues, and exacerbates the issue around the world, especially in areas with a colonial legacy and Indigenous or other land-connected groups.

We are also seeing more mining companies mature and get away from 'defensive sustainability' that is, focusing primarily on monitoring negative impacts and doing 'less bad' while failing to create social value or natural capital. To be truly successful, mining companies must reject the outdated trade-off mentality of thinking that anything ESG-related always costs more and adopt an approach that focuses on creating a sustainable culture that maximises social (and environmental) value while also addressing the expectations and needs of a wider audience, including local communities, governments, lenders, investors and downstream original equipment manufacturers (OEMs). Competent and responsible mining companies at all levels continue to make efforts to understand and creatively address the macro and micro socio-economic risks and impacts involved, yet many still struggle to succeed in social performance. This often worsens as companies have inadvertently also adopted an inappropriate decide-announce-defend (DAD) approach to dealing with community engagement. Historically the problem has typically not been a lack of good intentions. More commonly, it has been a lack of willingness to let go of control, too few experienced social professionals who can execute, and the appropriate internal structure to ensure effective and transparent lines of communication between community members, on-site personnel, corporate offices and ultimately the board and shareholders.

3. Deciphering the 'social licence to operate' concept

The term 'social licence to operate' (SLTO) was first coined by Jim Cooney, a former executive with Placer Dome. He used the phrase in a meeting with the World Bank in 1997 and it gained wider currency at a World Bank-sponsored meeting on mining and the community later that year. It was typically applied in countries that had real or perceived weak governance systems and huge internal power disparities between local communities in often remote areas near mining projects on the one hand and their governments and major business interests on the other. These communities traditionally experienced few sustained economic benefits from mining development, while bearing a disproportionate share of the environmental and social costs. In 2004 the World Bank Group's Extractive Industries Review (EIR)[4] definition of an SLTO started to create a greater influence within the mining industry. However, the EIR definition was not well consolidated, with criteria appearing sporadically throughout the report. Interestingly, the EIR also asserted that an SLTO may not be obtainable in all countries, citing operating difficulties and legal problems concerning Indigenous Peoples' rights.

SLTO is now well embedded in the mining industry vernacular. It refers to the tacit 'licence of legitimacy' sought by mining companies around the world as an objective beyond compliance for project approvals. It is a factual multi-party 'agreement' rather than a legal concept that is now widely used by industry, activists, commentators and political leaders alike. A company attempts to build and maintain an SLTO over time through meaningful local relationships and by being a steward for the environment, its employees and the community in which it operates – in short, by being accountable for its actions. An SLTO cannot be provided by regulatory authorities or by political structures nor can it be claimed to be a product of an internal corporate process such as an audit of company 'good practices'. It can only come from the

4 The World Bank, *Striking a better balance: the World Bank Group and extractive industries – the final report of the extractive industries review*, https://documents.worldbank.org/en/publication/documents-reports/documentdetail/961241468781797388/striking-a-better-balance-the-world-bank-group-and-extractive-industries-the-final-report-of-the-extractive-industries-review.

acceptance granted by the affected local communities and such acceptance is neither automatic nor unconditional.

For six consecutive years, SLTO has topped, or near topped, Ernst and Young's[5] risk listing for mining and metals as it is viewed as imperative for business continuity and profitability. Companies that do not act fairly towards host communities and fail to achieve the SLTO at the beginning of a mine's life cycle – or later lose it – will often face a multitude of challenges from costly and unexpected delays or closures, negative social media and reputational damage, limited access to capital, regulatory noncompliance, inability to attract or retain talent, and much more. The mine site community interface is where the real social performance happens and the SLTO is won or lost – and it is dynamic as socio-political issues and relationships can change in an instant. However, the loss of an SLTO can cause lasting damage to a company and, in some cases, the ramifications can be global. Notable examples include the catastrophic dam collapse at Vale's Corrego de Feijao mine in Brumadinho in Brazil, which ultimately led to the drafting of the Global Industry Standard on Tailings Management, and Rio Tinto's destruction of the 46,000-year-old sacred Aboriginal site at Juukan Gorge in Pilbara region of Australia, which resulted in a national enquiry and worldwide rethinking of how Indigenous Peoples are consulted and cultural heritage is assessed and managed. The mining industry's collective response to such public social performance challenges is increasingly coming under scrutiny from governments, host communities, investors and other civil society stakeholders.

It remains a metaphor to encapsulate values, activities and ideals that mining companies must espouse within society to ensure successful operation, but even metaphors require clear boundaries to make them meaningful. Hence, the SLTO concept has attracted notoriety from civil society and scholarly attention that has questioned its nature and utility and attempted to objectively define what it is (eg, legitimacy, credibility, community perceptions, social contract, ongoing approval, broad-based acceptance, ethical promise etc), how it can be conceptualised and enacted, and how it can be measured. Some critics claim the discursive use of SLTO is mere public relations spin covering up social irresponsibility by mining companies. The concept, its parameters and its legitimate modes of use are still vague and evolving, remaining an abstract idea that has no consensus on definition or application. Today SLTO is still politicised and highly ambiguous being used in different ways by different actors criticising the other usage, advocating their own preferred interpretation of what the SLTO means and implies, while delegitimising conflicting narratives.

---

5 EY Canada, "Top 10 business risks and opportunities for mining and metals in 2024", 10 October 2023, www.ey.com/en_ca/mining-metals/risks-opportunities.

Defining a metaphorical SLTO remains relatively murky and, as a consequence, the mining industry has attempted to address SLTO (or social acceptance) through a variety of 'precautionary principle' means, while often contextualising it as the aim or desired outcome of their sustainable development activities. In general, companies tend to define three broad areas of SLTO interest: environment, social and community issues (including health and education), and employment practices (including occupational health and safety and employee relations). However, critics claim it is all too capricious and ambiguous to be able to hold the industry to account constructively and fairly. Importantly, a gold mine in Kazakhstan, Peru or Ghana is not going to face the same set of social risks and issues as a copper mine in Canada, the Democratic Republic of Congo or Chile and, hence, measurement or theoretical comparison of an SLTO is rather ideological and academic. The fact is an SLTO is informal and unpredictable – it tends to be invoked in some contexts yet not in others. Nevertheless, and without inadvertently oversimplifying, three core principles are pretty much globally relevant across all cultures and jurisdictions. Host and Indigenous communities need to be listened to; be able to trust mining companies and their employees; and see meaningful and tangible benefits from the mining operations.

Many mining companies often promote their SLTO in formal sustainability/ESG-related disclosure without really defining what it means for their unique socio-cultural and socio-political circumstances. Because the criteria defining an SLTO remain relatively amorphous it dooms SLTO to the realm of intangible 'do-gooder' sentiments that are decoupled from business practice. Major gaps persist between theoretical ideals underpinning the SLTO, and how attainment is actualised on mine sites. In addition, many in the industry still fail to recognise the difference between a SLTO and actual social performance. The former is about the benefit to the company only and its desire to secure community acceptance to ultimately ensure business continuity. In contrast, the latter is about the benefit to communities and creating societal value through equitable benefit sharing and maximising local procurement and local employment. The fact is you will never hear a host community celebrate the presence of a SLTO – they need to see tangible benefits. Companies that successfully integrate sustainability/ESG into their core strategy understand this important difference between SLTO and social performance and can commit to upholding high standards of accountability and integrity towards both and create value beyond compliance. This is the essence of a social contract.

4. Moving towards a social contract

In an era when social media can turn a remote local conflict into an immediate global event, many of the past approaches to social performance, including the ever-popular SLTO, are fundamentally flawed and will simply not suffice. The mining industry needs to bridge the gap between theory and social performance practice – it needs to create a social contract with the wider community. While the criteria may be complicated, in the end, getting the 'S' right boils down to treating local and Indigenous communities or other rights holders with the respect and consideration we would want for our own communities, wherever we live – putting people first.

It is important to note that solutions to secure a social contract and improve performance do not have to be overly complicated, but they do need to be fully aligned with the company's objectives and attuned to the socio-cultural context. As a start, this means going slow with local stakeholders to eventually go fast to meet project demands and corporate expectations. One should never rush the process, or worse, create the impression of rushing a community into making an important decision about its future. Companies can benefit from taking time to develop plans at both the local and national levels to see how their activities could contribute to the host development trajectory and align with the strategic priorities of national governments. And after solutions are set out and agreed upon with stakeholders, timely follow-through on commitments is crucial. This also means bringing corporate policies to life and closing the gap between intent and action. It entails doing a more thorough job of properly identifying and mitigating social risks and impacts while capitalising on opportunities. Beyond that, a wider set of stakeholder concerns and expectations must also be identified, and managed, and socio-economic benefits distributed more equitably.

Codification of social performance management practices is maturing and there are a growing number of evolving international standards with associated guidance, coupled with country-level mechanisms, that are increasingly reflecting what is deemed to be 'good practice'. Key examples include:

- IFC Environmental and Social Performance Standards;
- EBR Environmental & Social Performance Requirements;
- International Council on Mining and Metals (ICMM) – Sustainability Framework and Principles;
- World Gold Council – Responsible Gold Mining Principles (RGMPs);
- Mining Association of Canada – Towards Sustainable Mining (TSM);
- Copper (Nickel, Zinc and Moly) Mark;
- Initiative for Responsible Mining Assurance (IRMA);
- UN Global Compact and Guiding Principles on Business and Human Rights; and
- Voluntary Principles on Security and Human Rights (VPSHR).

As a start, this will entail doing a more thorough job of properly identifying and mitigating social risks and impacts, while capitalising on opportunities. Beyond that, a wider set of stakeholder concerns and expectations must also be identified, and managed, and socio-economic benefits distributed more equitably. While verifiable and robust social performance assessment currently lags behind environmental assessment and associated disclosures, gains are being made as the social stakes are increasing for miners across the globe. Despite many positive strides, the mining industry still has a challenge that cannot be ignored, especially in the post-pandemic world, as we face a cluster of interconnected risks that has been termed by the World Economic Forum a 'polycrisis'.[6] Looking to the future, the mining industry will have to intensify its efforts to capture and track appropriate qualitative and quantitative social performance metrics to help key stakeholders from local communities, governments and company investors to make informed decisions.

Successful mining operators have been well versed in identifying and addressing the specific technical issues that might impact operations and are now increasingly adept at doing so for social risks to their operational and business continuity. But to minimise the mine's impact on community resiliency, there needs to be a more comprehensive and honest assessment of current and ongoing socio-economic risks and impacts generated by their operations, coupled with a deliberate focus on the more palatable opportunities. The types of direct and indirect risks that need to be considered are wide-ranging, dynamic and interrelated, and may include:

- undermining of fundamental human rights, often by heavy-handed public or private security agencies;
- social order disruption due to changes in local leadership dynamics and localised inflation;
- loss of traditional rights and ecosystem service amenities leading to food insecurity;
- involuntary physical or economic displacement through land acquisition or expropriation;
- more acute impacts felt by vulnerable, marginalised or Indigenous Peoples;
- reduced community physical and psychological health, safety and well-being;
- in-migration of mine and opportunistic labour placing increased demand on infrastructure/public services;
- gender-specific adverse impacts including gender-based violence and harassment (GBVH);
- increased negative anti-social behaviour, substance abuse, sex work, delinquency and criminality;
- intensified opportunity and motivation for local bribery and corruption;

---

6 World Economic Forum, "We're on the brink of a 'polycrisis' – how worried should we be?", 13 January 2023, www.weforum.org/agenda/2023/01/polycrisis-global-risks-report-cost-of-living/.

- influx of illegal and/or informal artisanal miners leading to safety, environmental and security risks;
- lack of community awareness and emergency preparedness (including for tailings management); and
- retrenchment and the socio-economic impact of mine decommissioning and eventual closure.

From society's perspective, just because a mining company is claiming to do no harm does not mean that it is doing good. Hence, to secure a social contract companies should assess whether they are cultivating meaningful stakeholder relationships, contributing to social value and creating economic value in a way that also creates value for society by addressing its needs and challenges – and making measurable positive impacts. While these impacts are local, their effects range much further: numerous examples have shown that lack of genuine attention to social risks and impacts – and failure to respond to community concerns, discontent and activism – will likely translate to costly delays, reputational damage, the inability to secure permits, operational disruptions and even complete shutdowns. Furthermore, such ramifications have knock-on effects for future mine developers, and by extension, the ability of the entire mining industry to build societal trust and meet the growing global demand for the critical metals and minerals vital to achieving global decarbonisation targets.

More explicit criteria regarding social issues would require companies to develop better means of capturing and reporting on social data that is more accessible, meaningful and potentially quantifiable to assess social issues, particularly those which seem more intangible. The fact is, local communities are never homogenous or singular, so mining companies need to conduct an appropriate socio-economic baseline and a predictive social impact assessment (SIA) to capture such quantitative and qualitative data. These assessments must go beyond simple geographical descriptions of an area with generic societal attitudes, and instead provide a real sense of the socio-political history and cultural context along with candid analysis of possible direct and indirect risks and impacts. Unfortunately, many SIAs often fail to meet this fundamental requirement and are justifiably undervalued. Done properly, a competent SIA can be a useful impact prediction mechanism that contributes to social performance management throughout the mine life cycle, from conception to post-closure. Importantly, this requires adopting a variety of social research techniques including: key informant interviews and consultations to demographic surveys; reviewing non-governmental organisation reports and social science/anthropology reports; listening to oral histories; and conducting various participatory group exercises (eg, participatory rural appraisal (PRA), which is an assessment and learning approach that emphasises empowering local people to assume an active role in analysing their own living conditions, challenges and opportunities to change their situation). Once the real (and perceived) direct/indirect impacts and opportunities are identified, mitigation and management plans can be drafted. However, the SIA stage is only one step in the social performance journey. Robust, sustained and impactful social performance involves more than mitigating and managing social risks and negative impacts – companies need to deliberately focus on capitalising on the socio-economic opportunities and deliver compelling and measurable positive social impacts, thereby helping to demonstrate the true impact of the mining industry, but importantly, with genuine humility, empathy and respect.

Armed with a better understanding of social risks and impacts, companies can then identify and understand what appropriate and pragmatic social performance 'good practices' are, and how to operationalise them through workable internal strategy and processes, operating standards and procedures that are integrated into broader company-wide risk and management operating systems. The management system must help prioritise, integrate and address the social performance goals of key internal and external stakeholders, including local employees, and host and Indigenous communities. This should include everything from proactive engagement planning and access to remedy (grievance management), honouring social commitments and maximising local content, to implementing community participatory monitoring and delivering on strategic social investments – remembering that a social contract cannot be secured through compliance or 'do no harm' mindset alone. In addition, companies must also focus on addressing respectful workplace behaviours, diversity, equity and inclusion, and apply the same rigour of existing health and safety regimes to psychological safety and employee well-being.

The systemisation of social performance approaches and practices are maturing and today there are many publicly available 'good practice' frameworks and toolkits that can help companies of all sizes draft and implement appropriate social performance management, systems plans and operating procedures. The resulting documents should be culturally attuned, workable and 'live', that is, continuously improved based on implementation experiences – but the real crux is in actual execution. Throughout the life of a mine, companies must continuously explore ways to understand host and/or Indigenous community aspirations and concerns (eg, through community perception surveys), make a positive difference in the quality of their lives and wellbeing, follow through on promises and commitments, and strive to leave a positive legacy – as this is the true measure of social value. Evidence has shown that robust social performance can play an important role in strengthening social and economic resilience in host communities. As the International Council of Mining and Metals has noted, if there is an overarching theme that one can apply to all situations, it is that companies should seek to create beneficial outcomes for local communities and wider society from their activities, engagements and commitments.

As an aside, while the appreciation of the importance of professional social performance is evolving (and arguably growing), there is regrettable 'competency greenwashing' (the practice of intentional or negligent misrepresentation of knowledge, skills, competencies or expertise relating to sustainability or ESG-related activities) coupled with a limited understanding of the role and responsibilities of the social performance function. Social performance is essentially an ongoing task that requires experienced and knowledgeable professionals who demonstrate flexibility, creativity and responsiveness. The function is typically charged with operationalising social performance policies and 'good practice' ESG standards through on-the-ground strategies of engagement, communication, negotiation, conflict resolution and development programming. Recent research conducted by the University of Queensland[7] suggests the function should focus on three main areas, namely:

- efforts by the mining company to understand local stakeholder and Indigenous perspectives;
- bridging local stakeholder/Indigenous and company perspectives to generate dialogue and mutual understanding; and
- facilitating necessary organisational change to continuously improve social performance.

To do so, the in-house social performance function (sometimes called 'community relations' or 'sustainability') must be adequately resourced and proportional to the identified social impacts, as well as the anticipated mining-induced changes. The research goes on to recommend that social performance be developed as a core competency connected to business planning. As with other established business support functions such as health and safety and human resources, the function should be appropriately positioned within the company hierarchy and properly supported, organised, managed and held accountable.

5. Decarbonisation and critical minerals

Although social performance largely comes down to local issues, the current stakes could not be more global. As the world strives to embrace a more circular economy through increased recycling, reuse and repurposing of secondary minerals – the irrefutable reality is that we simply must increase mining activity to produce the critical minerals needed for a clean-energy world. For many

7 Deanna Kemp and John R Owen, "Corporate affairs and the conquest of social performance in mining", *The Extractive Industries and Society*, Vol 7, issue 3, July 2020, pp835–837, https://doi.org/10.1016/j.exis.2020.06.012.

producing countries this could be an opportunity to drive economic growth and secure investment, jobs and government revenue – all of which contribute to achieving the United Nations' Sustainable Development Goals (SDGs). Decarbonisation provides opportunities for growth in the mining sector, entering emerging frontiers and encountering different host communities and rights holders, including Indigenous groups.

The importance of aligning with the Paris Agreement to help limit global warming is widely understood, but less so the social impact of the net zero transition. The G7 governments agree that failure to tackle ESG governance challenges head-on could make the energy transition a 'resource curse' rather than a blessing for many producing countries. The rapid transition to a low-carbon economy must not increase biodiversity loss, global inequality or injustice as a result. In 2019 the World Bank focused on "Climate Smart Mining".[8] In 2022, the United Nations and other agencies started to use the term 'a just transition': greening the economy in a way that is as fair and inclusive as possible to everyone concerned, creating decent work opportunities and leaving no one behind. In 2024 the UN Secretary-General established a Panel on Critical Energy Transition Minerals seeking to build trust between governments, local communities and industry, by addressing issues relating to equity, transparency, investment, sustainability and human rights. It builds on existing standards and initiatives, particularly the Working Group on Transforming the Extractive Industries for Sustainable Development and its flagship initiative, "Harnessing Critical Energy Transition Minerals for Sustainable Development",[9] to strengthen and consolidate existing efforts.

So as the demand for critical minerals grows, the mining industry can expect its social performance credentials to be more closely scrutinised by governments, host communities, investors and wider civil society, especially for its contribution to the well-being and quality of life of host and Indigenous communities. Already, the traceability of these critical minerals, and the ability to demonstrate the provenance with strong ESG performance, is deemed increasingly vital for end-users such as the battery, automotive and electronics industries. Without further innovation and efforts to increase transparency and robust ESG governance, the rapid demand for critical minerals is likely to drive economic instability, corruption and environmental and social harm – all of which could derail global efforts to fight climate change. That's why social 'S' and environmental 'E' performance for mining are inextricably linked – and

---

8 World Bank Group, "Climate-Smart Mining: Minerals for Climate Action", www.worldbank.org/en/topic/extractiveindustries/brief/climate-smart-mining-minerals-for-climate-action.

9 UN Secretary-General's Working Group, "Harnessing Critical Energy Transition Minerals for Sustainable Development: A UN Interagency effort on Critical Minerals", 29 August 2023, https://unemg.org/wp-content/uploads/2023/08/29-August-2023-Presentation-at-Nexus-Dialogue-EMG-Critical-Energy-Transition-Minerals.pdf.

learning from history to avoid the negative ESG impacts of previous commodity booms is so essential.

There may never be a perfect solution to such complex issues. However, with a comprehensive understanding of local social impacts and issues, effective lines of feedback and open communication, an experienced management team coupled with a knowledgeable board and shareholders who are all committed to adding social value, it is possible to find compromises all sides can live with while allowing the local community to enjoy the economic benefits that a mine can provide. It can be done, but if the effort is half-hearted, it will likely be disastrous – limiting the ability to avoid conflict, obtain permits, raise capital and ultimately protect assets from impairments. When done well, a robust social contract can be hugely positive and often transformational through economic multiplier effects. If the sector can get behind placing social performance at the centre of decision making, and the concept of a robust social contract for mining, it would be hugely positive for everyone. Miners would be better equipped to meet regulatory and ESG performance standard requirements and secure and maintain their much sought-after SLTO, which in turn brings the desired business continuity benefits. Investors would gain greater comfort during their due diligence processes and be more confident about the long-term viability of their investments. By actively partnering alongside responsible investors, governments, international development partners, host communities and NGOs, our industry can deliver extensive, lasting socio-economic developmental benefits that contribute to community resilience. Looking at humanity's future, if we want to decarbonise, mining is not a choice. How we mine is.

Extractive industries and human rights in Africa – the Democratic Republic of Congo as a case study

Yasmin Batliwala
Advocates for International Development (A4ID)

1. Introduction

The Democratic Republic of Congo (DRC), located in Central Africa, is the most populous Francophone country in the world with an estimated population of 112 million.[1] Rich in natural resources, the DRC has become a hub for extractive industries. It is the world's largest producer of cobalt and the sixth largest producer of copper.[2] According to the Extractive Industries Transparency Initiative (EITI) report of 2021,[3] the DRC relies heavily on its extractive industry, which contributes significantly to the government's revenue and accounts for 98.9% of the country's exports. This makes the extractive industries a crucial sector in the country's economy, profoundly affecting the socio-economic and cultural development of the citizens. Autesserre argues that the centrality of the extractive industries to the economy has made them a focal point for tension, crisis and conflict at all levels, from the individual to communal.[4] Autesserre further posits that historically land and the natural resources extracted from the land have been critical sources of instability and tension in Congo as land is seen as the 'key to survival' for individuals and families and a 'primary means of gaining social capital needed to integrate into local structures and secure natural resources'.[5]

Moreover, these natural resources have fuelled conflict and contestation due to the challenges of managing these resources for the 'public good of all' amid political, social, environmental and economic factors. Burnley notes that resource management is particularly complex in the DRC because of its

1 C Burnley, "Natural Resources Conflict in the Democratic Republic of the Congo: A Question of Governance", *Sustainable Development Law & Policy* (2011) 12 (7): 7–53.
2 S Katz-Lavigne, "Copper Stakes: Exclusion, Corporate Strategies, and Property Rights in the Democratic Republic of Congo", in N Andrews, A Grant and J Ovadia (eds), *Natural Resource-Based Development in Africa: Panacea or Pandora's Box?* (University of Toronto Press, 2022).
3 EITI, "Democratic Republic of the Congo", 2021, https://eiti.org/countries/democratic-republic-congo.
4 S Autesserre, "The Trouble with Congo: How Local Disputes Fuel Regional Conflict", *Foreign Affairs*, (2008) 87 (3): 94–110.
5 *Ibid*, p95.

historical background of political tension and conflict over its natural resources.[6] Rahm expands on this idea,[7] explaining that since Belgium's colonisation of the DRC in 1885, mining practices have progressed to involve deeper extraction as the superficial layers have been depleted. The capital-intensive nature of modern mining, which encompasses labour and safety measures, environmental management, exploration costs and infrastructure development, has led to allegations of labour exploitation, violations of community land rights and broader sustainability issues in mining operations. Additionally, there is a growing dependence on DRC cobalt – which accounts for 70% of cobalt available internationally – as it is an essential component in rechargeable batteries for electric vehicles and equipment in a range of industries, including medical and telecommunications devices.[8] This has led to increased cases of human rights breaches, including mass eviction and displacement of communities which has gone on unchecked due to the lack of accountability and corruption among local and corporate governance structures. Therefore, this chapter aims to examine the impact of the extractive industries in the DRC on human rights, with a focus on community rights violations and labour rights. It will then consider corporate environmental social and governance (ESG) practices and highlight what constitutes good practice for mining companies.

The structure of this chapter begins with a brief contextual discussion of the extractive industries in the DRC, and the legislative frameworks governing them. This is followed by an examination of existing literature on ESG and human rights. The historical impact of the extractive industries on community rights will be explored with a focus on land rights violations, environmental degradation, socio-economic disruption and cultural impact. A brief discussion of the methodological underpinning of the chapter follows. Subsequently, a discussion on what constitutes good practices within the mining industry will be extrapolated. The chapter concludes with thoughts and recommendations on improving global best practices in the extractive industry to achieve sustainability in mining.

2. Contextual background

The DRC's extractive industry has existed for over a century.[9] It has transformed

---

6 C Burnley, "Natural Resources Conflict in the Democratic Republic of the Congo: A Question of Governance", *Sustainable Development Law & Policy* (2011) 12 (7): 7–53.

7 S Rahm, "Mining the ESG Ground Research Paper: Assessing the Financial Component of Sustainability Strategies in the Mining Sector", Schroders, December 2013, https://mybrand.schroders.com/m/30fbae61466b2c7e/original/Mining_the_ESG_Ground_report_December_2013.pdf.

8 S Katz-Lavigne, "Copper Stakes: Exclusion, Corporate Strategies, and Property Rights in the Democratic Republic of Congo", in N Andrews, A Grant and J Ovadia (eds), *Natural Resource-Based Development in Africa: Panacea or Pandora's Box?* (University of Toronto Press, 2022).

9 H Ngalula and E Mbuyi, "Mining 2024: Democratic Republic of Congo", Chambers and Partners, January 2024, https://practiceguides.chambers.com/practice-guides/mining-2024/democratic-republic-of-congo.

over time to reflect the global standard of transparency and accountability in line with EITI principles, as the sector has been faced with accusations of corruption, exploitation and human rights abuses. The controversy surrounding these allegations is heightened due to the industry's importance to the economy of the country.[10] Therefore, the purpose of this section is to provide a brief contextual background to mining in the DRC, highlighting how the country's historical context continues to shape the industry. It addresses the broader assertion that the DRC is "a startling contradiction of one of the richest countries in the world in terms of natural resources" yet remains one of the poorest due to corruption, lack of governance and regulatory issues.[11] Additionally, key legislative frameworks governing the extractive industry will be examined to identify any existing gaps and suggest ways to strengthen them.

Mining in the DRC occurs at two levels: artisanal/small-scale mining and large-scale mining (LSM). Artisanal mining, an informal industry, practised by local communities, involves extracting resources such as cobalt from small mines and selling them into the larger supply chain. While this provides rare employment opportunities, the practice is unregulated and hazardous. Miners work with crude tools, such as spades and pickaxes, and have little to no safety measures in place.[12] Most miners in this sector are 'freelance', with no security regarding payment, hours or medical support. While artisanal mining is often considered less developed, Ngalula and Mbuyi[13] argue that within the DRC, it is "highly developed" and "employs hundreds of thousands of people, often in difficult, dangerous and illegal conditions". Artisanal mining provides direct income for communities seeking to improve their living conditions making it a widespread practice across the DRC.[14] Despite its developed nature, Maconachie[15] contends that the sector is characterised by labour exploitation, perilous working conditions and human rights abuses, leading to social and environmental problems.

On the other hand, LSM, conducted by the larger and more established mining companies, significantly impacts local and national economies and is governed by national and regional regulatory frameworks. LSM accounts for

10 *Ibid.*

11 JA Diemel and JM Hilhorst, "Unintended consequences or ambivalent policy objectives? Conflict minerals and mining reform in the Democratic Republic of Congo", *Development Policy Review*, 37(4): 453–469 at 455.

12 S Katz-Lavigne, "Copper Stakes: Exclusion, Corporate Strategies, and Property Rights in the Democratic Republic of Congo", in N Andrews, A Grant and J Ovadia (eds) *Natural Resource-Based Development in Africa: Panacea or Pandora's Box?* (University of Toronto Press, 2022).

13 H Ngalula and E Mbuyi, "Mining 2024: Democratic Republic of Congo", Chambers and Partners, January 2024, https://practiceguides.chambers.com/practice-guides/mining-2024/democratic-republic-of-congo.

14 C Huggins, "Is collaboration possible between the small-scale and large-scale mining sector? Evidence from 'Conflict-Free Mining' in the Democratic Republic of the Congo (DRC)", *The Extractive Industries and Society* (2023) 13, 101163.

15 R Maconachie, "'We miners die a lot'. Appalling conditions and poverty wages: the lives of cobalt miners in the DRC", *The Conversation*, 30 January 2024, https://theconversation.com/we-miners-die-a-lot-appalling-conditions-and-poverty-wages-the-lives-of-cobalt-miners-in-the-drc-220986.

about 80% of the cobalt in the DRC and 70% of the international cobalt supply.[16] The co-existence of both sectors often leads to conflict, as artisanal mining "activities increasingly intersect with LSM operations".[17] Factors such as the re-categorisation of mining sites by the state, and artisanal miners exploiting vacuums without formal permission from the state, are common issues across the DRC.[18] These conflicts, coupled with failed or fragile state institutions, have led to human rights abuses and exploitation within large-scale mining companies.[19] Furthermore, Katz-Lavigne argues that although LSM is considered a more acceptable and reliable form of mining than artisanal, significant cases of abusive and exploitative practices still persist.[20]

This is not a new phenomenon, as mining in the DRC has historically been rooted in exploitation.[21] According to Mazalto, the mining and extractive industries flourished under Belgian colonisation and the regime of Mobutu between 1971 and 1997. However, systematic large-scale corruption, weak regulatory institutions, territorial disparities and the contestation between the central government and states have plagued the extractive industries and have enabled human rights abuses. During colonialism, labour forces were pressured to work on a 'global scale' with minimum respect for human rights to serve foreign interests.[22] This exploitative practice continued even after independence. The conflicts and armed activities that followed independence perpetuated colonial-era human rights abuses, corruption and environmental degradation in the DRC's mining sector.[23]

Therefore, there is a need for systematic reform in the mining sector to advance and promote human rights. The DRC operates a civil legal system, closely modelled on Belgian law. Various pieces of legislation provide a framework for the extractive industries. This chapter focuses on key legal frameworks related to the environment, land ownership, mineral resources ownership and operational codes, which are crucial for regulating the extractive industry. Two primary sources of mining law can be found in the newly

---

16 S Katz-Lavigne, "Copper Stakes: Exclusion, Corporate Strategies, and Property Rights in the Democratic Republic of Congo", in N Andrews, A Grant and J Ovadia (eds) *Natural Resource-Based Development in Africa: Panacea or Pandora's Box?* (University of Toronto Press, 2022).

17 C Huggins, "Is collaboration possible between the small-scale and large-scale mining sector? Evidence from 'Conflict-Free Mining' in the Democratic Republic of the Congo (DRC)", *The Extractive Industries and Society* (2023) 13, 101163.

18 *Ibid.*

19 M Mazalto, "Governance, Human Rights and Mining in the Democratic Republic of Congo", in B Campbell (ed), *Mining in Africa: Regulation and Development* (Pluto Press, 2009).

20 S Katz-Lavigne, "Copper Stakes: Exclusion, Corporate Strategies, and Property Rights in the Democratic Republic of Congo", in N Andrews, A Grant and J Ovadia (eds), *Natural Resource-Based Development in Africa: Panacea or Pandora's Box?* (University of Toronto Press, 2022).

21 M Mazalto, "Governance, Human Rights and Mining in the Democratic Republic of Congo", in B Campbell (ed), *Mining in Africa: Regulation and Development* (Pluto Press, 2009).

22 J Peemans, "Capital Accumulation in the Congo Under Colonialism: the Role of the State", in P Duignan and L Gann (eds), *Colonialism in Africa 1870–1960* (Cambridge University Press, 1975).

23 M Mazalto, "Governance, Human Rights and Mining in the Democratic Republic of Congo", in B Campbell (ed), *Mining in Africa: Regulation and Development* (Pluto Press, 2009).

amended Mining Code of 2018, supplemented by Decree No 18/001 of 9 March 2018, and Decree No 038/2003 of 26 March 2003, relating to Mining Regulations, as amended and supplemented by Decree No 18/024 of 8 June 2018. These legal provisions address issues such as the management of the mining sector, conditions for obtaining mining rights and environmental protection.

The amended Mining Code has been commended for integrating the concept of Environmental and Social Impact Assessment (ESIA), which balances the social and environmental responsibilities of mining companies to communities affected by their activities, for rebalancing of state royalties.[24] Additionally, the revised Mining Code requires mining firms to contribute at least 0.3% of their turnover to the development of mine-affected communities. However, scholars and social critics have criticised the amended Mining Code for its lack of clarity regarding the management of funds intended for the benefit and development of communities. The code is not explicit on this issue and defers details to subsequent decrees by the Prime Minister.[25]

In addition, Article 9 and Article 202 point 36 litera f of the Congolese Constitution of 2006, as amended by Law No 11/002 of 2011, establish the fundamental principles for mining law in the DRC. The Mining Code and the Constitution serve as the core legislative frameworks governing the mining sector. Law No 11/022 of 2011 is notable for protecting and promoting the rights of Indigenous Peoples in relation to land, natural resources and development. This legislation is the first in the DRC to formally recognise and safeguard the rights of Indigenous Peoples, particularly their land rights, and to secure their land tenure. However, this legislation has been criticised for lacking effective enforcement mechanisms. Moreover, both the Mining Code and the Constitution have faced criticism for failing to provide transparency regarding the ownership and beneficiaries of mining rights.[26] Given the endemic corruption in the DRC and its impact on other vices, improving transparency in the allocation of mining rights and the management of the country's natural resources is vital for enabling the extractive industry to meet global operational standards.

---

24 L Koné, *Democratic Republic of the Congo: A Right-Based Analysis of Mining Legislation*, Forest Peoples Programme, July 2023, www.forestpeoples.org/sites/default/files/documents/DRC%20A%20rights-based%20analysis%20of%20mining%20legislation%20ENG.pdf.

25 See Herbert Smith Freehills, "The Democratic Republic of Congo's Revised Mining Code", 25 April 2018, www.herbertsmithfreehills.com/insights/2018-04/the-democratic-republic-of-congos-revised-mining-code.

26 Global Witness, "Global Witness' comments on DRC's revised Mining Code", 14 October 2013, www.google.com/url?sa=t&source=web&rct=j&opi=89978449&url=https://www.globalwitness.org/documents/18088/DRC-GW_mining_law_GW_comments_EN_-_October_2013.pdf&ved=2ahUKEwj_67i2zLqIAxV8UEEAHbUJKhwQFnoECBQQAQ&usg=AOvVaw03E9g1PRjrer7v2_edtUWS.

3. Literature review

The heightened focus on human rights has become central to corporate consciousness with the rise of corporate social responsibility (CSR) and ESG standards. While human rights are inherently part of the 'social' aspect, their impacts intertwine with the other ESG facets due to their interconnectedness.[27] This connection is especially evident in the extractive industry, where violations of protected rights, such as those outlined in the UN Declaration on the Rights of Indigenous Peoples (UNDRIP), often coincide with environmental harm caused by destructive mining practices. Such unregulated activities also reflect governance shortcomings by state authorities. The limited integration of the 'social' aspect within ESG, as highlighted in a 2016 review of oil, gas and mining company boards, poses a significant obstacle to corporate due diligence in the extractive sector.[28] Instances of slave and child labour in the Congolese mining sector, along with the disregard for community rights, highlight broader institutional weaknesses in accountability and compliance with mining regulations.[29]

Exploitation and bondage in the sector arise from the global pursuit of simplistic sustainability ideals. The significant reserves of copper and cobalt in the DRC make the extractive sector vital for clean energy technologies and rechargeable batteries.[30] However, achieving this goal often involves modern slavery, as evidenced by studies showing high rates of labour exploitation among the DRC mining workers.[31] Amnesty International's Secretary General, Agnes Callamard, emphasises the need for a "just transition" for climate justice, recognising the importance of renewable energy sources without compromising human rights.[32]

Boyd *et al*[33] argue that modern slavery and climate change represent concurrent crises, yet their interconnections are often overlooked. Since slave labour is prevalent in ecologically harmful industries, modern slavery exacerbates climate change as a "threat multiplier".[34] Indigenous communities,

27 Nishith Desai Associates, "ESG: The New Age Value Creator: Code of Governance for Start-Ups", 2023, https://nishithdesai.com/fileadmin/user_upload/pdfs/Research_Papers/ESG-The-New-Age-Value-Creator.pdf.

28 First Peoples Worldwide, "Social Performance and Corporate Governance in the Extractive Sector: A Review of Oil, Gas and Mining Company Board", 2016.

29 Free the Slaves, "Slavery in DR Congo Slavery in 'Conflict Minerals'", 2013, https://freetheslaves.net/our-work/where-we-work/dr_congo.

30 Amnesty International, "DR Congo: Huge Expansion in Cobalt and Copper Mining is 'Wrecking Live'", 2023, www.amnesty.org.uk/press-release/dr-congo-huge-expansion-cobalt-and-copper-mining-wrecking-lives-new-report.

31 Free the Slaves, "Slavery in DR Congo Slavery in 'Conflict Minerals'", 2013, https://freetheslaves.net/our-work/where-we-work/dr_congo.

32 Amnesty International, "DR Congo: Huge Expansion in Cobalt and Copper Mining is 'Wrecking Lives'", 2023, www.amnesty.org.uk/press-release/dr-congo-huge-expansion-cobalt-and-copper-mining-wrecking-lives-new-report.

33 D Boyd, B Jackson, J Wardlaw, G Foody, S Marsh and K Bales, "Slavery from Space: Demonstrating the Role for Satellite Remote Sensing to Inform Evidence-Based Action Related to UN SDG Number 8", *ISPRS Journal of Photogrammetry and Remote Sensing* (2018) 142: 380–388.

34 K Bales and B Sovacool, "From Forests to Factories: How Modern Slavery Deepens the Crisis of Climate Change", *Energy Research & Social Science* (2021) 77 (102096): 1–9.

among the most vulnerable groups, face disproportionate impacts because their territories often encompass untapped natural areas.[35] Despite accountability mechanisms, colonial legacies persist in extractive governance, leading to human rights abuses and severe consequences, including land loss, forced eviction and health risks.[36]

In response to the lack of oversight, grassroots-led Indigenous monitoring mechanisms have emerged to improve mining industry practices on Indigenous lands. Indigenous Community-Based Monitoring programmes (ICBM) track environmental changes and future trends, compensating for inadequate government monitoring efforts.[37] However, criticisms of ICBM highlight its potential to disconnect Indigenous observations from industrial practices, leading to the loss of Traditional Ecological Knowledge.[38] Natcher and Brunet,[39] citing Preuss and Dixon,[40] argue that ICBM has been criticised for patronage and struggling to integrate local traditional knowledge in a scientifically driven manner. In some cases, it employs scientific and technological tools that fail to recognise the inherent values of the communities. This issue highlights broader concerns regarding the accessibility and bias of government engagement with Indigenous communities.[41]

4. Methodology

This study is qualitative in nature making it well suited for understanding social issues. Creswell posits[42] that qualitative research methods allow researchers to comprehend social phenomena and gain insights into complex and profound issues. Therefore, this chapter uses an in-depth analysis of documents, primarily legislation, to understand ESG practices within the extractive industry in the DRC. A critical interpretative approach will provide insights into the realities of ESG in mining and its best practices in the DRC.

35 A Scheidel, B Fernandez-Llamazares, D Bene, D David-Chavez, E Fanari, I Garba, K Hanacek, J Liu, G Martinez-Alier, V Reyes-Garcia, B Roy, L Temper, D Thiri, M Walter and K Whyte, "Global Impacts of Extractive and Industrial Development Projects on Indigenous People, Lifeways, Lands, and Rights", *Science Advances* (2023) 9 (23): 1–9.

36 OHCHR, A/HRC/54/4: *Summary of the panel discussion on the negative impact of the legacies of colonialism on the enjoyment of human rights – Report of the Office of the United Nations High Commissioner for Human Rights.*

37 A Buckland-Nicks, "Keys to Success: A Case Study Approach to Understanding Community-Based Water Monitoring Uptake in Governmental Decision-Making", master's thesis, 2015, Dalhousie University.

38 D Natcher and N Brunet, "Extractive Resources Industries and Indigenous Community-Based Monitoring: Cooperation or Cooptation?", *The Extractive Industries and Society*, (2020) 7 (4): 1279–1282.

39 *Ibid.*

40 K Preuss and M Dixon, "Looking After County Two-Ways: Insights Into Indigenous Community-Based Conservation From the Southern Tanami", *Ecological Management & Restoration*, (2012) 13 (1): 1–15.

41 C Samson and E Cassell, "The Long Reach of Frontier Justice: Canadian Land Claims 'Negotiation' Strategies as Human Rights Violations", *The International Journal of Human Rights*, (2012) 17(1): 35–55.

42 J Creswell, *Educational Research: Planning, Conducting and Evaluating Quantitative and Qualitative Research* (Pearson, 2014).

5. What constitutes good practices for mining companies?

ESG in mining encompasses a wide range of issues that can impact communities and the environment both positively and negatively. Given the extensive scope of ESG, and its various components, it is not feasible to exhaustively examine all its aspects within this chapter. Instead, this chapter aims to highlight key social issues within the mining sector in the DRC and explore what constitutes good practice.

The discussion focuses on three main issues: community rights violation, workers' rights and working conditions, and stakeholders' engagement. These issues are particularly significant in the DRC's mining sector.[43] By situating the discussion within the broader context of best practices for mining companies, we can better understand how to address these challenges effectively.

6. Community rights violation

Over the years, there have been growing concerns regarding the rights of communities to their land and the exploitation of these lands and resources to the detriment of those communities.[44] Mazalto[45] argues that mining activities have increasingly displaced communities within the DRC from their lands. Therefore, Law No 22/030 on the Protection and Promotion of Indigenous Pygmy People's Rights[46] which safeguards 'indigenous peoples' rights to their land, is commendable. However, mining companies should engage with communities to obtain their free, prior and informed consent (FPIC) before commencing mining activities.

FPIC involves a process, and an outcome of engagement that is free from external manipulation, coercion and intimidation. It requires sufficient advance notice and full disclosure of information regarding all aspects of a proposed project or activity in a manner that is accessible and understandable to the people whose consent is being sought. This process acknowledges that the people have the right to approve or reject a project or activity at any point in the process and that the entities seeking consent will abide by and respect their decision.[47]

Each component of FPIC carries meanings that convey both the rights of the community and the obligations of the entities interacting with them.[48]

---

43 M Mazalto, "Governance, Human Rights and Mining in the Democratic Republic of Congo", in B Campbell (ed), *Mining in Africa: Regulation and Development* (Pluto Press, 2009).

44 *Ibid.*

45 *Ibid.*

46 The DRC is home to approximately 1.5 million Pygmy Indigenous People, who are recognised by the government and civil societies. They are sometimes referred to as the Mbuti, Baka and Batwa people (see IWGIA report, www.iwgia.org/en/democratic-republic-of-congo/5045-iw-2023-drc.html, and Central African Forest Initiative reports).

47 ICMM, "ICMM Human Rights Due Diligence Guidance", May 2023, https://internationalwim.org/wp-content/uploads/2023/07/guidance_human-rights-due-diligence-compressed.pdf.

48 Oxfam Australia, "Free prior and informed consent", www.oxfam.org.au/explore/mining/free-prior-and-informed-consent.

- *Free:* Engagement must be free from force, intimidation, manipulation, coercion or pressure by any government or company.
- *Prior:* Consent must be obtained before the government allocates land for specific uses and prior to approval of specific projects. Indigenous Peoples must be given adequate time to consider all the information and make an informed decision.
- *Informed:* The community must receive all relevant information to make an informed decision. This information should be in a language that the community can easily understand and must include access to independent information, not just information from the project developers or the government. The community should also have access to legal and technical experts, if requested, to help make their decision.
- *Consent:* The community must have the right to say 'yes' or 'no' to the project at each stage, following their decision-making processes. The right to give or withhold consent is a crucial distinction between the rights of Indigenous Peoples and other project-affected peoples.

FPIC aligns with the United Nations Declaration on the Rights of Indigenous People (UNDRIP), which, although not binding, expresses the commitment of UN member states to uphold a standard of treatment for indigenous persons and to foster the development of new international legal norms.[49] Article 32 of UNDRIP specifically mandates that states must "consult and cooperate in good faith with the indigenous people concerned through their own representative institutions in order to obtain their free and informed consent prior to the approval of any project affecting their lands or territories and other resources, particularly in connection with the development, utilisation or exploitation of mineral, water or other resources".[50] UNDRIP similarly requires FPIC prior to adopting and implementing legislative or administrative measures that may affect them.

Furthermore, the International Labour Organization (ILO) Convention No 169, which in contrast to UNDRIP is legally binding for countries that have ratified it, requires state parties to consult with communities to reach agreement or consent on proposed measures implemented under the convention.[51] The convention includes various provisions mandating that nations consult with or secure the cooperation of indigenous peoples.

These and other key UN bodies and instruments argue that international standards regarding FPIC apply equally to non-state actors, such as extractive

49 United Nations Declaration on the Rights of Indigenous Peoples (UNDRIP), 2007, https://social.desa.un.org/issues/indigenous-peoples/united-nations-declaration-on-the-rights-of-indigenous-peoples.

50 *Ibid.*

51 ILO, "C169 – Indigenous and Tribal Peoples Convention, 1989 (No. 169)", Article 6, www.ilo.org/dyn/normlex/en/f?p=normlexpub:12100:0::no::p12100_instrument_id:312314.

companies. These bodies include the UN Permanent Forum on Indigenous Issues,[52] the UN Working Group on the issue of human rights and transnational corporations and other business enterprises, the UN Special Rapporteur on the Rights of Indigenous Peoples, the UN Experts Mechanism on the Rights of Indigenous Peoples and several UN Human Rights Treaty Bodies.[53]

7. Human rights issues

One of the major criticisms of the mining industry in the DRC is the prevalence of human rights abuses in various forms. While many of these issues are not unique to the mining industry, the following are commonly associated with it.[54] These issues include workers' rights and wages; as the mining supply chain, particularly in construction and facilities management, is often characterised by a low-skilled workforce. This workforce may include seasonal or migrant workers sourced through contractors and subcontractors. Low-skilled workers are especially vulnerable to exploitation due to limited financial resources and lack of sustainable employment options. This vulnerability can lead to unfair treatment, such as improper hiring and firing practices due to temporary contracts, unpaid or underpaid wages, excessive working hours, substandard, overcrowded and unsanitary living conditions, and restrictions of workers' freedom of movement, including the illegal withholding or confiscation of passports or personal identification documents.

7.1 Forced labour

The shipping, cleaning, personal protective equipment and electronics equipment supply chains are particularly vulnerable to practices where recruitment agencies or intermediaries charge high fees to recruit workers resulting in debt bondage. Migrant workers often have their travel documents confiscated by their employers as a 'condition' of employment.

7.2 Trafficking/gender-based violence

Human trafficking and sexual exploitation, including sex trafficking, can be significant risks around mining sites due to the transitory nature of the workforce, the high influx of workers and the isolation of worksites. Construction activities may attract numerous job seekers, predominately male, creating a 'boom town' effect. This can lead to gender-based violence and sexual health issues, such as an increase in sexually transmitted infection/disease transmission between transient workers and local communities.

---

52 United Nations Permanent Forum on Indigenous Issues, "Frequently Asked Questions – Declaration on the Rights of Indigenous Peoples", www.un.org/esa/socdev/unpfii/documents/FAQsindigenousdeclaration.pdf.

53 OECD, *OECD Due Diligence Guidance for Meaningful Stakeholder Engagement in the Extractive Sector*, 2 February 2017, http://dx.doi.org/10.1787/9789264252462-en.

54 *Ibid.*

7.3 Environmental degradation

Extractive industry activities can significantly degrade soil quality and contribute to air and water pollution, threatening resources that people rely on for subsistence and harming biodiversity.

7.4 Physical security

Private security personnel and public security forces often use excessive force to remove landowners from sites required for mining or associated infrastructure. They may also forcibly remove communities protesting against the negative ESG consequences of those developments. Additionally, local human rights defenders, workers and community leaders may become targets of violence, particularly in conflict zones or areas with weak governance.

7.5 Gender discrimination and abuse

Men in a community may often gain access to employment and economic opportunities from which women are excluded, or in which they are subject to sexual harassment. An increase in the cash economy can lead to changing power dynamics within families.

7.6 Conflict

The discovery of natural resources can generate local conflict or regional conflict, leading to violence and forced migration. Existing conflicts may be exacerbated by extractive operations.

The risks should be integrated into a company's management of existing projects, and its due diligence for potential new projects. According to the Organisation for Economic Cooperation and Development,[55] mining companies should develop and implement a comprehensive strategy to address these identified risks. This strategy should include conducting a supply chain risk assessment, with findings reported to senior management and an independent ombudsman. Additionally, a risk management plan should be created and adopted. This strategy will enable the company to manage risk by either: (i) continuing trade while undertaking measurable risk mitigation efforts; (ii) temporarily suspending trade while pursuing ongoing measurable risk mitigation; or (iii) disengaging with a supplier after failed attempts or if risk mitigation is deemed unfeasible or unacceptable.

To determine the appropriate strategy, companies should review Annex II of the *Due Diligence Guidance*[56] and assess their ability to influence suppliers.

---

55 *Ibid.*

56 OECD, *OECD Due Diligence Guidance for Responsible Supply Chains of Minerals from Conflict-Affected and High-Risk Areas*, www.oecd-ilibrary.org/governance/oecd-due-diligence-guidance-for-responsible-supply-chains-of-minerals-from-conflict-affected-and-high-risk-areas_9789264111110-en;jsessionid=1gJzKln0ikc54CbhmqAKjllXOhMdlrJrc1rnPX79.ip-10-240-5-138.

Where necessary, they should take steps to build leverage over suppliers who can most effectively prevent or mitigate the identified risks. If companies decide to pursue risk mitigation while continuing or temporarily suspending trade, they should consult with suppliers and affected stakeholders, including local and central government authorities, international or civil society organisations and affected third parties. Together, they should agree on a strategy for measurable risk mitigation in the risk management plan. Companies may draw on the suggested measures and indicators under Annex III of the *Due Diligence Guidance*[57] to design strategies sensitive to conflict or high-risk and to measure progressive improvement.

8. Stakeholder engagement in addressing risks and key issues

The activities of the extractive industry impact a range of stakeholders, including both state and non-state actors. The OECD (2017) provides guidelines in its *Due Diligence Guidance for Meaningful Stakeholder Engagement in the Extractive Sector* report, emphasising best practices for engaging with stakeholders.[58]

Local communities are among the most critical stakeholders, and the OECD guidelines stress the importance of understanding the context in which they operate. In the case of the DRC, with its complex historical background, extractive industries should engage in extensive consultations with technical experts, local community leaders and legal professionals to clarify obligations regarding interactions with indigenous communities.

These consultations help mining companies identify domestic requirements to obtain FPIC and assess their potential impact. For example, they should consider factors such as migration patterns of local wildlife, harm to biodiversity that may affect cultural heritage, customary land tenure rights and historical marginalisation of certain communities.

Mining companies should also establish robust support systems for meaningful engagement with communities. Personnel engaging with Indigenous Peoples should receive training to show respect for their culture, way of life, governance systems, traditional knowledge, and rights to and special connection with their lands, territories and natural resources. Understanding the Indigenous community's language, even informally, can demonstrate respect.

Additionally, resources needed for effective engagement with Indigenous Peoples, such as technical and legal support, community capacity building, local facilitators and compensation for community participation, should be

---

57 *Ibid.*

58 OECD, *OECD Due Diligence Guidance for Meaningful Stakeholder Engagement in the Extractive Sector*, 2 February 2017, http://dx.doi.org/10.1787/9789264252462-en.

determined and agreed upon in consultation with Indigenous Peoples throughout the engagement process.

Also, the OECD has outlined six essential steps for implementing meaningful stakeholder engagement in the extractive sector:

- *Understanding the local context:* ensure that personnel leading the stakeholder engagement are well-versed in the local and operational context.
- *Identify priority stakeholders:* determine and prioritise key stakeholders and interlocutors relevant to the engagement process.
- *Establish support systems:* set up the necessary support infrastructure for effective stakeholder engagement.
- *Design engagement activities:* create and implement appropriate and effective activities and processes for engaging with stakeholders.
- *Ensure follow-through:* maintain a commitment to the engagement process and follow through on actions and agreements.
- *Monitor and evaluate:* continuously monitor and evaluate engagement activities, addressing any identified shortcomings and making necessary adjustments.

9. Conclusion and recommendations

In conclusion, the extractive industries in the DRC are crucial to the national economy but pose significant challenges to human rights, particularly regarding community land rights and labour rights. The persistent exploitation in the sector highlights the urgent need for comprehensive reforms to safeguard human rights and promote sustainable practices. While key legislative frameworks, such as the recently amended Mining Code and Law No 22/030 on the Protection and Promotion of Indigenous Pygmy People's Rights, offer a foundation for addressing these issues, persistent gaps in enforcement and transparency call for robust implementation mechanisms.

Good practices for mining companies should include strict adherence to the FPIC principles, ensuring that communities are well-informed and can consent to mining activities without coercion. Additionally, addressing human rights abuses in the sector requires companies to design and implement effective risk management strategies. This involves conducting thorough supply chain assessments and adopting effective mitigation plans. Meaningful stakeholder engagement is also essential; mining companies must proactively engage with local communities and other stakeholders to understand the local context and address concerns comprehensively and proactively.

The intersection of corporate ESG standards with human rights highlights the necessity for an integrated approach that addresses environmental sustainability, social equity and robust governance. As the global demand for cobalt and other minerals increases, particularly for clean energy technologies, it is crucial that mining practices in the DRC adhere to international human rights standards and sustainability objectives.

9.1 Call to action

It is essential for the DRC government, international bodies and mining companies to collaborate in reforming the extractive sector. Implementing and enforcing stringent regulatory frameworks, promoting transparency, and ensuring accountability are critical steps. Mining companies must prioritise ethical practices, respect for human rights and meaningful community engagement. By doing so, the extractive industry can contribute to the sustainable development of the DRC, ensuring that natural resources benefit all citizens equitably and responsibly.

This chapter was prepared by Ufuoma Akpojivi, PRL team; James Aiken, PBLS team; Patrick Karanja, African team; and Yasmin Batliwala, CEO of Advocates for International Development (A4ID), with support from a legal partner who preferred anonymity, and CMS, London.

Indigenous rights in resource development: an UNDRIP perspective

Sandra Gogal
David How
Cassels Brock & Blackwell LLP

1. Introduction

Indigenous Peoples are socially and culturally distinct groups who share collective ancestral ties to the lands and natural resources where they traditionally live and occupy. The lands and resources upon which they depend are inextricably linked to their identities, cultures and livelihoods, as well as their physical and spiritual well-being.

Globally, Indigenous Peoples live in over 90 countries and their traditional lands are often rich in natural resources, such as oil and gas and minerals. However, the lack of formal legal recognition of rights over their lands, territories and natural resources prevents their full participation in and ability to benefit from resource development. This lack of recognition is a source of much conflict and discourse, leading to legal uncertainty at a time when interconnectivity is unavoidable, and cooperation is an imperative. Climate change and the need for critical mineral development presents a unique opportunity to address the legacy of exclusion and focus on collaborative approaches to resource development.

Indigenous Peoples worldwide share similar stories of exclusion from industrial development and disproportionately experience the legacy of environmental harms that it causes. While the focus of this chapter is on Indigenous rights in Canada, the lack of recognition and protection of Indigenous rights is a global issue. Canada's constitutional framework has forged a path for increasing the participation of Indigenous Peoples in Canada through meaningful consultation and the negotiation of impact and benefit agreements with proponents. However, international instruments such as the United Nations Declaration on the Rights of Indigenous Peoples (UNDRIP)[1] is shaping a global response to Indigenous participation in the resource sector, one based on the premise that consent should be a prerequisite to project development.

1 UNGAOR, 61st Sess, 107th Mtg, UN Doc 61/295 (2007) (UNDRIP).

This chapter presents an overview of Indigenous rights in Canada and how they are recognised and protected within Canada's constitutional framework. The chapter then proceeds with a brief outline of Canada's relationship with UNDRIP and an analysis of how UNDRIP and its concept of free, prior and informed consent (FPIC) has been applied and interpreted in Canadian law. As noted, while Canada has a unique relationship with its Indigenous Peoples, developed because of its constitutionally entrenched protection of Aboriginal rights under the Constitution Act, 1982,[2] the underlying objection and opposition to mineral development by Indigenous Peoples in Canada reflects a similar Indigenous voice, no development without consent.

2. Indigenous rights in Canada

The Indigenous Peoples of Canada, known under the law as the "Aboriginal peoples of Canada", can be understood to fall under three distinct groups: the First Nations, the Inuit and the Métis. Canada's various First Nations and Inuit peoples occupied, used and acted as stewards of their traditional territories prior to, at and after European contact and settlement of Canada. The Métis emerged as a distinct Indigenous People of mixed ancestry following contact between European settlers and various First Nations groups. What is common to all of Canada's Indigenous Peoples is their connection to and interest in the land, including through historic use and occupation of traditional lands and from the reservation of land for their benefit under historic and modern treaties and following settlement of claims with the Crown.

European settlement did not terminate the interests and customary laws of Canada's Indigenous Peoples, rather they survived the assertion of sovereignty of the Crown and were "absorbed into the common law as rights, unless (1) they were incompatible with the Crown's assertion of sovereignty, (2) they were surrendered voluntarily via the treaty process, or (3) the government extinguished them".[3] However, it was not until Canada enacted the Constitution Act, 1982 that the pre-existing Aboriginal and treaty rights of Canada's Indigenous Peoples were crystallised and enshrined in Canada's constitutional framework, thereby elevating their status and protection to Canada's supreme law. Section 35(1) of the Constitution Act, 1982 states:

> *The existing aboriginal and treaty rights of the aboriginal peoples of Canada are hereby recognized and affirmed.*

Section 35(1) is characterised as the primary instrument through which the Aboriginal rights and the treaty rights of Canada's Indigenous Peoples are recognised and protected in Canadian law, but it is notably not their source; they existed prior to the enactment of the Constitution Act, 1982. Section 35(1)

---

2 Constitution Act, 1982, being Schedule B of the Canada Act 1982 (UK), 1982, c 11.
3 *Mitchell v Minister of National Revenue*, 2001 SCC 33 at paragraph 10.

recognises Aboriginal rights and treaty rights, both of which are characterised as *sui generis* rights.[4] Aboriginal rights are "those rights held by Aboriginal peoples that relate to activities that are an element of a practice, custom, or tradition integral to the distinctive culture of the Aboriginal group claiming such rights, and that have not otherwise been extinguished prior to [the enactment of the Constitution Act, 1982] or by treaty".[5] While Aboriginal rights are often tied to land, such as hunting and fishing rights, it is not a requirement that they be. Aboriginal title is a category of Aboriginal rights that encompasses the collective right of an Indigenous community to the exclusive use and occupation of the land to which it attaches and is often referred to as the "highest form of Aboriginal right".[6]

The Supreme Court of Canada (SCC), the highest court in Canada, has outlined the test for establishing the existence of Aboriginal rights and, once established, an Aboriginal right is constitutionally protected by Section 35(1) of the Constitution Act, 1982. However, this protection is not absolute, and governments must function and balance the interests of society as a whole when making decisions.

The Crown, however, must act honourably in its dealings with Indigenous Peoples. This principle grounds the honour of the Crown, a legal concept unique to Canada that derives from the special trust relationship and the responsibility of the government *vis-à-vis* Indigenous Peoples that is itself rooted in the Crown's assertion of sovereignty over Canada and the prior occupation of the land by Indigenous Peoples.[7] Flowing from the honour of the Crown are various duties owed to Indigenous Peoples, such as the duty to consult that arises where contemplated government decisions or action may adversely affect Aboriginal rights (duty to consult) and fiduciary duties that arise where the government assumes discretionary control over Aboriginal interests. While the honour of the Crown continues to develop as a legal concept, fundamentally, it is always at stake when the Crown deals with Indigenous Peoples.[8]

Another form of rights protected under Section 35(1) of the Constitution Act, 1982 are treaty rights. Treaty rights are "those rights that are contained in treaties entered into between the Crown and Aboriginal peoples and can include specific rights such as those relating to hunting, fishing, trapping, and gathering".[9] Treaty rights can derive from either historic or modern treaties, are

---

4 *Newfoundland and Labrador (Attorney General) v Uashaunnuat (Innu of Uashat and of Mani Utenam)*, 2020 SCC 4 at paragraphs 25, 29 and 34.

5 Thomas Isaac, *Aboriginal Law*, 5th edition (Thomson Reuters, 2016), p59.

6 *R v Marshall; R v Bernard*, 2005 SCC 43 at paragraph 77.

7 *R v Sparrow* [1990] 1 SCR 1075 at paragraph 1114.

8 *R v Van der Peet* [1996] 2 SCR 507 at paragraph 24; *R v Badger* [1996] 1 SCR 771 at paragraph 41; *Haida Nation v British Columbia (Minister of Forests)*, 2004 SCC 73 at paragraph 16 (*Haida*).

9 Thomas Isaac, *Aboriginal Law*, 5th edition (Thomson Reuters, 2016), p60.

afforded the same constitutional protections as Aboriginal rights, and may be subject to justified infringement by legislation where the test outlined by the SCC is met.

3. UNDRIP in Canadian legislation

UNDRIP is an international human rights document which sets "the minimum standards for the survival, dignity and well-being of the [I]ndigenous peoples of the world".[10] Drafted over two decades by the United Nations' Working Group on Indigenous Populations, the international community, Indigenous leaders and experts, and Indigenous Peoples' advocates, UNDRIP was adopted by the United Nations General Assembly on 13 September 2007 by a majority of 144 countries in favour, four against, and 11 abstentions.[11]

While UNDRIP is not a legally binding international treaty, convention or agreement, Canada was initially one of the four countries that voted against it, along with Australia, New Zealand and the United States. Canada's initial position on UNDRIP did not represent a refusal to protect Indigenous rights domestically, but rather its position that several key provisions of the international document were overly broad and could be interpreted as being fundamentally incompatible with the country's legal regime.

Of particular concern, which is explored later in this chapter, were the provisions regarding the principle of FPIC. Canada considered the principle to be broad, unduly restrictive and capable of being interpreted as prohibiting state action on any legislative or administrative matter that may affect Indigenous Peoples in the absence of FPIC. Interpreted in this manner, the principle would represent a "complete veto power" and would thus be "fundamentally incompatible" with Canada's legal regime, which provides for a strong consultative process but not one with a complete veto power for any particular group.[12]

Canada eventually reversed its objection to UNDRIP, endorsing it with qualifications in a statement of support in 2010[13] and formally and fully endorsing it without qualification in 2016.[14] In removing its objector status, Canada stated it would adhere to UNDRIP in a manner consistent with

---

10 UNDRIP, Article 43.

11 United Nations General Assembly, "General Assembly Adopts Declaration on Rights of Indigenous Peoples: 'Major Step Forward' towards Human Rights for All, Says President", 13 September 2007, www.un.org/press/en/2007/ga10612.doc.htm.

12 Thomas Isaac and Grace Wu, "British Columbia's Enactment of the Declaration on the Rights of Indigenous Peoples Act: A Step Towards Reconciliation?" in Thomas Isaac, ed, *Key Developments in Aboriginal Law, Volume 2* (Thomson Reuters, 2021), p128.

13 Indigenous and Northern Affairs Canada, "Archived – Canada's Statement of Support on the United Nations Declaration on the Rights of Indigenous Peoples", 12 November 2010, www.aadnc-aandc.gc.ca/eng/1309374239861/ 1309374546142.

14 Government of Canada, "Canada Becomes a Full Supporter of the United Nations Declaration on the Rights of Indigenous Peoples", 10 May 2016, www.canada.ca/en/indigenous-northern-affairs/news/2016/05/canada-becomes-a-full-supporter-of-the-united-nations-declaration-on-the-rights-of-indigenous-peoples.html.

Canadian law. The legal and moral ambiguity created by this position has unfortunately added to the conflict and discourse in its dealings with Indigenous Peoples.

In 2021, Canada enacted the United Nations Declaration on the Rights of Indigenous Peoples Act (UNDRIP Act)[15] with two stated purposes:

(a) affirm [UNDRIP] as a universal international human rights instrument with application in Canadian law; and

(b) provide a framework for the Government of Canada's implementation of [UNDRIP].[16,17]

The UNDRIP Act also requires government to develop and implement an action plan to achieve the objectives of UNDRIP and to prepare annual reports on the progress made in respect of these objectives.[18]

In 2023, Canada released the United Nations Declaration on the Rights of Indigenous Peoples Act Action Plan,[19] which outlines the 181 measures that Canada will adopt and which in turn reflect the priorities and proposals identified by Indigenous Peoples, contribute to achieving the objectives of UNDRIP, and align with specific topics covered by the UNDRIP Act.[20] It includes both broader, general commitments, such as exploring options for providing UNDRIP training to the judiciary, as well as more specific initiatives, such as establishing an independent Indigenous rights monitoring, oversight, recourse or remedy mechanism with detailed functions and requirements.[21]

However, given its broadly worded commitments, Canada's Action Plan falls short of addressing the uncertainty around the legal effect of the UNDRIP Act, nor how Canada intends to align its laws with UNDRIP.

4. UNDRIP in Canadian jurisprudence

Canadian courts have begun to wrestle with the role UNDRIP plays in Canadian law. The question of whether UNDRIP has become part of Canadian law such that Canada's laws must be in conformity with its obligations or whether it is

15 United Nations Declaration on the Rights of Indigenous Peoples Act, SC 2021, c 14.

16 *Ibid*, Section 4.

17 The first UNDRIP-related statute in Canada was enacted by the province of British Columbia in 2019, Declaration on the Rights of Indigenous Peoples Act, SBC 2019, c 44, which Canada's UNDRIP Act was modelled after. In 2023 the territorial government of the Northwest Territories also enacted the United Nations Declaration on the Rights of Indigenous Peoples Implementation Act, SNWT 2023, c 36 (UNDRIPIA) with similar stated purposes as the Canada and British Columbia UNDRIP-related statutes.

18 Of note in the British Columbia legislation is the ability of government to enter into agreements with Indigenous governing bodies for the purposes of implementing the legislation and furthering the process of reconciliation, including agreements respecting the joint exercise of statutory decision-making power or Indigenous consent prior to the exercise of a statutory decision-making power.

19 Government of Canada, "The Action Plan", 21 June 2023, www.justice.gc.ca/eng/declaration/ap-pa/index.html (UNDRIP Act Action Plan).

20 In 2022, British Columbia released its Declaration on the Rights of Indigenous Peoples Act Action Plan containing 89 priority actions and including collectively identified goals and outcomes that form the long-term vision for implementing UNDRIP in British Columbia. The Northwest Territories has yet to release an action plan under UNDRIPIA.

21 UNDRIP Act Action Plan, pp28–29.

merely an interpretive aid Canadian courts may rely on when undertaking a statutory interpretation exercise, is still a live question.

At one end of this debate, the Superior Court of Québec has held that UNDRIP should be given the same weight as a binding international instrument when interpreting Section 35 of the Constitution Act, 1982, reasoning that Canada enacted the UNDRIP Act, therefore demonstrating an intention to make UNDRIP binding.[22]

At the other end, several Canadian courts have held that UNDRIP does not have legal force in Canada and is only applicable as an interpretive aid, requiring that statutes be interpreted in conformity with UNDRIP or where multiple interpretations are possible, an interpretation that best conforms to UNDRIP is favoured.[23] This is the position adopted by most courts in Canada.

The SCC has ruled that UNDRIP is not a binding treaty in Canada and the UNDRIP Act lacks clear and explicit intent to bind Canada to UNDRIP and to implement it.[24] However, the SCC held that UNDRIP "has been incorporated into the country's domestic positive law" and, therefore, federal statutes "must be interpreted in light of UNDRIP".[25] Furthermore, the UNDRIP Act creates several positive obligations binding on Canada, including an obligation to take all measures necessary to ensure that the laws of Canada are consistent with UNDRIP.[26]

5. FPIC and the duty to consult

The legal effect of UNDRIP in Canadian jurisprudence is critical to understanding the integration of UNDRIP's FPIC provisions within Canada's existing jurisprudence on the duty to consult. The duty to consult flows from the honour of the Crown and imposes a duty upon the Crown to consult with Indigenous Peoples when it is contemplating a decision or action that has the potential to adversely impact an Aboriginal or treaty right.

The threshold for triggering the duty to consult is a low one, the Crown's contemplated action or decision need not have an immediate effect on the Aboriginal or treaty right or interest, nor does the Aboriginal or treaty right or interest have to be explicitly recognised by a court.[27] Instead, there only needs to be a potential for an adverse effect on the right or interest asserted for the duty to be triggered, although the adverse effect must be appreciable.[28]

---

22 *White v Montour*, 2023 QCCS 4154 at paragraphs 1201–1202.

23 See *Gitxaala v British Columbia (Chief Gold Commissioner)*, 2023 BCSC 1680 at paragraph 417; *Wesley v Alberta*, 2022 ABKB 713 at paragraphs 145 and 147; *East Prairie Metis Settlement v Alberta*, 2021 ABQB 762 at paragraph 35; *Watson v Canada*, 2020 FC 129 at paragraph 351; *Ross River Dena Council v Canada*, 2017 YKSC 59 at paragraphs 302–303; *Nunatukavut Community Council Inc v Canada (Attorney General)*, 2015 FC 981 at paragraph 104.

24 *Reference re An Act respecting First Nations, Inuit and Métis children, youth and families*, 2024 SCC 5 at paragraphs 4 and 15.

25 *Ibid* at paragraphs 4, 15, 59 and 85.

26 *Ibid* at paragraphs 15 and 85.

27 *Haida* at paragraph 37.

28 *Rio Tinto Alcan Inc v Carrier Sekani Tribal Council*, 2010 SCC 43 at paragraphs 40–41, 44 and 46.

The 'depth' of consultation required in any given situation will depend on the strength of the asserted Aboriginal or treaty right or interest and the potential adverse effect on those rights.[29] The SCC has described the Crown's duty to consult as existing along a spectrum, with deeper consultation being owed where rights are established and the impact severe.[30] However, the courts have been clear that the duty to consult does not represent a veto by the Indigenous community being consulted, nor does it require that the Crown and the Indigenous community reach an agreement.[31] Rather, it is a commitment to a meaningful consultation process that is conducted in good faith.[32]

The Crown must determine, after completing consultations, whether it should proceed with its contemplated decision or action and, if so, whether some accommodation is warranted. The Crown must also balance Indigenous rights and interests with any competing rights and interests of the broader Canadian society.[33]

Is the principle of FPIC consistent with Canadian jurisprudence? The answer is not easily ascertainable, but clarity may be found in the purpose and language used in UNDRIP. The principle of FPIC is contained in six articles in UNDRIP, with the most focused debate centred around Article 32(2) which reads:

> *32(2) States* ***shall consult and cooperate*** *in good faith with the [I]ndigenous peoples concerned through their own representative institutions in* ***order to obtain*** *their free and informed consent prior to the approval of any project affecting their lands or territories and other resources, particularly in connection with the development, utilization or exploitation of mineral, water or other resources* [emphasis added].

In the context of resource development, Article 32(2) has often been cited as requiring the consent of Indigenous Peoples prior to any project approval. However, this interpretation begs scrutiny considering the mandatory language found in Articles 10 and 29(2) of UNDRIP. By contrast, Articles 10 and 29(2) require states to obtain FPIC in cases where Indigenous Peoples are forced to relocate or upon the disposal of hazardous materials on their lands.

> *10 Indigenous peoples shall not be forcibly removed from their lands or territories. No relocation shall take place without the free, prior and informed consent of the [I]ndigenous peoples concerned and after agreement on just and fair compensation and, where possible, with the option of return.*

---

29 *Haida* at paragraphs 43–45.

30 *Ibid* at paragraphs 43–44.

31 *Ibid* at paragraphs 48–49; *Ktunaxa Nation v British Columbia (Forests, Lands and Natural Resource Operations)*, 2017 SCC 54 at paragraphs 80 and 83; *Behn v Moulton Contracting Ltd*, 2013 SCC 26 at paragraph 29; *Taku River Tlingit First Nation v British Columbia (Project Assessment Director)*, 2004 SCC 74 at paragraph 2.

32 *Haida* at paragraphs 46, 48 and 50.

33 *Haida* at paragraphs 47 and 50; *Mikisew Cree First Nation v Canada (Minister of Canadian Heritage)*, 2005 SCC 69 at paragraph 66; *Chippewas of the Thames First Nation v Enbridge Pipelines Inc*, 2017 SCC 41 at paragraph 59.

29(2) States shall take effective measures to ensure that no storage or disposal of hazardous materials shall take place in the lands or territories of [I]ndigenous peoples without their free, prior and informed consent.

An interpretation imposing a more general obligation to consult with the Indigenous group in order to obtain their consent, as found in Article 32(2), would be consistent with Canadian jurisprudence in the context of the Crown's duty to consult. As noted previously, the SCC has held that this does not mean Indigenous Peoples hold a veto over project development. In fact, the government of Canada has stated that FPIC does not constitute such a 'veto' power over government decision making but rather should be likened to the duty to consult where the parties work together in a good faith partnership with different processes being required depending on the circumstances.[34] Whether such a position is tenable remains to be determined by Canadian courts. In any case, as a part of UNDRIP, FPIC itself is not legally binding in Canada.

In what context then should a project not proceed where the consent of the Indigenous community has not been obtained? What does consent mean if it has no persuasive authority to determine whether a project proceeds or not? While it is ultimately left to the courts to determine, the answer may lie in the degree of impact a project may have on the lands and territories held by the Indigenous Peoples. As in the case of relocation, where their lands are removed, or the case where hazardous materials are disposed of, rendering the lands useless in terms of exercising harvesting rights, such impacts are significant and irreversible. If FPIC is to serve any purpose, should projects which have an equally devastating impact on lands and resources or would constitute an irreversible infringement of rights, be held to this higher standard of obtaining consent? It can be argued that the Crown's duty to consult already imposes such a higher standard in analogous contexts in Canada.

6. Summary

The imperative for global cooperation in the context of climate change and the need for critical mineral development requires a transformative change in the way in which extractive sectors address Indigenous rights to lands and resources. Climate-related disasters and impacts on the environment have a direct and disproportionate effect on their way of life and survival such that their participation in the decision making and the entitlement to be accommodated for any impacts to their lands and rights is just, if not legally required.

While Canada's constitutional and common law framework applicable to protecting the rights of Indigenous Peoples may be considered more developed

34 Government of Canada, "Backgrounder: *United Nations Declaration on the Rights of Indigenous Peoples Act*", 19 July 2021, www.justice.gc.ca/eng/declaration/about-apropos.html.

and sophisticated than that of any other country, it faces equal criticism and opposition from Indigenous communities in the context of resource development. Developing a collaborative approach to critical mineral development, whether grounded in law or fairness principles, will go further in creating legal certainty and minimising conflict and discourse. The lack of legal certainty and enforceability of UNDRIP in Canada and in other signatory countries presents a unique opportunity for industry to forge a practice of Indigenous participation and inclusion to a degree commensurate with the degree of intrusion and impact to Indigenous rights, lands and resources.

Anti-bribery and corruption considerations and transparency in dealing with governments

Eoin O'Shea
CMS Cameron McKenna Nabarro Olswang LLP

There has always been wealth to be found in mining and mineral extraction. A particular risk faced by the mining and extractive sector globally is the fact that the right to extract valuable material from land on an industrial scale, and/or control of the means of doing so, is almost always controlled by government bodies. Such bodies are prone to corruption, especially in countries where there is relatively weak governance and transparency and where law-enforcement institutions are themselves likely to be affected by corruption.

This problem is as prevalent in relation to industrial commodities such as lithium, cobalt, aluminium and copper as it was (and, of course, remains) for precious metals, gemstones and coal.

It is hard to exaggerate the consequences of corruption. This chapter is no place for a thesis on this complex topic; however, there can be little doubt that widespread corruption has a deleterious effect on the stability and development of states. Corruption inevitably affects the proper functioning of institutions concerned with social and economic decision making. It causes loss of trust in government, incites local conflicts and undermines the rule of law and local and national security interests.

Such consequences also create very significant risks for corporations. Even corporates which do not engage in corruption can be harmed by the economic and social instability which tends to affect countries undermined by widespread corruption, and ethical corporates can be prejudiced in their own dealings with corrupt governments. For corporates that engage in or tolerate corruption relating to their own business interests, the effects can be very grave. There will be few countries, if any, which do not criminalise domestic corruption. Moreover, many countries now also criminalise corruption overseas, in particular when it is connected with business or commercial interests.[1] In many cases, disclosure of corruption investigations or even allegations can have a material effect on corporate reputation, share price, recruitment and retention. That is to say nothing of the damage to the reputations and careers of individuals.

Globally, over the past decade or more, as part of the environmental, social and governance (ESG) movement, we have seen anti-bribery and corruption playing a prominent role in government policies. Jurisdictions across the globe now enforce anti-bribery legislation with extra-territorial reach.

There are numerous international initiatives, the purpose of which is to prevent or deter corruption. Initiatives promulgated by international /intergovernmental organisations include:

- the Organisation for Economic Co-operation and Development (OECD) Anti-Bribery Convention;
- the United Nations Convention Against Corruption (UNCAC);
- the African Union Convention on Preventing and Combating Corruption (AUCPCC);
- the Inter-American Convention Against Corruption (IACAC); and
- the Council of Europe's Criminal Law Convention on Corruption G20 Anti-Corruption Working Group.[2]

There are also initiatives espoused by private sector or trade associations, with less emphasis on legislation and more on practical measures which companies can adopt. These include model codes of conduct and procedures, lists of recommended good practice, suggested training programmes, and, in some cases, collective action platforms for reporting or risk-sharing.

Among these are:

- Transparency International's Business Principles for Countering Bribery;
- International Chamber of Commerce (ICC) Rules on Combating Corruption;
- World Economic Forum's Partnering Against Corruption Initiative (PACI);
- TRACE International's anti-bribery compliance solutions;
- OECD Guidelines for Multinational Enterprises;
- United Nations Global Compact's 10th Principle against corruption;
- Extractive Industries Transparency Initiative (EITI);
- Maritime Anti-Corruption Network (MACN); and
- Wolfsberg Principles (for banking sector).

In summary, it is clear that the risk of corruption in dealing with

---

1 For example, the United States is an enthusiastic enforcer of the Foreign Corrupt Practices Act 1977 (FCPA). The United Kingdom has dramatically increased enforcement activity in relation to the Bribery Act 2010. The French 'Loi Sapin II' considerably extends the jurisdiction of the French courts for corruption by companies overseas. There are several other examples.

2 Although the G20 does not produce legally binding instruments, its initiatives influence international standards and practices in the fight against corruption. The Group collaborates with various international organisations, including the OECD, UNCAC and the Financial Action Task Force (FATF), to promote global anti-corruption efforts.

governments is likely to be very significant for companies in the extractive sector. A robust approach to anti-bribery and corruption will be a vital tool in risk management and corporate governance. There is no shortage of authoritative material to which companies can look for guidance.

1. Typical risk factors (cross-sector)

A consistent theme of model codes and guides to good practice[3] is the need for effective risk assessment as regards bribery and corruption.

The following generic risk factors are likely to apply to almost all companies doing business internationally whether or not in the mining /extractive sectors.

1.1 Geographic risk

Operations in countries where there is a history of corruption in relation to the extractive sector and/or which rank low on various indices of international corruption[4] must be seen as having a higher risk of bribery and corruption.

Of course, any published 'league tables' may have methodological flaws or biases and should not be seen as determinative of the risks of a particular project. Nevertheless, their ubiquity is such that they cannot be ignored as important indicators of potential risks. Operations in a high-risk country should automatically prompt greater vigilance across all affected parts of the business, even more so when dealing with government bodies.

1.2 Strength of regulatory environment

Where anti-corruption laws, though they may exist, are not regularly enforced or any enforcement is arbitrary or connected to political factors, this tends to increase the risk of bribery.

1.3 Number/importance of government interactions

There will be few mining projects which do not require some interaction with government agencies and officials. However, a higher than average level of 'bureaucracy' in certain countries tends to provide officials with more opportunities to seek bribes and tempt companies to skip the queue by illicit means.

1.4 Low transparency societies

"Sunlight is the greatest disinfectant" is a well-known aphorism.[5] There is a greater risk of opacity and lack of accountability in public contracting, and thus a greater risk of bribery and corruption, in countries which place significant

---

3 For example: OECD FAQs "How to address bribery and corruption risks in Mineral Supply Chains", the OECD Anti-Bribery Convention, the UNCAC and the OECD MNE Guidelines.

4 Such as the Transparency International Corruption Perceptions Index, published annually.

5 Louis Brandeis, *Other People's Money And How the Bankers Use It* (1914).

limits on reporting on government contracting, political scrutiny and on the free press generally.

1.5 Common use of third-party intermediaries

There are some countries where it is very common for external companies to make use of the services of third-party agents in order to win business or to interact with government agencies on topics such as licensing, taxation or other regulatory matters. The use of such agents is generally seen as a risk factor due to the lack of control which the principal tends to have over the activities of the agent. The agent may engage in bribery on behalf of the principal in order to win business or gain some other advantage, and thus to earn commissions or bonuses. The position under the legal systems of several countries (eg, the United States and the United Kingdom) is that companies may be liable for bribery by their agents as long as the bribery was done to benefit the principal.

1.6 Project-specific characteristics

There is likely to be greater bribery risk to projects with the following characteristics:

- Larger and/or more valuable projects or contracts, given the greater incentives involved;
- Projects with significant impacts on local communities (eg, environmental effects, need for significant infrastructure or resettlement). Such projects tend to have more stakeholders and involve more disparate interests. As a result, there is a greater potential for conflicts of interest which may be less clear than in other circumstances; and
- Projects which may, directly or indirectly affect the standing, funding or popularity of particular political parties or politicians, ethnic, linguistic or social groups. Where projects or contracts are politically sensitive or consequential there will be more pressure on officials and investors to cut corners and bypass governance processes and other safeguards.

2. Typical risks: mining/extractive sector

2.1 Procurement/contracting with governments

(a) Awards of rights

Countries award exploration and mining rights in different forms. They may be called leases, titles, licences, concessions or tenements. The methods used to allocate the rights also differ. In some countries, rights are granted on a first-come-first-served basis, in others through a tender or competitive bidding process or via negotiated agreements.

The awarding of mining or extraction or processing rights/contracts is particularly vulnerable to corruption, given the significance and likely value of such awards. One in four corruption cases in the extractive sector are believed to occur at this initial phase.[6]

Red flags of vulnerability to corruption when rights are being awarded include:

- unrestricted decision-maker discretion;
- deviations from the law;
- no or unclear fixed timeframe;
- no or limited documentation requirements;
- no clear decision maker;
- multiple decision makers;
- lack of independence of decision maker;
- conflicting duties of decision maker;
- prevalence of workarounds;
- face-to-face contacts the norm rather than written communications; and
- needlessly complex structuring, whether for tax or other reasons.

Companies may be faced with demands for bribes, either explicit or disguised. The ways in which this may happen are too numerous to list, but typical examples include demands for cash payments, demands for unnecessary services from third parties, demands for unnecessary extraneous work such as infrastructure projects or demands for specific outcomes as regards sub-contracting or local participation.

(b) *Public consultations*

Issues also arise from opaque processes for converting and opening land for mining/extraction. The corruption risk can arise because of a lack of clear, binding guidance on the process and principles for the consultation process, because the consultation occurs too late in the approval process, or because only the local elite or specific groups are consulted. The scope for public consultation should be clearly defined and criteria set out. Clear records of all such consultations should be kept and, if possible, made subject to independent scrutiny or verification. Where there are conflicts of interest, for example between the rights of landowners and mining authorities, a clear legal framework is required, to set out how these issues should be addressed.

---

6 OECD, *Corruption in the extractive value chain: Typology of risks, mitigation measures and incentives*, 18 August 2018, www.oecd.org/en/publications/corruption-in-the-extractive-value-chain_9789264256569-en.html; Transparency International, *Mining Awards Corruption Risk Assessment Tool*, https://knowledgehub.transparency.org/assets/uploads/kproducts/2017_MACRA_Tool_EN.pdf.

(c) ***Permits, planning and licences***

Licences or permits will inevitably be under the control of public agencies and officials. In the mining sector the area of land to be exploited/explored, infrastructure, service-provision to the site, building and planning, environmental requirements and reporting and control commitments can all be subject to the discretion of corrupt individuals or of agencies under the control of corrupt individuals.

Risks can also arise when the relevant authority has a conflicting mandate, for example, the licensing authority is also responsible for promoting investment in mining. As a result of a focus on securing the investment in mining, other interests, such as economic, environmental and social interests may suffer.

(d) ***Contracting/joint ventures with state-owned entities***

It is often the case in the mining sector that the state will have its own commercial entities with an interest in mining or refining or processing mined commodities. It may be commercially attractive, or even legally required, to partner with such state-owned enterprises (SOEs). However, doing so may increase bribery risks. In general, SOEs tend to be somewhat opaque and more subject to political influence than purely privately held commercial entities.

Joint ventures with other local partners can also present risks – it is not unheard of for such entities to be owned by senior government officials (often via opaque ownership structures) or by parties acting on their behalf.

(e) ***Operations***

Ongoing operations also provide opportunities for solicitation of bribes or other corrupt activity. Examples include:

Safety and labour issues: Mining tends to be labour-intensive and involves considerable health and safety hazards. Inspection and certification of operations as safe and compliant with standards can carry the risk of bribery in cases where agencies or officials deliberately delay or withhold, or threaten to delay or withhold, certification. Even more serious would be the case where certification is not justified but is offered in any event in exchange for a bribe.

The same risks attend dealings with organised labour representatives or officials charged with ensuring compliance with labour laws (eg, as regards overtime, holiday pay, breaks etc).

Shipping, customs and transport: Of course, goods and materials have to be shipped to and from a mining site. Shipping material across national boundaries (eg, state lines) and international borders often involves dealing with officialdom. Tax and customs duties and other import/export formalities are classic occasions on which officials can seek to extract bribes by means of illicit 'fees' or charges in exchange for clearances or release of goods.

Environmental issues: Mining projects frequently have significant impacts on the environment, the regulation of which is a matter for government. Approval of the project or some aspect of it will often involve assessing the potential environmental (and social) impacts of the proposed extraction plan and developing a plan to manage and mitigate these. These processes are often referred to as environmental and social impact assessments (ESIAs).

In some countries, the review of ESIAs is carried out by private consultants, who are often recruited for short fixed-term contracts. This creates the risk of potential conflicts of interest and connected risks of bribery.

Clear and transparent criteria are required to ensure that ESIAs are properly verified and to control the discretion of public officials, and to ensure that their decisions about whether to approve the content of ESIAs and associated management plans are not subject to political interference or improper economic incentives.

The same principles of course apply to all other environmental work which requires government approval, including mitigation processes or carbon-reduction commitments, among others.

Taxation: Mining projects, or the revenue derived from them, are typically subject to taxation in the country in which the project is located. A demand to pay a bribe can sometimes also be dressed up as the payment of tax, although not destined for the government of that country but for the personal benefit of an official. Tax officials can also make demands for bribes in order to show leniency in assessing taxes, withholding enforcement actions or accepting a particular tax treatment.

Entities should therefore consider public disclosure of all information on taxes, fees and royalties that are paid to governments for mineral extraction, trade and export to mitigate these risks.

3. Outline anti-bribery and corruption (ABAC) policy

The discussion below outlines a structure for such policies and procedures which tend to be seen across various sectors, however, there is no one-size-fits-all as regards ABAC policies and procedures. Each company's risk-profile and resources will be different.

3.1 Code of ethics

A code of ethics usually covers topics considerably wider than just ABAC, taking in personnel issues, health and safety, whistleblower protection, quality control, conflicts of interest, accuracy in books and records, confidentiality, anti-trust and numerous other topics. However, such a code should be very clear that ABAC is a central facet of the company's approach to doing business. It should make clear reference to the bribery policy and procedures.

Transparency International recommends that all directors and employees should be required to sign a declaration annually to state that they have read and understood the applicable code. This serves the dual purpose of a reminder to staff of their duties when it comes to bribery and corruption and to reinforce the top-level commitment to ethical business conduct.

3.2 ABAC policy and procedures

The UK government guidance on the Bribery Act 2010 outlines six principles on which to establish good ABAC governance. Although directed at compliance for UK organisations and those doing business in the United Kingdom, these principles can be seen as reflecting generally recognised good practice and providing a solid foundation for any approach to ABAC for companies operating in Western markets. The principles are as follows.

(a) Proportionate procedures

An effective risk assessment (discussed below) will identify which areas of business pose the greatest risk, and this will inform the implementation of procedures, both in terms of prevention polices and the means of implementing them.

The procedures should seek to ensure there is a practical and realistic means of achieving the organisation's stated anti-bribery policy objectives across all of the organisation's functions. Typical elements of the policy will address at least the following:

- provision of gifts, hospitality and promotional expenditure, facilitation payments or political and charitable donations or contributions;
- direct and indirect employment, including recruitment, terms and conditions, disciplinary action and remuneration;
- governance of business relationships with all other associated persons including pre- and post-contractual agreements;
- financial and commercial controls such as adequate bookkeeping, auditing and approval of expenditure;
- transparency of transactions and disclosure of information;
- decision making, such as procedures for delegation of authority, separation of functions and the avoidance of conflicts of interest;
- enforcement, detailing disciplinary processes and sanctions for breaches of the entity's anti-bribery rules;
- the reporting of bribery, including 'speak up'/'whistleblowing' procedures; and
- implementation plans, ie, how policy will be applied to individual projects and to different parts of the organisation.

The policy should include a risk management plan. If the identified risks arise, how will these be managed? Will the entity continue to trade with the offending party throughout the course of risk mitigation efforts, temporarily suspend trade while pursuing ongoing risk mitigation or disengage with a supplier either after failed attempts at mitigation or where the company deems mitigation not feasible or the risks unacceptable?

(b) Top-level commitment

An anti-bribery stance must be communicated/adopted from the most senior members of the organisation/entity and cascaded down. The individuals running an organisation are best placed to foster a culture in which bribery is unacceptable. This should be communicated both internally and externally – how this is done will depend on the size and nature of the entity. Consideration should be given to how best to draw this to people's attention, whether this is done on a periodic basis, through a statement on the entity's internet site and/or its intranet site. Such a communication is another opportunity to reinforce the anti-bribery policy/commitment and the company's code of ethics, and can cover such points as:

- a commitment to carry out business fairly, honestly and openly;
- a commitment to 'zero tolerance' towards bribery;
- the consequences of breaching the policy for employees and managers;
- for other associated persons, the consequences of breaching contractual provisions relating to bribery prevention (eg, a cascading of the anti-bribery commitment, and that the entity will not work with others who don't make the same anti-bribery commitment);
- articulating the business benefits of rejecting bribery (reputational, customer and business partner confidence);
- reference to the range of bribery prevention procedures the entity has or is putting in place, including protection and procedures for confidential reporting of bribery;
- key individuals and departments involved in the development and implementation of the entity's bribery prevention procedures; and
- reference to the organisation's involvement in any collective action against bribery in, for example, the same business sector.

Where a training programme is being rolled out, entities may wish to involve top-level managers as part of this to demonstrate the anti-bribery commitment. Similarly, their active involvement in risk assessments and the development and oversight of anti-bribery polices may be appropriate. A presence on sectoral organisations and engaging with relevant external bodies is particularly relevant in the mining and minerals sector, for example as a Supporter of the Extractive Industries Transparency Initiative, a member of the

International Council on Mining and Metals (ICMM) or other commodity-specific or national organisations, which have ABAC and other governance standards and commitments.

(c) *Risk assessment*

An entity must assess the nature and extent of its exposure to potential external and internal risks of bribery. The risk assessment should be both outward and inward looking. It should enable the entity to accurately identify the risks it may face and how to prioritise them.

The ABAC risk assessment should be documented and reviewed periodically to ensure it remains current. Risks do not remain static. For example, a change of government or an environmental incident can influence the risks, whether by eliminating, altering or creating a new one. While a periodic review should be diarised, there should also be allowance for reactive reviews, such as on a change of government or the occurrence of a natural disaster.

Whether the ABAC risk assessment is standalone or is contained within a broader risk assessment will depend on the size of the entity and the nature of its business. There is an interface with any practices relating to customer, supplier or employee due diligence, as these also are designed to identify risks and mitigate against their occurrence.

As part of the risk assessment process, good governance principles advocate that the following are addressed as part of the risk assessment process:

- oversight of the process/sign off by top-level management;
- appropriate resourcing to ensure the assessment is done properly;
- identifying internal and external information sources to be considered to enable full assessment of the risks to be reviewed;
- due diligence enquiries; and
- accurate and appropriate documentation of the risk assessment and its conclusion.

Risks can be categorised into five broad groups.

- *Country risk:* What is the perceived level of corruption in the country? Guidance is available from FATF and Transparency International.[7] Does the country in which the entity is transacting have effectively implemented anti-bribery legislation? Does the government, media, local business community and civil society promote transparent procurement and investment policies?
- *Sectoral risk:* Undoubtedly the mining and mineral extraction sector carries higher risk than many others for many of the factors outlined above.

---

7 Transparency International runs an annual Corruption Perceptions Index which ranks every country by its perceived levels of public sector corruption, see www.transparency.org/en/cpi/2023.

- *Transactional risk:* Certain types of transactions give rise to higher risks, for example, charitable or political contributions, licences and permits, and transactions relating to public procurement.
- *Business opportunity risk:* Such risks might arise in high-value projects or with projects involving many contractors or intermediaries; or with projects which are not apparently undertaken at market prices, or which do not have a clear legitimate objective.
- *Business partnership risk:* Certain relationships may involve higher risks, for example, the use of intermediaries in transactions with foreign public officials; consortia or joint venture partners; and relationships with politically exposed persons where the proposed business relationship involves, or is linked to, a prominent public official.

Bribery risks can exist internally as much as externally. Relevant internal factors include:

- deficiencies in employee training, skills and knowledge;
- bonus culture rewarding excessive risk taking – could tempt bonus-eligible staff to engage in bribery/corruption in order to win business for the entity and thereby boost their bonus;
- lack of clarity in internal policies on, and procedures for, hospitality and promotional expenditure, and political or charitable contributions;
- lack of clear financial controls – an efficient system of financial controls should immediately flag any unusual/excessive payment which can be a red flag for a bribe having been paid/received; and
- lack of a clear anti-bribery message from senior management.

(d) Due diligence

Due diligence is widely seen as central to good corporate governance. Due diligence specifically relating to bribery prevention is both a form of risk assessment and a means of mitigating a risk.

In keeping with the theme of the guidance, the due diligence should be proportionate to the identified risk. It can be done internally or by external consultants.

A commonly encountered situation that carries particular due diligence implications is a merger of commercial organisations or acquisition of one by another. Often it is in these situations that bribery risks are uncovered and require a self-report to be made.

The Bribery Act states that an entity's employees are assumed to be persons associated with that entity, for the purposes of the Bribery Act requirements, and this assumption is likely to be common across legal systems. Therefore, recruitment and human resources procedures should be reviewed to ensure that an appropriate level of due diligence is carried out for new recruits – the appropriate level of due diligence will be based on the risk associated with the post in question, with lower risk posts unlikely to require due diligence.

(e) ***Communication (including training)***

Internal and external communication are central to ensuring that an entity has embedded its bribery prevention policies and procedures and that they are understood by those who need to.

Consideration should be given to who in the organisation would most benefit from these messages and how to best communicate them. Content, language and tone of communications for internal consumption may vary to that for external use. Consider if translations are required.

Internal communications should convey the 'tone from the top' but also focus on the implementation of the organisation's policies and procedures and the implications for employees. Employees should be clear in where they can access the policy and procedure on things such as decision making, financial control, hospitality and promotional expenditure, facilitation payments, training, charitable and political donations and penalties for breach of these rules. Also central to the internal communication is the 'whistleblowing' procedures. Each entity should have in place a secure, confidential and accessible means for internal and external parties to raise concerns about bribery on the part of associated persons, to provide suggestions for improvement of bribery prevention procedures and controls, and where they can seek advice.

Training needs will depend on the nature and role of the work undertaken by the entity – consideration should be given to mandatory general training for all new employees or agents as part of the induction process. However, those roles involving higher risk functions such as purchasing, contracting, distribution and marketing and/or those working in high-risk countries may require more bespoke training. Again, this should be regular and reviewed to ensure it remains current and takes account of any evolution in the bribery risks the entity may face. It is essential that attendance at training is insisted on by the organisation's leadership and is recorded diligently.

(f) ***Monitoring and review***

Bribery risks can change over time and the nature and scale of an entity's commercial activities may evolve. As a result, companies will wish to monitor and evaluate the effectiveness of their bribery prevention procedures and adapt these where necessary.

Although a periodic review is advocated, it is also observed that other factors may trigger a review, such as governmental changes, an incident of bribery or press reporting of the same.

External verification or assurance of effectiveness of anti-bribery procedures: Some organisations offer gap-analysis and other services which evaluate the effectiveness or otherwise of existing ABAC programmes. Depending on circumstances these may be worth considering.

It may also be possible to apply for certified compliance with one of the independently-verified anti-bribery standards maintained by industrial sector associations or multilateral bodies.[8] It must be borne in mind, however, that such certification does not necessarily mean that a commercial organisation's bribery prevention procedures are 'adequate' for all purposes when considering a Section 7 offence.[9]

3.3 Outline supporting policies

(a) Ownership of ABAC policy and procedure (eg, central legal or compliance department)

In keeping with good corporate governance, the ABAC policy and procedures should clearly define who takes responsibility for these. If the entity has a legal department, it recommended that they take ownership of the policy and procedure and ensure that they are kept up to date.

(b) Training and record-keeping

Training should be provided to internal staff and relevant staff of subsidiaries and joint ventures. It may also be appropriate to offer such training to suppliers in high-risk supply chains, supplement their existing training or work with suppliers to develop training specific to the supplier. As noted above, training needs will depend on the nature and role of the work undertaken by the entity. In addition to mandatory general training for all new employees or agents, additional training should be considered for those in higher-risk roles such as government relations, permitting, purchasing and contracting and/or those working in high-risk countries may require more bespoke training. Again, this training should be regular and regularly reviewed to ensure it remains current and takes account of any evolution in the bribery risks the entity may face.

(c) Screening of third parties (eg, supply chain, senior employees, joint venture partners – add ABAC to screening priorities)

Desk-based research is a good place to start with screening of third parties – beginning with internet, database and media searches, including sanctions lists

---

8 For example, the ISO 37001 standard.

9 Section 7 of the Bribery Act 2010 is the corporate offence of failure to prevent bribery. It is a defence for entities to show that they had in place 'adequate procedures' to prevent the bribery.

and politically exposed persons (PEP) screening. This should quickly identify publicly known problems.

Screening questions should include: Does the entity have previous proven experience in the sector? Or conversely, does the entity have a record for failing to meet health and safety/environmental responsibilities? Has it changed/disguised its name over time to hide political connections or distance itself from allegations of misconduct?

This can be supplemented with a questionnaire provided to the supplier, with particular attention to:

- internal oversight and independence of ethics and compliance policies, programmes or measures;
- appropriate disciplinary procedures etc to address ABAC conduct and ensuring that this policy is implemented;
- payment information and contractual relationship information between the supplier and government entities;
- payment information, ownership and governance arrangements between supplier and its state shareholders for state-owned enterprises (SOEs); and
- beneficial ownership information of the supplier or of any of its third parties potentially linked to risk (joint venture, subcontractor, sub-supplier etc).

Depending on the nature of the third party, it may be necessary to consider screening of senior employees – have they worked with or for the government or appear to be closely connected to the political elite?

Depending on the value of the contract/exposure to risk, it may be appropriate to engage independent accountants and/or lawyers to either carry out this assessment or to advise the entity on implementing their own effective ABAC procedures.

Aligned with the screening of third parties, consideration should be given to including specific anti-corruption clauses in contracts that give buyers the right to audit revenue flows that raise concerns.

(d) Whistleblowing

Whistleblowing refers to the situation where someone who works in or for an organisation raises a concern about possible criminal conduct or danger or serious risk that could threaten colleagues, customers, shareholders, the public or the environment or damage the organisation's reputation. In many jurisdictions, including the United Kingdom, workers who make a disclosure under whistleblowing legislation are protected from dismissal or detriment by dint of their status as a whistleblower.

Employers should create an open, transparent and safe working environment where workers feel able to speak up. The creation of a whistleblowing policy demonstrates that commitment.

It is a recognised principle of good ABAC risk-management that companies should have a whistleblowing policy in place, which encourages workers to 'speak up' and provides a safe mechanism through which they can report allegations of wrongdoing.

Corporate governance, disclosure and reporting considerations

Ben Lepley
SLR Consulting

1. Introduction

Stakeholders and rights holders in mining and minerals projects are demanding that environmental, social and governance (ESG) issues are considered at every stage of mineral project evaluation and development. In response, project developers, sponsors and investors are working to develop and implement strategies to ensure ESG aspects are part of everyday operations and that words are converted to actions. A key pillar of this shift is the creation of a robust corporate governance framework to ensure that key environmental and social risks, sustainability plans, policies and goals are identified, prioritised and controlled in a timely manner, with roles, responsibilities and accountabilities clearly defined. Perhaps more than any other industrial sector, governance in mining should also extend to leadership, ethics and culture, with the aim of creating a sustainable business with respect for human rights and sustainable development at the centre. The requirements for reporting on results of these actions are also evolving rapidly, reflecting the changing pressures applied by stakeholder and rights holder groups.

ESG is new in name only – the core principles have existed for decades in different forms, including corporate social responsibility (CSR), health, safety, environment and community (HSEC) and sustainability. ESG was coined by the financial community to capture emerging and evolving and traditionally under-represented environmental and community-related risks, that may be material to financial decision making. The nuance of ESG is having an umbrella term for all risks and opportunities that could impact the environment and communities and that are considered holistically and reported on transparently to uphold accountability of those responsible. It also involves thinking laterally about value – not only considering financial value of the company and products, but also the value of the environment (natural capital) and people (social and human capital). Who companies consider as stakeholders has also evolved, from being internal-centric (management and shareholders) and legally required (regulators), to local and Indigenous communities and, more recently, to supply chain actors and consumers. The term 'rights holders' has been introduced to capture the role of Indigenous Peoples and communities that have traditional rights and important knowledge over lands that are now being developed for resource extraction.

The mineral exploration and mining industry may receive more attention than most industries due to the inherent nature of mining – invasive, intense and localised. The geographical location cannot be moved; geological endowment of a region has been fixed, sometimes for billions of years, by discreet mineralisation events. Also, many populated places globally are located around mining districts as a direct result of the economic opportunities they create. As mining is a temporary land use, mines inevitably close, often causing widespread social issues when the once-dominant industry dies. It also means that, as districts are depleted of resources, new areas are required to fill the void – often in remote and wild places. As we venture further into the unexplored, we start to overlap with Indigenous Peoples' territories that have often been managed using sustainable practices through generations. A recent study[1] suggested that over half of the world's mines and exploration projects for energy transition materials (such as copper, nickel and lithium) are located on or close to Indigenous Peoples' traditional lands. These overlapping land uses have historically caused conflict and social unrest, and underline the importance of strong governance to ensure we have genuine sustainable development in harmony with sustainable land management and environmental stewardship.

In the next section we outline some of the more important stakeholder and rights holder groups, the types of ESG requirements they place on minerals and mining companies, and the governance systems and processes these companies need to help manage ESG risk.

2. Stakeholder influence

The governance of an organisation is determined by a number of factors, as illustrated in Figure 1.

Each of these variables influences the number and variety of stakeholders whose rules, regulations and expectations should be considered when developing governance frameworks. As an example, consider a diversified mining company headquartered in London, listed on a public stock exchange, operating exploration and mining projects across several continents, and extracting and processing a variety of commodities.

1 JR Owen, D Kemp, AM Lechner, J Harris, R Zhang and É Lèbre, "Energy transition minerals and their intersection with land-connected peoples", https://doi.org/10.1038/s41893-022-00994-6" (2023) *Nature Sustainability*, 6 203–211.

Figure 1. The governance of an organisation

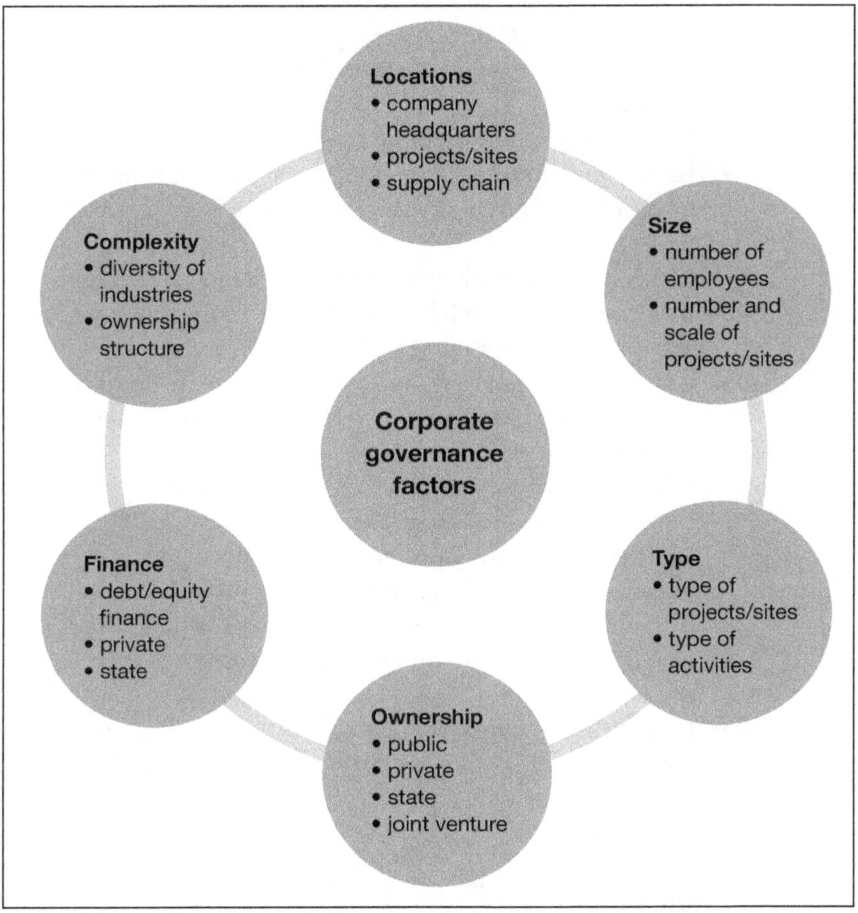

A (non-exhaustive) list of the potential stakeholders is as follows.

- Internal – board of directors, management and employees.
- Governments – United Kingdom (headquarters) as well as all countries where extraction, transport and refining are conducted and countries receiving their products. This includes regional blocs such as the European Union. Each country or state has its own legal system and legislative requirements.
- Regulatory bodies – United Kingdom as well as all countries where extraction, transport and refining are conducted or where the product is sold. This includes environmental, financial, health and safety, and administrative regulators.
- Multilateral organisations (such as the United Nations, World Bank and the International Labour Organization) – through treaties and

international agreements with the various countries and states involved, and also through lenders (eg, multilateral development banks, Equator Principles Association).

- Financial institutions – stock exchanges, trading platforms, insurance companies.
- Investors – institutional or private.
- Local communities – communities that are directly impacted or affected by operations, including those downstream/river of project sites or other land users.
- Rights holders – landowners and other rights holders for projects/sites, including but not limited to Indigenous Peoples with traditional rights and knowledge over project lands.
- Ecosystems – ecosystems, biodiversity and the environment (represented by regulatory bodies, environmental organisations and local campaigners).
- Value chain actors – all other companies upstream and downstream in the mineral and metal products supply chain, that may influence environmental and social footprint such as transport and logistics, refineries and smelters, manufacturers, distributors.
- Consumers – of end-product and intermediate products.
- Non-governmental organisations (NGOs) and activists – opposition to the company.
- Contractors – companies that are contracted to perform work on the project, including but not limited to consultants, advisers, construction companies, camp operators, etc.
- Media outlets.

Clearly all these parties cannot have an equal say in how a company is governed and what is reported; however, a responsible company should at least develop and maintain a list of interested parties and consider the potential number and scale of risks and opportunities of their business on these stakeholders and rights holders, and also of the stakeholders and rights holders on their business. This is the concept of 'double-materiality', where both inside-out (ie, impacts of a business on external actors, generally considered as environmental and social impacts) and outside-in (ie, impacts from external factors on the business, generally considered as financial impacts) impacts are assessed. The assessed materiality (relevance and scale) of each impact can then be used to guide governance frameworks and/or be reported on (disclosed). A governance structure should be designed that best reflects the operating environment, ensuring legal requirements are at the forefront alongside human rights and sustainable development.

3. Governance considerations

Governance frameworks set out the expected processes and procedures, organisational structure, roles and responsibilities and reporting and documentation requirements for successful operation of a business. They provide structure to management and staff within an organisation with the main aim of ensuring key stakeholders and rights holders' requirements are met. They should cover all aspects of an organisational footprint, including financial and non-financial (environmental and social) aspects.

There are several organisations globally that have been created with the aim of helping countries and governments create national-level governance frameworks to effectively manage mineral resources and assist operating companies. The International Resource Panel – part of the United Nations Environment Programme – produced a guidance document in 2020 on mineral resource governance.[2] This document sets out a vision for mining to be a central part of sustainable development and coined a new term of 'sustainable development licence to operate'. The Intergovernmental Forum on Mining, Minerals, Metals and Sustainable Development regularly produces guidance documents with the aim of promoting good governance and raising standards globally. The Organisation for Economic Cooperation and Development (OECD) is another multilateral organisation aiming to improve global standards and promote sustainable development, including in the mining and minerals sector. The main role of these organisations is to assist governments to understand the evolving landscape and ensure their country is developing their mineral resource sector with sustainable development at the core. They may influence legislative change and should (especially for multinational corporations with projects and operations in multiple jurisdictions) impact company-level corporate governance.

Some key areas expected to be considered in corporate governance frameworks are described below.

3.1 Accountability and directors' duties

Accountability is central to good governance and incentivises performance. It ensures that top management including company directors are held accountable for operationalising plans, processes and procedures. Commitments from top management to execute effective plans and embed sustainability practices within operations are essential but must also be paired with repercussions should commitments not be kept; there must be accountability. This can take the form of performance-related bonuses or renumeration packages, along with disciplinary action.

---

2 ET Ayuk, AM Pedro, P Ekins, J Gatune, B Milligan, B Oberle, P Christmann *et al*, *Gearing extractive industries towards sustainable development*, International Resource Panel, 2020, United Nations Environment Programme.

3.2 Legal and other requirements

Understanding the legal requirements of all operating locations is fundamental to good governance. Ensuring the company operates in compliance with relevant laws and regulations represents the most basic aspect of governance. Rules and regulations are many and varied, differ by jurisdiction, and are subject to regular revision and amendment. This can be complex in the example of a company operating across multiple jurisdictions and with an integrated supply chain. Other (non-statutory but potentially binding) requirements also need to be identified, understood and evaluated for impact on the business. These 'other' requirements may include expectations imposed by rights holders, investors, customers, certification bodies etc.

3.3 Goals and targets

Setting goals and targets for the company allows for strategies and plans to be developed and tracked. The selection of goals and targets will be heavily influenced by the expectations and requirements of key stakeholders and rights holders, again underlining the importance of early identification and mapping of these interested parties. Goals and targets can be based on various sources, including global goals, declarations and treaties, such as:

- **United Nations**
  2007 UN CEO Water Mandate;
  2008 UN Declaration for the Rights of Indigenous Peoples;
  2011 UN Guiding Principles on Business and Human Rights;
  2015 UN Sustainable Development Goals (UNSDGs); and
  2018 UN Declaration on the Rights of Peasants and Other People Working in Rural Areas.
- **Other**
  1989 International Labour Organization Indigenous and Tribal Peoples Convention (ILO Convention 169);
  1992 Convention on Biological Diversity;
  2000 Voluntary Principles for Security and Human Rights;
  2016 Paris Climate Agreement and related climate targets; and
  2018 OECD Due Diligence Guidance for Responsible Business Conduct.

Additionally, collaborative industry organisations such as the International Council on Mining and Metals (ICMM) and national mining associations, such as the Mineral Council of Australia and Mining Association of Canada (MAC) set their own goals and targets which their member organisations must adhere to. The ICMM's performance expectations as well as MAC's Towards Sustainable Mining initiative are well-regarded as industry-leading tools promoting sustainability principles.

3.4 Management systems

Management systems and plans provide the foundation for good governance, creating the structure for a company to deliver on its goals and targets. A thoughtfully designed and well-implemented management system, structured around continuous improvement, will facilitate the identification, prioritisation and control of material risks and opportunities that face the company. A management system will set out rules and expectations for employees to follow and managers to track performance of compliance obligations (which can be both mandatory and voluntary). A management system will outline the key corporate policies and processes including responsibilities and accountabilities, and establish programmes and plans to meet legal and other requirements, and fulfil identified targets and goals. Good management systems require dedicated resources to implement and can be time intensive. They can also cover a range of topic areas depending on the focus of the management (again driven by stakeholder expectations). Some common management systems include environment (including greenhouse gas emissions), social/community responsibility, quality, energy, occupational health and safety (OHS/OSH), water quality and circular economy. Management systems following an internationally recognised standard (eg, the International Organization for Standardization or ISO standards) are written to facilitate integration of aspects, wherein all of the (for example) environment, social/community, quality, energy and OHS/OSH aspects of the business can be managed in an integrated manner.

Core to management systems is the concept of 'plan-do-check-act', where systems are not static but are constantly being updated and tweaked to reflect changes in the organisation and external factors. Effective systems should include training and education for company employees to ensure roles and responsibilities are understood. ISO is one of the main providers of certifiable standards for management systems, which provides a level of consistency and minimum standards.

Management plans (MPs) are perhaps the most important element of the management system. These documents describe the way that the company ensures operational control over its most important (material) risks. MPs are more specific and target key areas requiring detailed processes and procedures to manage. Common aspects covered in MPs include:

- environmental protection – pollution prevention and control, biodiversity management, water stewardship, air emission management, greenhouse gas emission management, waste and effluent management;
- social engagement – stakeholder engagement and communication, grievance mechanisms, socio-economic development, indigenous peoples' interaction, resettlement procedures; and
- cultural protection – cultural monument protection, cultural awareness training.

3.5 Audits and inspections

Audits and inspections are an effective way of ensuring legal and other requirements (compliance obligations) are being met, management systems are fit for purpose, and goal and targets are being achieved. They can and should be conducted by both internal (staff) and external (third party) teams of experienced individuals. For example, international standards such as ISO 14001 (environmental management systems) require internal and external audits at specific intervals. Audits are generally comprehensive and involve a detailed evaluation of performance against a defined set of criteria. For example, a customer or a certification body may decide to audit a company's performance against one of its compliance obligations, through site observations, interviews and document review to establish evidence of conformance (or lack thereof). Inspections are generally less rigorous and may include spot checks of project or operator compliance with specific standard operating procedures or plans. For example, a company may implement an inspection programme to conduct regular visual observations of the containment dams and dykes around a tailings storage facility.

3.6 Financial institutions

Institutions providing or enabling finance to minerals and mining companies have their own set of governance and reporting requirements. These are again highly variable but all have the same aims of promoting responsible operation and sustainable development. A number of the institutions and their key requirements in this area are as follows.

- World Bank – group of five financial institutions aiming to provide finance to sustainable development projects with a focus on embedding good ESG practices. Requirements to be followed by recipients of financial backing from World Bank institutions include various guidelines and standards pertinent to minerals and mining, as summarised in the environmental and social framework (latest version released in 2017). These focus on numerous ESG topics with the aim of assisting sustainable development.
- Equator Principles Association – financial institutions that are signatories to the Equator Principles aim to provide finance to projects embedding good ESG practices. Requirements include 10 principles required to be followed by recipients of financial backing from EP institutions (latest version of principles' guidance, EP4, 2020). These relate to broad ESG topics and include specific requirements for environmental and social impact assessment, action plans, stakeholder engagement and grievance mechanisms, reporting and transparency.
- International Financial Corporation (IFC) – private investor hub and part of the World Bank. Requirements include eight performance standards

(latest version of standards, 2012) required to be followed by recipients of financial backing from financial institutions that are signatories to the Equator Principles. The topics covered are similar to the Equator Principles but with additional focus on Indigenous Peoples, biodiversity, health and safety, labour rights and cultural heritage.

- Principles for Responsible Investment (PRI) – voluntary organisation created and run by private investors. Requirements include six principles required to be followed by signatories of the PRI. These include considering ESG issues in decision making, developing processes and procedures to manage ESG risk, disclosing information and collaborating with other signatories of the PRI.
- Sustainable Stock Exchange Initiative – providing guidance to stock exchanges on embedding ESG reporting criteria in filing documentation. Information is provided in their guidance document: *Model Guidance on Reporting ESG Information to Investors: A Voluntary Tool for Stock Exchanges to Guide Issuers* (2015).

3.7 Communication

Another key factor when considering governance frameworks is the communication and dissemination of information. Why, what, how, when and where information is communicated is important and varies for different stakeholders and rights holders. This also includes two-way communication, with functional systems to allow for dialogue between the company and stakeholders. Effective communication should include whistleblowing channels (for employees) and grievance mechanisms (for external stakeholders).

3.8 Reporting

One of the most notable recent changes in corporate governance is the explosion of reporting and disclosure standards, again as a result of stakeholder demands. Companies are feeling pressured into transparency and are rushing to report on ESG performance, often without really understanding the what, the how and the why of information disclosure. Disclosure needs to be specific, factual/reliable, relevant, timely and accessible. Companies must also recognise that disclosure is forever – once data and information is released it is difficult to control and the internet facilitates instantaneous dissemination. Disclosure is also complicated by multiple financial and sustainability rating schemes.

Reporting on financial performance and results has long been an expectation of shareholders; the change is the expectation to report on non-financial (environmental and social) performance. Disclosure and reporting of performance is driven by the need for transparency in order to gain the trust and confidence of stakeholders. The varying types of ESG disclosure standards and their reporting requirements is a direct result of stakeholder expectations, as discussed in the following section. Management must ensure that the standards mandated by law or voluntarily entered into and committed to are embedded in company practices and management systems.

4. ESG disclosures

The landscape of reporting and disclosure of ESG considerations is evolving rapidly. While this is certainly a boost for sustainability and social acceptance of the industry, minerals and mining companies are finding this onerous and resource-intensive, increasing with each new expectation from stakeholders. Many of the disclosure and reporting standards and initiatives are voluntary or a requirement of membership of specific organisations; however, a new wave of mandated requirements for reporting is emerging, particularly driven by the European Union.

Investors and other stakeholders are promoting the adoption of a uniform set of ESG reporting standards – so that disclosures are more comparable – and regulators are mandating them. For example, in the United Kingdom, listed and large private companies are already required to report climate risks and opportunities under the framework of the Task Force on Climate-related Financial Disclosures (TCFD), and the scope of the new Corporate Sustainability Reporting Directive (CSRD) and related Corporate Sustainability Due Diligence Directive (CS3D) extend to listed small and medium enterprises (SMEs) and also some non-EU companies based on their EU operational footprint.

4.1 Global initiatives

The United Nations is behind many of the developments in governance of mineral and mining projects and the UN Global Compact is the United Nations' answer to disclosure. It is not industry specific and is designed around the UNSDGs along with other key UN initiatives and declarations. It is also not mandatory, but nevertheless has been adopted by a number of mineral companies who wish to align themselves with the UNSDGs. It is based around 10 basic principles relating to human rights, labour issues, environmental issues and anti-corruption and bribery (ABC). Along with the United Nations, other notable organisations with disclosure requirements include the OECD, whose due diligence standards around conflict and high-risk areas are ubiquitously referenced across other sustainability initiatives.

4.2 Responsible mining and sourcing

The concept of responsible mining and sourcing of minerals was developed based on supply chain demands, often stemming from manufacturing organisations whose customers are demanding higher standards across the board. Look far enough upstream and every supply chain starts with mining and minerals. For many products and organisations, mines represent the highest environmental and social risk. In some cases, responsible mining initiatives were developed from within the industry – being generated by concerned members of mining associations such as MAC and ICMM along with the Prospectors and Developers Association of Canada. In other cases, third-party, independent organisations were developed from multi-stakeholder interest groups, such as the Initiative for Responsible Mining Assurance. In between industry and multi-stakeholder-led initiatives, are others that are supply-chain led and often commodity-specific, such as the Responsible Minerals Initiative, Copper Mark (and associated frameworks for nickel, zinc, lead and molybdenum), Responsible Gold Mining Principles, Aluminium Stewardship Initiative, Responsible Steel, Responsible Jewellery Council Code of Practices and Better Coal.

These initiatives are all focused on improving sustainability practices across the industry but vary significantly in terms of reporting requirements, internal governance, certification and assurance processes, market uptake and ultimately the goals of each standard, as governed by the affected stakeholders. All are currently voluntary and uptake depends on stakeholder expectations as outlined at the start of the chapter (depending on, for example, jurisdiction, commodity, scale and complexity of company/projects). Stakeholder trust in reporting is a key factor in successful uptake for these standards, that is, will reporting to a certain standard fulfil the requirements of the affected stakeholders? However, some standards require more detailed reporting across a higher number of ESG topic areas and are seen as more onerous; the resources required to undertake assessments and reporting may therefore be restricting uptake. It is noteworthy that, at the time of writing, a number of organisations are working together to simplify this responsible mining standards landscape through consolidating their individual standards into a single standard and multi-stakeholder oversight system (described in section 4.6 below).

A comparison of the main aspects of the current leading responsible mining standards is provided in Table 1.

Table 1. Comparison of main responsible mining standards (at time of writing, June 2024)

Category	ICMM performance expectations	Copper Mark	Towards Sustainable Mining Initiative	IRMA Standard
General info	ICMM is an industry group that unites 25+ major global metal producers and traders, such as Anglo American, Rio Tinto and Glencore. All company members are represented on ICMM's Council by their CEOs, and on various committees and working groups by nominated representatives. All ICMM members are required to meet its performance expectations (PEs). The ICMM PEs were last updated in 2023.	Copper Mark (CM) is an industry-led initiative which was founded and initially developed by the International Copper Association. The CM assurance framework aims to promote responsible practices across the copper, molybdenum, nickel and zinc value chains. Companies adopting the CM are expected to fully meet all 33 Risk Readiness Assessment (RRA) criteria along with requirements of the Joint Due Diligence (JDD) Standard within two years from commitment. CM/RMI RRA Version 3.0 was published in 2023. JDD last updated 2022.	MAC established the Towards Sustainable Mining (TSM) initiative in 2004. Participation in TSM is mandatory for all MAC members. Since its establishment, TSM has been adopted by more than 10 mining associations around the world (including but not limited to Australia, Botswana, Brazil, Finland, Mexico, Norway, Spain). TSM was last updated in early 2024, with protocols periodically updated.	The Initiative for Responsible Mining Assurance (IRMA) is a multi-stakeholder-led organisation whose governance is equally shared by civil society, communities, and organised labour alongside the private sector. The IRMA decision-making process requires a consensus between the six different groups. IRMA is currently the most comprehensive and ambitious mining standard with over 400 requirements for participating members. IRMA Standard version 1 (2018) is the latest and only version; V2 is in development and due in 2024.
Governance	Industry-led	Industry-led with stakeholder participation	Industry-led with stakeholder participation	Multi-stakeholder
Supply chain tiers	Mining and processing	Mining and processing	Mining	Mining (next version will cover exploration and processing)

continued on next page

Category	ICMM performance expectations	Copper Mark	Towards Sustainable Mining Initiative	IRMA Standard
Material coverage	All minerals	Copper mainly – also available for nickel, zinc and molybdenum producers	All minerals	All minerals
Number of requirements	PEs: 39 Position statements: nine	RRA Requirements: 33	Indicators: 34 Protocols: nine (10 in Finland)	Requirements: 400+ Chapters: 26
ESG scope	Environment Human Rights Community Rights Governance	Environment Human Rights Community Rights Governance	Environment Human Rights Community Rights Governance	Environment Human Rights Community Rights Governance
Geographic focus	Global	Global	Global*	Global

**Only companies based in the following countries can be verified (companies in other countries can use TSM standard as guidance only). TSM participants (as of June 2024): Argentina, Australia, Botswana, Brazil, Canada, Colombia, Finland, Guatemala, Mexico, Norway, Philippines and Spain.*

4.3 Disclosure standards

Sustainability disclosure standards are designed to provide standardised reporting around material topics, to increase transparency in companies and operations. They have mainly evolved from industry-agnostic third-party independent bodies and have gained relevance and importance due to the interests of the investment community. The sustainability disclosure space is seeing rapid shifts towards streamlining the reporting process to enable consistency and comparability in reporting, and decrease the burden on companies that are subject to multiple standards and reporting requests.

A key marker in this global shift towards streamlining is the launch of the International Financial Reporting Standards (IFRS) Sustainability Disclosure Standards published by the International Sustainability Standards Board.[3] The first two standards, IFRS S1 and IFRS S2, came into effect in 2024 with the aim to provide robust, streamlined, comparable and verifiable sustainability reporting, by consolidating several key reporting frameworks, including the TCFD, Sustainability Accounting Standards Board Standards, Climate Disclosure Standards Board Framework, Integrated Reporting Framework, and metrics from

3 See www.ifrs.org/news-and-events/news/2023/06/issb-issues-ifrs-s1-ifrs-s2/.

the World Economic Forum. Several jurisdictions have declared their intent to introduce ESG disclosure requirements that are aligned with the IFRS S1 and S2, including Australia, the United Kingdom, Japan, Canada and the European Union.

While there has been significant consolidation of global reporting standards into the IFRS, the Global Reporting Initiative (GRI) remains a distinct standard. In early 2024, GRI published a new reporting standard and guidance for the mining sector, GRI 14,[4] which members of the ICMM are required to comply with. While remaining separate entities, GRI and IFRS are collaborating to harmonise reporting requirements between their standards, making it easier for companies to adhere to both GRI and IFRS standards.

4.4 Issue and topic-themed requirements

In addition to the mandatory and voluntary reporting standards and initiatives described above, some ESG aspects are particularly high risk and require their own guidance and standards. High-risk topics include tailings and waste, radioactive materials, cyanide, artisanal and small-scale mining and occupational health and safety.

A leading example is the Global Industry Standard on Tailings Management (GISTM). This includes a comprehensive set of reporting requirements for both the engineering as well as environmental and social aspects of tailings management facilities. This standard was developed in response to the high-risk nature of tailings, combined with a number of recent high-profile catastrophic (and fatal) tailings dam failures. GISTM was created and is governed by a multi-stakeholder group representing various stakeholder groups including investor groups, industry and NGOs. It is adopted by and a mandatory requirement of membership in ICMM.

4.5 Mineral resources and reserves reporting

Accurate reporting of mineral resources and reserves is an imperative for any minerals and mining company. It will have direct impacts on the valuation and financial viability of a company. Particularly for companies with a limited portfolio of projects, an updated statement of resources and/or reserves can have a profound effect. A project may be the sole asset of the company on which the fate of the organisation rests. Should the resource/reserve suddenly increase or decrease significantly, share prices or valuations will mirror the positive/negative trend, which can result in success or demise, respectively. It can also have far-reaching consequences for other stakeholders. For example, positive results may improve the likelihood of an exploration project coming to fruition and developing into a mining operation, which brings positive impacts

---

4 See www.globalreporting.org/standards/standards-development/sector-standard-for-mining/.

such as employment opportunities and tax revenues, but may also increase negative environmental and social impacts. These material impacts on company success or failure mean the reporting of resources and reserves is duly scrutinised in detail. The definitions of both mineral resources and mineral/ore reserves[5] are provided below from the Committee for Mineral Reserves International Reporting Standards (CRIRSCO) Reporting Template (2019):[6]

A Mineral Resource is a concentration or occurrence of solid material of economic interest in or on the Earth's crust in such form, grade or quality and quantity that there are reasonable prospects for eventual economic extraction ... Mineral Resources are subdivided, in order of increasing geological confidence into Inferred, Indicated and Measured categories.
A Mineral Reserve is the economically mineable part of a Measured and/or Indicated Mineral Resource. It includes diluting materials and allowances for losses, which may occur when the material is mined or extracted and is defined by studies at Pre-Feasibility or Feasibility level as appropriate that include application of Modifying Factors.

Along with the imperative to standardise the methods used to quantify the tonnage and grade of mineralised material in the ground, reporting of resources and reserves has also evolved as a direct result of market shocks from negligent and criminal behaviour. In a number of well-documented cases, investors and other stakeholders were misled by company representatives for financial gain, resulting in disastrous consequences. The Poseidon nickel and Bre-X gold scandals are two high-profile cases, with the latter immortalised in the Hollywood movie *Gold* in 2016 (with artistic licence exaggerating some aspects). To counteract potential criminal behaviour and to harmonise reporting of mineral resources/reserves, reporting codes with rules for reporting results of mineral exploration and mining activity were developed in the 1980s and 1990s and have since evolved to reflect changing stakeholder sentiment.

The Joint Ore Reserves Committee (JORC) of Australia published the first JORC Code in 1989. This was an early trend-setter that other organisations of resource-rich countries used to kickstart their own codes and guidelines. To assist with standardising and aligning standards, the CRIRSCO was created to act as an umbrella organisation for national reporting organisations wishing to collaborate. As of 2024, CRIRSCO includes representatives from Australia (JORC), Canada (Canadian Institute of Mining, Metallurgy and Petroleum, CIM), Europe (Pan-European Reporting Code, PERC), South Africa (South

---

5 All reporting codes with the exception of the JORC Code use the term Mineral Reserve; the JORC Code uses Ore Reserve. They are considered equivalent.

6 CRIRSCO, "International Reporting Template for the Public Reporting of Exploration Results, Mineral Resources and Mineral Reserves", 2019.

African Mineral Resource Committee, SAMREC), the United States (Society for Mining, Metallurgy and Exploration, SME), Chile (Comision Minera), Russia (OERN), Mongolia (MPIGM), Brazil (CBRR), Kazakhstan (KAZRC), Indonesia (KCMI), Columbia (CCRR), Turkey (UMREK), India (NACRI) and the Philippines (PMRCC).

These reporting codes provide companies with a set of rules and instructions for reporting results of exploration campaigns, mineral resources and reserves. They do not provide prescriptive requirements of how exploration must be conducted, or how resource/reserve estimates must be completed. They do provide rules for what must be disclosed so that informed potential investors can complete their assessment on a level playing field. The codes that align with CRIRSCO have three core governing principles: transparency, competency and materiality, as described in the latest CRIRSCO template:[7]

> ***Transparency:*** *requires that the reader of a Public Report is provided with sufficient information, the presentation of which is clear and unambiguous, so as to understand the report and not to be misled.*
> ***Materiality:*** *requires that a Public Report contains all the relevant information which investors and their professional advisers would reasonably require, and reasonably expect to find in a Public Report, for the purpose of making a reasoned and balanced judgement regarding the Exploration Targets, Exploration Results, Mineral Resources and/or Mineral Reserves being reported.*
> ***Competence:*** *requires that the Public Report be based on work that is the responsibility of a suitably qualified and experienced person (referred to herein as a Competent Person) who is a member of a Professional Organisation (PO) with an enforceable code of ethics and disciplinary process, which includes the powers to suspend or expel a member.*

Disclosure requirements in these codes include a wide range of topics, with the key items listed below:

- Project outline: including location, description of exploration and/or mining activities, history of project, legal and permitting aspects, liabilities.
- Geological setting and mineralisation style: describing how the mineralised deposit formed and its geological context.
- Exploration: non-invasive (mapping, geophysics, grab sampling) and invasive (drilling, trenching, pitting) sampling methods, quality and results.
- Estimation of exploration results, mineral resources: geological

7 CRIRSCO, "International Reporting Template for the Public Reporting of Exploration Results, Mineral Resources and Mineral Reserves", 2019.

modelling, grade and tonnage estimation methodology, reasonable prospects for eventual economic extraction (RPEEE[8]), classification (resource/reserve category) techniques, reporting methodologies (including economic constraints).

- Technical studies: study level, mine design methodologies, metallurgical and processing testwork, infrastructure requirements, environmental and social setting, market studies and economic criteria, risk analysis and economic assessment.
- Estimation of mineral reserves: estimation and modelling techniques, classification criteria, reporting methodologies (including assessment of modifying factors[9]).

Disclosure of ESG factors affecting mineral resources and reserves has been a requirement since the first iterations of these reporting codes. However, only in the most recently updated reporting code, the PERC Standard (2021), has the term ESG been introduced. Prior to this, the CRIRSCO 2019 template included 'sustainability considerations' and previous iterations included topics referred to as 'environmental, social and governmental' factors. It is expected that an updated version of the early pioneer JORC Code (expected during 2024) will have significant changes to the reporting of ESG aspects in line with the latest CRIRSCO template and PERC Standard.

It is also important to note that there are distinctions between the reporting codes that reflect the reporting jurisdiction. In some cases, reporting codes are mandated by stock exchanges; this is the case, for example, for the Australian Stock Exchange, where the JORC Code is mandated. The Toronto Stock Exchange (TSX) and TSX Venture exchange is another example, where the National Instrument 43-101 and accompanying policies are mandated to be used for disclosure (using guidance from the CIM). National Instrument 43-101 requires the disclosure of relevant ESG aspects of the project. Other examples are the S-K1300 (using guidance from SME) for US-based exchanges regulated by the Securities and Exchange Commission and SAMREC for the Johannesburg Stock Exchange. In Europe, there is currently no stock exchange that mandates using the PERC Standard, which is also reflected in the title referred to as 'Standard' and not a 'Code'. Likewise, the CRIRSCO template is only a template and is not used by any jurisdiction for reporting – it is designed to act as an overarching guide for other standard-setting organisations.

---

8 RPEEE – a judgement by the competent person on the future viability of economic extraction of the mineralised material based on a preliminary assessment of the modifying factors.

9 Modifying factors – considerations used to convert resources to reserves, including mining, processing, metallurgical, infrastructure, economic, marketing, legal, environmental, social, governance (ESG) and regulatory factors (from PERC, 2021).

4.6 Future of reporting and disclosure

There are calls from across the industry to reduce the number and complexity of reporting and disclosure standards. There has been a proliferation in the late 2010s and 2020s that has led to frustration and confusion as to which standards to use, which topics to disclose and which tools to use for disclosures. In addition, the complexity of the reporting and disclosure landscape, added to a lack of coherent oversight, has led to calls to strengthen public bodies to act as independent regulators to ensure responsible mining is not optional or voluntary, as described succinctly in a recent paper.[10]

A tool was developed to assist companies wishing to report using multiple standards simultaneously. The M3 Integrated Assessment Tool attempts to allow users to input reporting data and fulfil requirements from TSM, IRMA and the RJC standards. Further developments are underway, where, based on pressure from reporting companies, a number of leading organisations have announced a collaboration starting in spring 2024 where they will attempt to merge their separate standards into one. The Consolidated Mining Standard Initiative (CMSI) includes the TSM, CM, ICMM PE and RGMP. It has started discussions and engagement with various stakeholder groups and aims to have a new standard developed in 2025.

Presently, many of these standards are voluntary and not mandated unless part of a membership organisation; however, this is changing. Mandatory reporting using sustainability standards/initiatives will be driven by fast-evolving legislation such as the EU Critical Raw Materials Act (CRMA). The CRMA refers to sustainability standards collectively as sustainability certification schemes. Details of which standards will be certified for use are not yet available at the time of writing (June 2024).

5. Conclusions

Governance refers to the structures, systems and practices an organisation has in place to:

- assign decision-making authorities, define how decisions are to be made, and establish the organisation's strategic direction;
- oversee the execution of its mission, the implementation of its policies, plans, programmes and projects, and the monitoring and mitigation of its key risks; and
- report on its performance in achieving intended results and use performance information to drive ongoing improvements and corrective actions.

10 D Murguía and A Bastida, "The elephant in the mine: Why voluntary sustainability standards are insufficient to ensure responsible mining", The Extractive Industries and Society, 2024, 101485.

We have described in this chapter some of the key components of effective governance for minerals and mining companies and have highlighted some of the challenges that face firms in this complex and fast-evolving area. Companies are facing pressure from a long list of stakeholders and rights holders to improve sustainability performance and improve disclosure of material ESG issues and risks. This is driving transparency and higher standards across the industry; however, the uptake and use of predominantly voluntary reporting and disclosure standards is highly variable. The number and complexity of standards is also causing issues in industry through onerous resource-intensive requirements and ever-evolving materiality of topics. The risk of greenwashing is also a key consideration for all stakeholders that must be identified and prevented. Information placed in the public domain lasts forever, and so it is imperative that information and data that is disclosed is complete, correct and appropriate. Reporting and disclosure set benchmarks and baselines which any areas of concern must be constantly assessed against to ensure progress is made and commitments are not empty promises.

Good governance is imperative to ensure we collectively have responsible practices embedded in our mineral-intensive world. The energy transition must be powered by minerals that have been explored for, extracted and processed using practices with the lowest practicable negative impact and highest possible positive impact on both the environment and communities. Transparency of material issues and risks will also ensure ongoing social licence to operate and help new mines develop in a timely manner through higher acceptance of a much maligned but essential industry.

The author would like to thank James Hartshorn for his contribution to this chapter.

The origins, evolution and direction of ESG regulation in mining

Tatiana Londoño Camargo
Daniela Vergel-Riascos
CMS Rodríguez-Azuero

1. Introduction

The evolution of environmental, social and governance (ESG) corporate management has been a fast-paced, at times confusing and convoluted journey. Over the past few decades, corporate ESG has evolved from the occasional voluntary commitment (and even then mostly based on corporate social responsibility (CSR)), to an increasingly controlled area within a sometimes politically charged, rapidly developing global regulatory landscape. Companies and practitioners alike must ensure they are permanently up to date and anticipating upcoming legislative processes and market requirement trends that may prove fundamental to their businesses, to avoid potentially heavy sanctions, reputational and legal risks, and to identify, assess and capitalise on major competitive advantages.

This chapter does not attempt to cover the complete breadth of the rapidly evolving ESG regulatory landscape, as in all probability it would then become outdated within just a few months. It instead seeks to describe the passage of ESG from an often ignored or opposed set of considerations, to a good-to-have trend, to an area of self-regulation and soft law for adverse impact management, to national or regional regulation on specific issues, and finally to a widely regulated area, not only regarding specific topics but also including the process of due diligence for adverse risk management. The chapter then seeks to envision a roadmap for further regulatory evolution in years to come, particularly as it pertains to the mining industry.

2. Origins and evolution of ESG regulation

The history of ESG regulation may be traced back to the industrial revolution, in which the unbridled search for profit and corporate competition generated serious adverse impacts within today's 'S' social category, such as dangerous, precarious and undignified working conditions, as well as upon the environmental 'E', with an uncontrolled use of available natural resources, and correlated environmental impacts from factory and industry waste, including noise, air and water pollution, among others.[1] This near complete lack of corporate management obligations in relation to the welfare of society has been labelled as *laissez-faire* capitalism,[2] where the sole aim of businesses was the generation of shareholder profit, often to the clear detriment of other stakeholders' fundamental rights.

During the 1950s and 1960s, an academic debate arose regarding the purpose of corporations, and how they should be held to ethical standards in their operations *vis-à-vis* shareholders and society, which became known as CSR, and is arguably where modern ESG management finds its roots. This foundational pillar of ESG finds its origins in influential academic and journalistic articles which put pressure on businesses to self-regulate and act responsibly towards society. ESG originally arose from this self-regulation, which emerged from social disapproval, which would eventually be channelled into political and formal regulatory processes addressing the avoidance of adverse impacts.

Doctrine widely considers the book *Social Responsibilities of the Businessman* by US economist Howard R Bowen[3] as one of the earliest influential academic writings that introduced the notion that companies hold responsibilities for their conduct towards society, including ethical behaviour towards their stakeholders. CSR was the expression of fundamental morality in the way businesses behaved towards different interest groups.

Prominent economists reacted against this idealistic notion of companies as accountable for the welfare of societies, and contrastingly advanced the notion that the aim of businesses should be to achieve material gain while operating in good faith.[4] Theodore Levitt, for instance, published in 1958 an article on "The Dangers of Social Responsibility" in the *Harvard Business Review*.[5]

This same critical idea was subsequently and most notably furthered by Milton Friedman in his 1970 *New York Times* article,[6] where he established what

---

1 L Davoudi, C McKenna and R Olegario, "The Historical Role of the Corporation in Society" (2018) 6 (suppl) *Journal of the British Academy* 17–47.

2 Suzanne Konzelmann, Victoria Chick and Marc Fovargue-Davies, "Shareholder Value or Public Purpose? From John Maynard Keynes and Adolf Berle to the Modern Debate", Centre for Business Research, University of Cambridge, Working Paper No 520, June 2020, www.jbs.cam.ac.uk/wp-content/uploads/2023/05/cbrwp520.pdf.

3 Howard R Bowen, *Social Responsibilities of the Businessman*, University of Iowa Press, 2013, www.amazon.co.uk/Responsibilities-Businessman-University-Faculty-Connections/dp/1609381963#:~:text=Bowen's%20Social%20Responsibilities%20of%20the,planning%20and%20managerial%20decision%2Dmaking.

4 Kimberlee Josephson, Foundation for Economic Education, "A Brief History of Corporate Social Responsibility", 23 May 2021, https://fee.org/articles/a-brief-history-of-corporate-social-responsibility-and-why-it-must-stop/?gad_source=1&gclid=Cj0KCQjwmMayBhDuARIsAM9HM8eA759gYQ8KCPgHWmHTLbxDiwfWmy7wu0XJaJjqRgx5qZotDDd5xr4aApnDEALw_wcB.

5 Theodore Levitt, "The Dangers of Social Responsibility" (September–October 1958) *Harvard Business Review* 41–50, http://57ef850e78feaed47e42-3eada556f2c82b951c467be415f62411.r9.cf2.rackcdn.com/Levitt-1958-TheDangersofSR.pdf.

6 Milton Friedman, "A Friedman Doctrine – The Social Responsibility of Business is to Increase its Profits", *The New York Times*, 13 September 1970, www.nytimes.com/1970/09/13/archives/a-friedman-doctrine-the-social-responsibility-of-business-is-to.html.

came to be known as the Friedman Doctrine: "The social responsibility of business is to increase its profits". In this famed work, Friedman denounces those who promote the concept as preaching "pure and unadulterated socialism".

Despite this counter-movement to the concept that companies were expected to be responsible members of society, other influential works were published during these years, finally making ground and instilling in large swaths of modern society the notion that, even though the main purpose of corporations is, indeed, profit, their earnings must be acquired in a manner that does not deprive the planet of its resources and strip society, including workers and communities, of their basic rights. Among such works we can find Rachel Carson's "Silent Spring", published in 1962,[7] and *The Limits to Growth*,[8] about the implications of continued uncontrolled worldwide growth, which would render the planet as uninhabitable by 2100.[9]

Derived from the concepts introduced by these works, most modern ESG regulation, both at international and regional or national levels, and most specifically within the 'E' component, seeks to limit the adverse impacts of corporate operations on the environment, in order to achieve a desired state of 'sustainability', a topic which is closely intertwined with ESG.

On the other hand, the 'S' component has evolved in a somewhat parallel manner. This chapter has already mentioned the squalid and dangerous working conditions which prevailed during the industrial revolution, and during most of the following centuries, labour conditions for many millions were not significantly improved. Moreover, even though the Universal Declaration of Human Rights and the subsequent International Covenants on Civil and Political Rights and Economic, Social and Cultural Rights clarified that states had among their primary obligations to enforce compliance with human rights by all actors within its territory, it was only when a series of social disasters stemming from corporate operations moved public opinion, that it was unambiguously recognised that companies were also obliged to respect the human rights of their stakeholders.

Some of the most significant of these disasters occurred within the mining sector. Accidents like the Monongah mine explosion in West Virginia in 1907 in which 350 mostly young boys died, or the 1942 Benxihu Colliery disaster in Liaoning, China, which is believed by some[10] to be the worst mining disaster in

---

7 Rachel Carson, "Silent Spring", 1962. See www.newyorker.com/magazine/1962/06/16/silent-spring-part-1.

8 Donella H Meadows, Dennis L Meadows, Jorgen Randers, William Behrens III, *The Limits to Growth: A Report for the Club of Rome's Project on the Predicament of Mankind*, 1972, https://collections.dartmouth.edu/content/deliver/inline/meadows/pdf/meadows_ltg-001.pdf.

9 *Ibid.*

10 John Retzer, "Ten Worst Mining Disasters", Bogey Media. Archived from the original on 18 April 2010. Retrieved 17 May 2014. See https://web.archive.org/web/20100418115719/http:/www.epicdisasters.com/index.php/site/comments/the_ten_worst_worldwide_mining_disasters.

history, and claimed the lives of 1,549 miners. In 1962, the Luisenthal mine disaster in Völkingen, Germany, took 299 lives, the collapse of the Aberfan colliery spoil tip in Wales in 1966, destroyed a school and left 144 dead, including 116 children, and in India in 1975, the Chasnala mining disaster is claimed to have taken the lives of 700. It is a litany of horror and unnecessary death, but eventually, from the accumulation of these tragedies and resulting public outrage only in the face of these repeated tragedies, emerged the shoots of a regulatory trend, fundamental today, of mine safety, which is enshrined in almost all national legislation, as well as in international sectoral self-regulatory initiatives.

Other notorious accidents from outside the mining industry have also shaped the landscape of corporate regulation, such as the Bhopal gas tragedy which in 1984 cost the lives of an estimated 3,787 victims, is considered as the deadliest industrial accident in history. Bhopal is considered a landmark case, which sparked the movement towards adequate industrial safety regulation on a global scale.

The 'S' within ESG not only focuses on internal stakeholders, like workers, but on external stakeholders as well, including neighbours, communities and, most notably, Indigenous, ethnic or otherwise vulnerable populations residing within companies' areas of influence or which are otherwise impacted by corporate operations.

In 1909, the British magazine *Truth* published American Walter E Hardenburg's articles which scandalised early 20th-century society by accusing Peruvian entrepreneur and politician Julio César Arana del Águila of massive slavery, rape, torture and genocidal abuses of natives in the Casa Arana and later the Peruvian Amazon Company's rubber plantations in the Colombian and Peruvian jungle, in what became known as the Putumayo Genocide.[11] Some estimate that between 50,000 and 100,000 people, who were the inhabitants of the area at that time,[12] were enslaved by the head of the Arana family and his henchmen.

It was only many years later, in 1989, that the International Labor Organization Indigenous and Tribal Peoples Convention No 169 was established, which aims to protect Indigenous populations from such abuses and to recognise their rights in relation to their native lands. The convention consecrates the right to consultation of ethnic peoples in relation to extractive operations and other types of developmental projects which could significantly impact their cultures and livelihoods.[13] Regulatory trends for what are generally considered as the 'social' component of ESG have generally followed this

11 See Greg Grandin, "Empire of Savagery in the Amazon", *The New York Times*, 12 February 2010, www.nytimes.com/2010/02/14/books/review/Grandin-t.html.

12 Andrea Díaz Cardona, BBC News Mundo, "El Paraíso del diablo: las atrocidades del 'holocausto del caucho' en la Amazonía de Colombia", 26 August 2022, www.bbc.com/mundo/noticias-america-latina-60922508.

13 International Labor Organization, "Indigenous and Tribal Peoples Convention", No 169, 1989.

tendency to respond to massive or otherwise notorious incidents that have steered public opinion, to mould local or national political legislative responses.

The regulation of corporate supply chains has not been oblivious to this trend. On 24 April 2013, the Rana Plaza eight-storey building collapsed in Dhaka, Bangladesh, killing 1,134 people and leaving thousands more maimed or permanently injured. Cracks had been discovered in the structure, but workers were forced to carry on with their labour. At least 29 well-known global brands had recent orders with one of the five garment factories in the Rana Plaza building.[14] Factories in Bangladesh were frequently preferred by international buyers as suppliers, for they provided exceedingly inexpensive textile products, in part due to grossly inadequate employee remuneration and working conditions.

Since this incident, important self-regulatory sector-wide certifications and, more recently, regulatory initiatives, have focused heavily on creating corporate responsibilities to supervise actors within value chains and other upstream and downstream business partners, in order to prevent, mitigate and respond to adverse human rights and environmental impacts, and the mining sector is a clear example of this.

3. Mining sector regulatory trends

Nowadays, there is a proliferation of standards and certifications focused on the mining sector, mainly created by the industry itself and each with different approaches and targets. For instance, the Towards Sustainable Mining standard was launched in 2004 by the Mining Association of Canada to support mining companies in the management of environmental and social risks through the adoption of 10 performance protocols focused on communities and people, environmental stewardship and energy efficiency, under four principles: transparency, credibility, accountability and measurability.[15]

In the same line, the International Council on Mining and Metals (ICMM) is an industry initiative seeking to establish best practices for the responsible management of natural resources focused on environmental resilience, social performance, governance and transparency, as well as innovation in sustainability for the mining and metal industry. Members of ICMM make a commitment to work towards the goals set as the organisation's strategy and action plan. This initiative is neither a standard nor a certification, but nonetheless aims to support mining companies to achieve ESG criteria within their operations.[16]

---

14 Clean Clothes Campaign, "Rana Plaza", https://cleanclothes.org/campaigns/past/rana-plaza.

15 The Mining Association of Canada, "Towards Sustainable Mining; TSM 101: A Primer", https://tsminitiative.com/assets-images/SPARK-MAC-TSM-PRIMER-2022-ENG.pdf.

16 ICMM, "Mining Principles", updated June 2023, www.icmm.com/website/publications/pdfs/mining-principles/mining-principles.pdf?cb=59962.

On the other hand, there are many certification and standard-setting initiatives promoted by diverse actors such as community organisations, environmentalists, business representatives and certification specialists. One example is the Alliance for Responsible Mining founded in 2004, which aims to transform artisanal and small-scale metal mining projects "into a socially and environmentally responsible activity, while improving the quality of life of artisanal miners, their families and communities".[17]

Another example is the Initiative for Responsible Mining Assurance (IRMA) Standard for Responsible Mining. This standard is focused on the social impacts of the mining projects at site, grouped under four principles: commercial integrity, social responsibility, planning for positive legacy and environmental responsibility. When a project adopts this standard, IRMA runs an external and independent audit which includes the participation of social actors such as workers, community and local authorities and the reports are made publicly available.[18]

4. Current ESG regulatory trends – the road from 'nice to have' to 'must have'

All of the abovementioned initiatives are self-regulatory, voluntary standards that have emerged over the last couple of decades. Alongside this self-regulation, national legislation regulating environmental and social negative impacts by companies has also been evolving throughout the world, beginning in countries with stronger records of societal protection and respect for individual rights such as Europe and the United States. However, ESG regulation has now spread more widely and evolved to include regional harmonisation of standards, international and global soft-law standards. These more recent norms cover not only specific topics and risks, but also corporate risk-management processes, such as reporting standards and due diligence. National legislation remains one of the fundamental pillars of ESG, which companies must analyse and comply with wherever they operate around the world.

The last category of ESG regulatory trends that originated with a wave of condemnatory public opinion, is the application of minimum international rules to subsidiaries of multinational corporations in all territories where they operate, potentially imposing higher standards than the applicable national laws.

In 1976, the Organization for Economic Cooperation and Development (OECD) adopted the "Declaration on International Investment and

17 Alliance for Responsible Mining, "About the Alliance for Responsible Mining", www.responsiblemines.org/en/history-2/.

18 Initiative for Responsible Mining Assurance, *IRMA Standard for Responsible Mining IRMA-STD-001*, June 2018, https://responsiblemining.net/wp-content/uploads/2018/07/IRMA_STANDARD_v.1.0_FINAL_2018-1.pdf.

Multinational Enterprises".[19] The revised version published in 2000 became known as the OECD Guidelines for Multinational Enterprises on Responsible Business Conduct.[20] Under that declaration, OECD-based multinationals were for the first time encouraged to follow the OECD Guidelines wherever they operated, and not exclusively in member countries. This set the basis for the concept of minimum international standards for corporations in issues related to responsible business conduct, composed mostly of ESG-related topics demarcated by the OECD: labour standards, environmental care and elimination of forced and child labour. For the first time, the Guidelines also introduced best practices related to ESG's 'G' component of transparency, stipulating companies should not offer or demand bribes, and introduced the topics of minimum consumer protection standards, anti-competitive behaviour, tax evasion and desired technology transfer.[21]

5. The rise of human rights respect and due diligence as a core regulatory pillar within ESG frameworks

The concept that multinational enterprises must comply with minimum international standards on certain matters, including environmental safeguards and human rights, follows the outlined ESG regulatory tendency of originating in self-regulation, best practice and soft-law instruments, only recently evolving into 'hard law' in the European Directive on Corporate Due Diligence on Sustainability, for example.[22] Judicial decisions also contributed by confirming parent company liability for the acts of omissions of foreign subsidiaries in concerns related to ESG, as portrayed in the 2021 UK Supreme Court decision in the case of *Okpabi and others v Royal Dutch Shell*.[23]

After the establishment of the OECD Guidelines, another vital ESG global soft-law initiative was engendered at the heart of the United Nations. In 1999, the United Nations Global Compact was created as a non-binding pact, the purpose of which is to encourage companies around the globe to adopt sustainable and socially responsible processes and publicly report on their performance, adopting the Ten Principles dedicated to environmental, social and good governance matters.

The UN Global Compact set out in its first two principles the notion that

---

19 Organization for Economic Cooperation and Development, "Declaration on International Investment and Multinational Enterprises", Adopted 1976, Amended 2023, https://legalinstruments.oecd.org/en/instruments/OECD-LEGAL-0144.

20 OECD, *OECD Guidelines for Multinational Enterprises on Responsible Business Conduct*, 2023 Amendment, www.oecd-ilibrary.org/docserver/81f92357-en.pdf?expires=1717084038&id=id&accname=guest&checksum=E7A643A365A0670804A81C9A96855778.

21 *Ibid.*

22 European Parliament, European Parliament legislative resolution 24 April 2024 on the proposal for a directive of the European Parliament and of the Council on Corporate Sustainability Due Diligence and amending Directive (EU) 2019/1937 (COM(2022)0071-C9-0050/2022-2022/0051(COD)), P9_TA(2024)0329, April 2024, www.europarl.europa.eu/doceo/document/TA-9-2024-0329_EN.pdf.

23 *Okpabi and others v Royal Dutch Shell plc and another* [2021] UKSC 3, Case UKSC 2018/0068, www.supremecourt.uk/cases/uksc-2018-0068.html.

companies should: (i) support and respect the protection of internationally proclaimed human rights; and (ii) make sure that they are not complicit in human rights abuses.[24]

Until then, corporate management of adverse environmental and social impacts had been addressed as a responsibility more than an obligation, and national laws had only ventured as far as regulating specific topics, mostly in the areas of environmental protection and labour issues. Remaining environmental and social corporate performance was considered as a voluntary and self-regulatory 'responsibility', treated alongside charitable donations in CSR initiatives. And this, in turn, created the unwelcome effect of an uneven competitive playing field between those companies observant of stakeholders' rights, including non-regulated environmental protection, and those employing lower standards of conduct and solely abiding by national legal mandates, which often fell short of accepted minimum international standards.

The failure, from the outset, to unambiguously identify companies as bound by human rights laws, led to the common misconception that prevailed until recently, that respect for human rights also lies within the spectrum of voluntary corporate social responsibility. Companies in all countries that have ratified core international human rights instruments such as the International Covenants on Civil and Political Rights and on Economic, Social and Cultural Rights have been (often unknowingly) bound by national implementing legislation for more than five decades, but adverse impacts were largely dealt with on a case-by-case, specific topic basis. In fact, most laws relating to the elimination of forced or child labour, minimum wages, gender-based rights in the workplace, ethnic rights to territory and culture, or to the elimination of discrimination, have been tackled independently, and not recognised as core matters of respect for human rights. In fact, the 'S', as it evolves around workers and communities, can be considered as a matter of human rights, at heart. And this recognition, which may be argued to have begun with the UN Global Compact, is a vital ESG soft- and hard-law global regulatory trend, which is having a major impact on the current global corporate landscape, involving, in a very direct manner, the mining sector.

In 2011, the United Nations Human Rights Council[25] unanimously endorsed the Guiding Principles on Business and Human Rights[26] (UNGPs), the principal soft-law international standards which dominate this area today. For the

---

24 The United Nations Global Compact, "Corporate Sustainability in the World Economy", January 2014, https://d306pr3pise04h.cloudfront.net/docs/news_events%2F8.1%2FGC_brochure_FINAL.pdf.

25 John Ruggie and Tamaryn Nelson, "Human Rights and the OECD Guidelines for Multinational Enterprises: Normative Innovations and Implementation Challenges", Working Paper No 66, A Working Paper of the Corporate Social Responsibility Initiative, John F Kennedy School of Government, Harvard University, May 2015, www.hks.harvard.edu/sites/default/files/centers/mrcbg/programs/cri/files/workingpaper.66.oecd.pdf.

26 United Nations Human Rights, Office of the High Commissioner, *Guiding Principles on Business and Human Rights: Implementing the United Nations 'Protect, Respect and Remedy' Framework*, 2011, www.ohchr.org/sites/default/files/documents/publications/guidingprinciplesbusinesshr_en.pdf.

creation of the UNGPs, a pilot project was conducted in 2009–2010 to test the establishing of internal corporate grievance mechanisms. For this pilot project, Colombian company Carbones del Cerrejón represented the mining sector,[27] which gave important support to the applicability of this important tool within the sector, and supported the creation of corporate internal human rights remediation mechanisms in general.

The UNGPs have three basic pillars, under the 'Protect, Respect and Remedy' framework. Pillar II, 'Respect', established the "independent corporate responsibility to respect human rights, which means that business enterprises should act with due diligence to avoid infringing on the rights of others and to address adverse impacts with which they are involved".[28] Guiding Principles 11 to 24, which constitute the pillar, clarify step by step how companies can fulfil their obligations to respect human rights as derived from national legislation implementing human rights treaties. It is important to note that the UNGPs are not a binding regulation, treaty or otherwise hard-law instrument, but soft-law principles, intended to guide companies in complying with their existing obligations to respect human rights.[29]

Principle 15(b) establishes that companies should implement "a human rights due diligence process to identify, prevent, mitigate and account for how they address their impacts on human rights".[30] Principles 17 to 21 then continue to describe in a detailed manner how this due diligence process should be carried out. It is here that the concept of due diligence for adverse risk management, now applicable to sustainability and a new concept to many, 13 years after its creation, was engendered.

Later, in 2011, the *OECD Guidelines on Multinational Enterprises* was updated, including a new human rights chapter, consistent with the UN Guiding Principles on Business and Human Rights. The new Guidelines also extended the Principles' due diligence approach to other concepts of responsible business conduct, including environmental risk management.[31]

---

27 Caroline Rees, *Piloting Principles for Effective Company-Stakeholder Grievance Mechanisms: A Report of Lessons Learned*, 2011, p5, https://media.business-humanrights.org/media/documents/files/media/documents/ruggie/grievance-mechanism-pilots-report-harvard-csri-jun-2011.pdf.

28 John Ruggie and Tamaryn Nelson, "Human Rights and the OECD Guidelines for Multinational Enterprises: Normative Innovations and Implementation Challenges", Working Paper No 66, A Working Paper of the Corporate Social Responsibility Initiative, John F Kennedy School of Government, Harvard University, May 2015, www.hks.harvard.edu/sites/default/files/centers/mrcbg/programs/cri/files/workingpaper.66.oecd.pdf.

29 "Nothing in these Guiding Principles should be read as creating new international law obligations, or as limiting or undermining any legal obligations a State may have undertaken or be subject to under international law with regard to human rights". United Nations Human Rights, Office of the High Commissioner, *Guiding Principles on Business and Human Rights: Implementing the United Nations 'Protect, Respect and Remedy' Framework*, 2011, p1, www.ohchr.org/sites/default/files/documents/publications/guidingprinciplesbusinesshr_en.pdf.

30 *Ibid*, p16.

31 Organization for Economic Cooperation and Development, OECD, *OECD Guidelines for Multinational Enterprises*, 2011 Edition, www.oecd-ilibrary.org/docserver/81f92357-en.pdf?expires=1730132058&id=id&accname=guest&checksum=E50994E6C78A14EA786F6CA0214F1945.

It should be noted, however, that in both the UNGPs themselves[32] and the United Nations' Pillar II Interpretive Guide of 2012,[33] impacts on the environment have been classified as impacts on human rights, lying within the subject matter which companies should address within their due diligence processes. Impacts on the environment were first addressed indirectly as affecting other rights such as those regarding health, life and the right to an adequate standard of living.[34] However, the UN recognition in 2023 of the right to a healthy environment as a human right,[35] the decision of the European Court of Human Rights recognising[36] climate change as an impact on human rights, and the recent decision by the Inter-American Court of Human Rights in *Habitantes de La Oroya v Peru*[37] that directly recognised adverse environmental impacts as human rights impacts, constitute another noteworthy trend towards integrating environmental matters with human rights.

In 2017, France became the first country in the world to adopt a law, known as the *Loi de Vigilance*,[38] or Corporate Duty of Vigilance Law, to mandate corporate due diligence in human rights and environmental performance, and publish an annual 'vigilance plan', all in accordance with the due diligence process set out in the UN Guiding Principles. This law obliges companies to adopt measures to identify and prevent or mitigate impacts in its own operations, those of its subsidiaries, and direct and indirect business partners as well. Several lawsuits have already been filed against French companies under the *Loi de Vigilance*, including TotalEnergies, BNP Paribas, Danone and Casino Group – some regarding the companies' own operations, others involving suppliers or subsidiaries. The sanctioning of this law, the first to integrate human rights and environmental risks and to focus on due diligence processes to adequately manage risks, rather than specific ESG issues, set the stage for the most recent and significant regulatory trend in the area, as will be seen.

In 2018, the OECD released its document *OECD Due Diligence Guidance for Responsible Business Conduct*,[39] the objective of which was to "support enterprises

32 United Nations Human Rights, Office of the High Commissioner, *Guiding Principles on Business and Human Rights: Implementing the United Nations 'Protect, Respect and Remedy' Framework*, 2011, pp5, 20, www.ohchr.org/sites/default/files/documents/publications/guidingprinciplesbusinesshr_en.pdf.

33 United Nations, Office of the High Commissioner of Human Rights, *The Corporate Responsibility to Respect Human Rights: An Interpretive Guide*, 2012, www.ohchr.org/sites/default/files/Documents/publications/hr.puB.12.2_en.pdf.

34 See Geneva Environment Network, "Update: Human Rights and Environment", 13 May 2024, www.genevaenvironmentnetwork.org/resources/updates/human-rights-and-the-environment/.

35 United Nations, General Assembly, "Resolution adopted by the General Assembly on 28 July 2022" A/RES/76/300, https://digitallibrary.un.org/record/3983329?ln=en&v=pdf#files.

36 European Court of Human Rights, "Verein KlimaSeniorinnen Schweiz and Others v. Switzerland – 53600/20", Judgment April 2024, https://hudoc.echr.coe.int/eng#{%22itemid%22:[%22002-14304%22]}.

37 Corte Interamericana de Derechos Humanos, Caso Habitantes de La Oroya vs. Perú, Sentencia de 27 de noviembre de 2023, www.corteidh.or.cr/docs/casos/articulos/seriec_511_esp.pdf.

38 Republique Française, *Journal Officiel* "LOI No 2017-399 du 27 mars 2017 relative au devoir de vigilance des sociétés mères et des entreprises donneuses d'ordre", NOR: ECFX1509096L, www.legifrance.gouv.fr/jorf/id/JORFTEXT000034290626/.

39 OECD, *OECD Due Diligence Guidance for Responsible Business Conduct*, 2018, https://mneguidelines.oecd.org/OECD-Due-Diligence-Guidance-for-Responsible-Business-Conduct.pdf.

on the implementation of the OECD Guidelines for Multinational Enterprises". The guidance constitutes another soft-law, self-regulation instrument which provides concrete, clear instructions for companies on how to manage and respond to their adverse ESG-related impacts and risks.

6. Supply chain due diligence obligations – on the road towards global regulation?

From this date forth, national legislation mandating sustainability or human rights due diligence aligned with the UNGPs began emerging as hard law in other European countries, such as Germany, with the German Supply Chain Due Diligence Act[40] enforceable from 2023, and Norway, with its Transparency Act from 2022.[41] Meanwhile, topic-specific ESG legislation has emerged in other jurisdictions, such as the United Kingdom, Canada, Australia and the Netherlands, often focusing on supply chain accountability and supervision of core human rights matters such as forced labour,[42] child labour[43] and modern slavery.[44] This, in turn, has spawned the last ESG trend of significance, which is the hard-law mandate of norms requiring companies to ensure compliance with human rights and environmental protection from their supply chains around the world, generating a cascading effect of hard-law regulation to other regions in the planet. Although this trend has roots in public clamour for better human rights and environmental protection, it should also be noted that it serves the economic agendas of developed consumer nations by levelling the playing field and restricting unfair competition from countries with lower ESG standards.

Specifically in the mining sector, hard laws have emerged both at national and regional levels mandating due diligence for supply chains, generating the aforementioned cascade effect to mining companies around the world. The most prominent of these legislations is EU Regulation 2017/821.[45] This rule specifically mandates the implementation for certain minerals of the OECD *Due Diligence Guidance for Responsible Supply Chains of Minerals from Conflict-Affected*

---

40 German Bundestag, Act on Corporate Due Diligence in Supply Chains – Lieferkettensorg – faltspflichtengesetz LkSG, 16 July 2021, www.bmas.de/SharedDocs/Downloads/ DE/Internationales/act-corporate-due-diligence-obligations-supply-chains.pdf?__blob=publication File&v=3.

41 Norway, Act Relating to enterprises' transparency and work on fundamental human rights and decent working conditions (Transparency Act), 2022, www.regjeringen.no/contentassets/c33c3faf340441faa 7388331a735f9d9/transparency-act-english-translation.pdf.

42 European Parliament legislative resolution of 23 April 2024 on the proposal for a regulation of the European Parliament and of the Council on prohibiting products made with forced labour on the Union market (COM(2022)0453 – C9-0307/2022 – 2022/0269(COD)), www.europarl.europa.eu/doceo/ document/TA-9-2024-0309_EN.html.

43 Swiss Confederation, 221.433 Ordinance on Due Diligence and Transparency in relation to Minerals and Metals from Conflict-Affected Areas and Child Labour, DDTrO, 3 December 2021, www.fedlex.admin.ch/ eli/cc/2021/847/en.

44 United Kingdom, Modern Slavery Act 2015 c 3, www.legislation.gov.uk/ukpga/2015/30/contents.

45 *Official Journal of the European Union* L1 30/1, Regulation (EU) 2017/821 of the European Parliament and of the Council of 17 May 2017 laying down supply chain due diligence obligations for Union importers of tin, tantalum and tungsten, their ores, and gold originating from conflict-affected and high-risk areas, https://eur-lex.europa.eu/legal-content/EN/TXT/PDF/?uri=CELEX:32017R0821.

and High-Risk Areas, providing another example of the ESG regulatory trend from self-regulation to soft-law instruments, to eventual transformation into formal legislation.

Another recent regulation is the EU Carbon Border Adjustment Mechanism (CBAM), which aims to reduce carbon leakage by incentivising the decarbonisation of non-EU production processes, initially for cement, steel, iron, electricity, hydrogen and fertilisers, with full implementation expected by 2026. Under this regulation, information on embedded emissions should be communicated to EU importers by non-EU producers so they can purchase digital certificates reflecting the carbon emissions embedded in the products, on a mandatory basis. Importers must declare the quantity of goods and their embedded greenhouse gas (GHG) emissions imported into the European Union and surrender CBAM digital certificates corresponding to the amount of GHG emissions embedded in imported products.

For producers of the listed goods, CBAM represents an opportunity to improve their manufacturing processes to address low or net carbon goals, because from 2026 onwards, embedded carbon emissions will be a significant factor in the competitiveness of these goods within the European Union.

The latest and most important example of legislation with extra-territorial reach is the recently approved EU Corporate Sustainability Due Diligence Directive (CSDDD)[46] which mandates due diligence on human rights and environmental protection aligned with UNGP and OECD standards for qualifying large European corporations, including special measures for their subsidiaries and supply chains. Even though the companies directly subject to the directive are limited, the fact that they must supervise business partners and their processes to identify, prevent, mitigate and eliminate adverse impacts[47] will create a ripple effect around the world. It is likely that all companies in these industries worldwide that integrate with European supply chains will be impacted by this regulation.

This directive complements the Corporate Sustainability Reporting Directive (CSRD), which also seeks to ensure consistency of due diligence reporting with international instruments such as the *UN Guiding Principles* and *OECD Guidelines and Due Diligence Guidance*.[48] The CSRD expands on one of the due diligence process's steps, which is the public communication of corporate risk management performance and includes human rights and environmental performance.

---

46 European Parliament legislative resolution 24 April 2024 on the proposal for a directive of the European Parliament and of the Council on Corporate Sustainability Due Diligence and amending Directive (EU) 2019/1937 (COM(2022)0071-C9-0050/2022-2022/0051(COD)), www.europarl.europa.eu/doceo/document/TA-9-2024-0329_EN.pdf.

47 *Ibid*, Article 15.

48 *Official Journal of the European Union* L322/15, Directive (EU) 2022/2464 of the European Parliament and of the Council of 14 December 2022 amending Regulation (EU) No 537/2014, Directive 2004/109/EC, Directive 2006/43/EC and Directive 2013/34/EU, as regards corporate sustainability reporting, https://eur-lex.europa.eu/legal-content/EN/TXT/PDF/?uri=CELEX:32022L2464.

The United States has so far abstained from approving mandatory due diligence legislation, but in April 2024 published the *United States Government National Action Plan on Responsible Business Conduct*,[49] another self-regulatory soft-law document, setting the expectation that all US companies conduct human rights due diligence on their own operations and their supply chains in line with UNGPs and OECD standards.

7. Conclusions – on the journey from soft law to hard law

In conclusion, although it has been a long and painful journey, ESG has come a long way since the industrial revolution, and its initial focus on addressing specific risks in national legislation, normally after a significant human tragedy. Self-regulation and soft law are progressively giving way to hard law with extra-territorial reach, which treats ESG as a core of interrelated concerns based on human rights and sustainability, to be addressed systemically and on a global basis. The ESG regulatory trends that are currently setting the corporate performance stage may be identified as the following:

- Even though there is still national and regional legislation emerging on specific ESG issues, such as forced labour,[50] deforestation,[51] green claims[52] and carbon emissions,[53] these obligations will need to be coherent with due diligence processes set by formal legislation both in human rights and environmental protection.
- Regional and national due diligence regulations mandate corporate supervision of business partners' operations, which will flow down corporate supply chains spanning the globe. As mining is a global business with high risk and a long history of negative human rights and environmental impacts, it is very likely that mining companies will in the short term, if not already, be required by regulation to demonstrate proper due diligence processes aligned with UNGP and OECD standards. In fact, the market is already demanding this. Buyers of minerals and

---

49 *United States Government National Action Plan on Responsible Business Conduct*, 2024, www.state.gov/wp-content/uploads/2024/03/2024-United-States-Government-National-Action-Plan-on-Responsible-Business-Conduct.pdf.

50 European Parliament legislative resolution of 23 April 2024 on the proposal for a regulation of the European Parliament and of the Council on prohibiting products made with forced labour on the Union market (COM(2022)0453 – C9-0307/2022 – 2022/0269(COD)), www.europarl.europa.eu/doceo/document/TA-9-2024-0309_EN.html.

51 *Official Journal of the European Union* L150/206, Regulation (EU) 2023/1115 of the European Parliament and of the Council of 31 May 2023 on the making available on the Union market and the export from Union of certain commodities and products associated with deforestation and forest degradation and repealing Regulation (EU) No 995/ 2010, https://eur-lex.europa.eu/legal-content/EN/TXT/PDF/?uri=CELEX:32023R1115.

52 European Commission, Proposal for a Directive of the European Parliament and of the Council on Substantiation and Communication of explicit environmental claims (Green Claims Directive), 2023/0085, 2023, https://eur-lex.europa.eu/legal-content/EN/TXT/PDF/?uri=CELEX:52023PC0166.

53 *Official Journal of the European Union* L130/52, Regulation (EU) 2023/956 of the European Parliament and of the Council of 10 May 2023 establishing a carbon border adjustment mechanism, https://eur-lex.europa.eu/legal-content/EN/TXT/PDF/?uri=CELEX:32023R0956.

metals, especially those based in Europe, are requiring mining companies, particularly those operating in regions such as Latin America, Asia and Africa, to guarantee and support the implementation of best practices on ESG standards within their operations, in order to mitigate litigation and reputational risks.

- Current sustainability due diligence hard law covers human rights and environmental management, which have been recently considered by several different court decisions as integrated issues. These two topics have been effectively brought together under the general umbrella of sustainability.
- Most ESG regulatory instruments, both hard and soft law, are aligned with the *UN Guiding Principles on Human Rights* and with the *OECD Guidelines for Multinational Enterprises*, as well as its *Guidance for Due Diligence*.
- It is expected that, especially for the mining sector which, as mentioned, is considered as high risk for human rights and environmental adverse impacts, new regulations will be implemented worldwide, directly mandating due diligence processes aligned with UNGP and OECD standards, as well as dealing with specific ESG issues on topics such as fundamental labour rights, forced labour, child labour, climate change and additional environmental protection norms. It has been a defining trend that what was once nice-to-have, and then became a matter of soft law and self-regulation, will quickly be transformed into hard, formal law in the years to come.

Leveraging effective ESG due diligence to unlock value in mining investment

Kevin PCJ D'Souza
KD Consulting

1. The rising importance of ESG

The biggest and most engaging media stories that shape the narrative around mining today are, by and large, negative impacts: environmental pollution, injuries and fatalities, bribery, corruption, human rights abuses, tailings dam failures, workplace harassment, sexism and racism, artisanal mining, conflict minerals and the destruction of cultural heritage. In this interconnected and image-dominated era, these controversies stay fresh in the minds of the public, governments and investors who look to the industry's recent past in the hope of gaining confidence for the future. These controversies often demonstrate that legal obligations are no longer a reliable proxy for ethical ones. Culture and leadership matter. In addition, the old-fashioned reputational management playbook pushed by many public relations/communications consultants that relies on quotidian messaging, deflection and neutralisation will no longer suffice. The eventual impact of all this controversy is wide-ranging and includes:

- the fracturing of public attitudes towards mining;
- host and Indigenous community resentment and opposition;
- regulatory delays and permit rescindments;
- government expropriation;
- an inability to attract and retain new talent;
- the spreading of misinformation; and
- frustrating undervaluations and being shunned by investors.

Meanwhile, although the trendiness, and use, of the environmental, social and governance (ESG) acronym may already be fading, ESG continues to dominate the investment and governance landscape. Several key institutional investors have now publicly committed to taking ESG factors into account when making investment decisions. The list includes key mining investors like Blackrock, Vanguard, Van Eck and State Street Global Advisors, as well as pension, endowment and sovereign wealth funds. In February 2023, Norway's sovereign wealth fund, the world's largest investor, announced it would vote against re-electing the boards of approximately 80 companies including Apple,

Microsoft, Nestlé and Samsung because they failed to set or meet ESG targets. They also cautioned other company directors that they would vote against their re-election if they did not extend their efforts on issues like climate change, human rights and diversity. Furthermore, prescriptive ESG regulations, institutional investor stewardship and corporate governance codes and ESG matters are increasingly under the watch of national securities regulators and listing agencies. Additionally, mandatory disclosure standards and proxy voting guidelines progressively require companies to articulate and demonstrate the roles and responsibilities concerning oversight of ESG.

The mining industry is far from immune from all this intensified activity. ESG ranked at the top spot in the 2024 EY[1] mining risks survey for the second consecutive year, followed by licence to operate and climate change. Within the mining industry, ESG issues are being advanced in many ways – new legislation; increasing stakeholder proposals and activism; and growing geo-political, protectionist and resource nationalism agendas. This manifests itself in several ways, from societal distrust and reputational damage to more tangible actions including permit revocation, shareholder proposals, proxy fights and even divestments and litigation. There may be some headwinds, particularly in the United States where ESG has been weaponised and fallen prey to undemocratic and partisan agendas, but ESG remains a fiduciary duty and its prominence with investors and in mining company boardrooms will continue to evolve at an accelerating pace. This will be a challenging time welcomed by some and eschewed by others.

It is worth reminding ourselves that the constituents of ESG (or whatever we choose to call it – perhaps preferably 'responsible mining' or 'sustainability') are certainly not new to the mining industry. Indeed, the mining industry has been a leader in many areas for decades, but part of the ongoing challenge is that ESG issues will never be static. They change and evolve with time, politics and societal beliefs and expectations. Some issues may be long term, others short term, and not every ESG topic is relevant to every jurisdiction, mine site or company. The breadth of what is now considered ESG is staggering, and the list keeps growing. This is one of the reasons it is impossible to define one set of perfect ESG 'best practices' for the industry; rather, there are a variety of constantly evolving 'good practices'. In truth, the mining industry has tended to develop its ESG expertise by responding to friction and when faced with existential challenges in a variety of areas from water stewardship, cultural heritage, biodiversity, mine closure, climate change, tailings management, occupational health and safety, human rights, Indigenous relations, conflict management, labour relations, revenue transparency and anti-corruption, to

---

1 EY Canada, "Top 10 business risks and opportunities for mining and metals in 2024", www.ey.com/en_ca/mining-metals/risks-opportunities.

diversity, equity and inclusion (DEI). The industry has made tremendous strides in many ESG areas, but this does not detract from the undeniable fact that there is still plenty of room for continuous improvement.

Until recently, most in the mining M&A and investor space treated ESG as an acceptable risk since the associated legal risks remained somewhat hypothetical. Many believed the risk of doing nothing was less than the risk of doing something – and the pain simply was not worth the gain. This is no longer the case as witnessed by Vale after the devastating failure of the tailings dam at Brumadinho in Brazil, Rio Tinto after the destruction of the 46,000-year-old sacred Aboriginal site at Juukan Gorge in Australia and Shell for allegedly mismanaging climate resilience. Such pivotal events are an affirmation that we are beyond the tipping point. The potential financial and reputational impact of failing (or being perceived to fail) when it comes to ESG stewardship, can be far reaching. Following in the footsteps of the US Securities and Exchange Commission, the Australian and Canadian securities agencies have already warned investors against making overly promotional ESG disclosures. Today investors can and are being held personally liable for ESG performance and stewardship shortcomings. Internal corporate development teams and external investors are being forced to reassess their ESG risk appetite and resilience in the face of this increasing disruption and question whether they have considered the cost of getting it wrong.

ESG has become a priority in financial transactions and investors (both equity and debt) are increasingly seeking to integrate ESG factors throughout their investment processes given their potential as value levers and to determine whether value is created, destroyed or preserved. In addition, a growing number of investments are moving from ESG integration screening strategies, which require a review of ESG factors as part of their overall investment analysis, towards negative screening strategies, whereby companies which do not uphold specific ESG principles would be *prima facie* excluded. Throughout the investment life cycle, investors ordinarily need to ensure material ESG factors are proactively identified, defined, understood and appropriately integrated into all investment decisions. However, the level of influence and control that investors have over their portfolio companies varies significantly, depending on the investment structure and contractual rights. The materiality of different ESG considerations, probability and magnitude of risk, investors' risk appetite and holding period, as well as their level of control and influence are all critical and interrelated factors. Many investors are now signatories to the UN Principles for Responsible Investment (PRI) which urges them to integrate ESG factors into their investment analysis, due diligence, decision making and active ownership policies and practices. The PRI was developed by an international group of institutional investors, reflecting the increasing relevance of ESG issues to investment practices.

2. Avoiding the many pitfalls

Due diligence (DD) is defined as a comprehensive investigation or audit of a potential investment or acquisition to confirm all the facts, which includes reviewing financial records, assessing risks, evaluating legal and operational issues, and generally ensuring that the investment or acquisition is sound and beneficial. Historically, most ESG-related DD approaches fell rather short, and little effort was made to improve their effectiveness. This resulted in ESG assessments being incomplete, superficial or biased.

Traditionally, DD focused on a narrow set of value-related legal, technical and commercial factors, while ESG due diligence tended to focus on compliance and reporting. This primarily revolved around trying to address potential controversial conduct while meeting the existing regulatory requirements and the basic standards related to ESG practices. It involved ensuring that a mining company adhered to the established regulatory guidelines and reported its performance by reference to those. Most often it emphasised short-term goals and meeting immediate obligations especially to secure regulatory permits and authorisations. Furthermore, it was based on the premise that the target company basically engaged in ESG 'activities' to avoid legal repercussions or to maintain a positive public image, without necessarily delving deeply into the long-term strategic implications. Consequently, the typical approach to ESG-related DD was simply an attempt to identify and somehow quantify reputational and legal risk relating to past practices of the target mining company.

It will always be imperative to assess legal compliance and legacy liabilities, such as environmental remediation obligations, mine closure costs or unresolved legal disputes. Contingent risks associated with legal claims, regulatory fines or contractual obligations must be proactively identified and objectively assessed. In addition, there has and will always be a need to verify actual licence and permit conditionality, contractual obligations and existing financing covenants. This is all without question. However, as previously mentioned, legal obligations have not always provided a reliable proxy for ethical ones, and the absence of controversy does not necessarily indicate robust ESG performance. Moreover, the sole focus on past ESG performance is akin to investing in a company solely based on historical production and financial results – a practice no savvy corporate development team or investor would rightly endorse. ESG DD needs to be forward-looking. The traditional approach also misguidedly assumes that a mining company can somehow accumulate reputational capital despite the fact that reputational risk always arises from negative impacts. Managing reputational risk has tended to involve treating corporate messaging as an end in itself – divorced from ESG performance and ethics. Meanwhile, history has demonstrated that neglecting ESG may lead to short-term profit maximisation but at the expense of environmental degradation, social conflict and erosion of trust with a wide variety of stakeholders.

ESG-related DD is a vital part of the asset acquisition cycle, yet it is often siloed or is an afterthought. Frequently DD processes have started long before the ESG specialists are engaged. In many instances an investment strategy has been formed and target screening has commenced. Financial, legal and technical DD processes have been initiated and preliminary negotiations have begun before ESG is considered. The time left for the ESG-related DD is frequently insufficient as parties have agreed to a timetable without regard to the true ESG impacts and risks. This results in a rushed timeline and narrowing of the scope of DD to only certain aspects while neglecting other potentially critical areas, with insufficient time for thorough research, analysis and validation of any findings. Initially, a potential acquirer or investor may request a 'technical review' to uncover any fatal flaws, with little understanding of the time required to properly define the ESG impacts and risks of the project. Such checklist reviews offer a cursory or initial insight and provide only an early-stage and general assessment. Unfortunately, these preliminary reviews are often substituted for a full ESG-related DD and expose the would-be acquirer or investor to higher levels of risk.

In the euphoria of making the 'deal', ESG issues often get deliberately 'softened' despite their ability to lead to unanticipated costs, operational disruptions and impairment of asset value, affecting shareholder returns and investor confidence. For instance, environmental liabilities, especially concerning realistic financial surety for mine closure, can be downplayed leading to 'unforeseen' cost escalation post-acquisition. This can happen when conflicts of interest to influence the due diligence process are not recognised or addressed. Sometimes the DD does not thoroughly or objectively examine permit and regulatory compliance processes and associated bureaucratic hurdles, underestimating the true timelines, which in turn can lead to unexpected delays and related legal or financial liabilities. Host communities and regulators are repeatedly frustrated and exhausted with projects changing ownership and having to rebuild trust and relationships. Despite this reality, it is common to see DD processes neglect to assess or disregard community, Indigenous groups, and other key stakeholder relationships; social and financial obligations in community benefit agreements; human rights risk exposure; supply chain risks; or the true quality of asserted 'social licence to operate', which again can all lead to growing opposition, social unrest, protracted legal disputes and more costly project delays.

Other ESG-related mistakes include overestimating post-investment synergies and not impartially assessing the cultural compatibility between the acquiring/investing and target companies. Both mistakes can impede integration efforts, leading to employee dissatisfaction, decreased morale and hindered productivity. In truth, cultural clashes are not uncommon and undermine post-investment synergy realisation, increase employee turnover and weaken local community and stakeholder relationships, ultimately undermining the success of the investment. Such issues may arise when ESG-related DD findings have for whatever reason not been effectively communicated to decision makers, leading to uninformed or misguided decisions.

More recently, M&A-related DD approaches have concentrated on derisking, with a focus only on mitigating the negative impacts through a 'do no harm' mindset. Many believed that legal permitting alone would derisk a project combined with the existence of adequate ESG policies. This 'confirmation bias' approach is not uncommon but undermines the process with a focus on information that confirms preconceived notions or desired outcomes concerning ESG while ignoring contradictory evidence. It results in a flawed analysis and makes assumptions without verifying their accuracy or validity through independent research or expert consultation. Such complacency is exacerbated as it is easy to talk about ESG, but in the mining industry the devil lurks in the 'how'. Indeed, there is often a disconnect between a company's ESG rhetoric and its on-the-ground reputation and performance – the 'say-do' gap. Companies often have wonderfully scripted corporate ESG policies, management plans and operating procedures that are not properly, or consistently, executed on their mine sites. In addition, they dedicate significant time and resources to producing detailed ESG reports which tend to offer distracting narratives with terse commitments, forgettable pledges and amorphous confusing jargon – projecting ESG breadth over depth. This is all impression management, where the onus is on defensive public relations and managing the ESG messaging, rather than the real issues or impacts with operational substance particularly on increasingly complex issues such as climate change, human rights or biodiversity management. Evidence of those behaviours should be a big 'red flag' in a DD process.

Another common pitfall has been the fixation with ESG ratings. At least 160 specialised companies have emerged virtually overnight that rate company performance. Wishful thinking contends that strong ESG ratings can somehow miraculously help mining companies develop both 'brand' awareness and build confidence with different stakeholder groups, even helping secure a 'social licence to operate'. However, one simply does not get the whole story when relying on inscrutable ESG ratings that are data-driven or derived by overlaying qualitative factors – and where there is still no single source of truth given the huge biases and inconsistencies of the ESG rating agencies' approaches and scores. The simple fact is that *bona fide* ESG comparability is unattainable in the mining industry without proper context and narrative, which will facilitate more meaningful interpretation and help support informed decisions about investments and capital allocation. There is no shortcut, and it is nonsensical to be judged against some random standardised criteria and then awarded a score. In 2021 Bloomberg[2] investigated one of the major rating agencies that scores a lot of mining companies and exposed that their ratings "don't measure a company's impact on the earth or society. In fact, they gauge the opposite: the potential impact of the world on the company and its shareholders". To well-meaning but less savvy investors these ESG ratings may appear to be a convenient stamp of approval during a DD exercise, but they are wide open to manipulation and subjectivity. ESG is not a competitive sport where the score is the only thing that matters. Circumventing process is inadvisable as an effective DD requires gaining a complete picture through first-hand insights into a company's ESG culture, strategy, risks, operational practices and jurisdictional nuances from mine sites to the corporate office.

Lastly, as decarbonisation goes mainstream, mining companies are hopping on the bandwagon and increasingly branding their products as 'critical minerals' for the clean energy economy. What is equally worrying is the growth of undifferentiated virtue signalling – from pledges on 'net zero' to being 'nature-positive' – which most often wildly outpaces genuine commitment and tangible actions on the ground. Therefore, ESG-related DD processes need to ensure that companies are not deliberately or mistakenly using greenwashing tactics such as distracting one-off sustainability initiatives and 'green' marketing to avoid meaningfully integrating ESG throughout operations.

3. Effective due diligence

ESG is increasingly becoming a deal driver, and when done well it is the 'black hat thinker'[3] in the diligence suite as defined by Edward de Bono's parallel thinking theory. Whether it is for corporate business development, royalty/streaming transactions, private equity investment, International Funding Institution (IFI) or bank debt or credit financing, the primary purpose of ESG-related DD is to determine the most likely business case and to identify and understand the risks and opportunities which surround that case. But today we live in a fast-moving, interconnected, image-dominated era where polarisation and misinformation flourish and there is no reliable way to avoid scrutiny and criticism – all of which create so many new challenges but also opportunities for mining companies and investors alike.

2 Bloomberg, "The ESG Mirage", www.bloomberg.com/graphics/2021-what-is-esg-investing-msci-ratings-focus-on-corporate-bottom-line/.

3 The Six Thinking Hats (Hats) is a tool for decision-making, problem-solving, new idea generation, or effective meetings. Developed by Dr Edward de Bono, the Hats are the cornerstone of parallel thinking theory: separate thinking to ensure participants work in parallel (together) to achieve the optimal solution. The Hats are imaginary 'thinking hats' that strive to separate thinking to avoid arguments and develop issues more thoroughly. Each hat represents a specific thinking role, ensuring participants focus on one role at a time. The black hat is the driver for critical thinking within the Hats and focuses on concerns, cautions and problems. The black hat is not negative. It is about ensuring a topic or problem is properly dissected.

The modern mining investment landscape is changing rapidly as ESG factors become an essential component of investing strategies. Due to regulatory requirements like the EU Sustainable Finance Disclosure Regulation (SFDR) the importance of ESG due diligence has been further amplified. The demand from European investors in particular for green investments, the proliferation of ESG in due diligence and requests for proposals have made it clear that those seeking to access capital will need to continue to weigh ESG in their decision-making processes. Therefore, ESG-related DD needs to be increasingly forward looking and strategic. It must seek to understand and address long-term sustainability issues that might affect the company's performance and reputation over time.

So, what should savvy acquirers and investors seek to do when approaching pre-investment ESG-related DD? How can DD ensure that ESG-related impacts, risks and innovative opportunities that could create, protect or enhance long-term value are both identified and then objectively assessed? Essentially how should ESG DD be approached so it shifts from a fatal flaw mechanism into delivering perspicacious insights?

Although there is a growing integration of ESG data into the decision-making processes of conventional corporate development teams of investors, many are still struggling to approach ESG as a strategic value driver in corporate valuations, instead treating it as a reporting, compliance and – regrettably – a marketing issue. They continue to rely on the completion of parochial responsible investment due diligence questionnaires that are relatively shallow and incomplete. These provide limited insight into a mining company's real ESG strategy and ethics, operational risks, impacts or opportunities, primarily due to a lack of contextualisation and informed analysis. Therefore, to provide that critical understanding the first (albeit often overlooked) DD step must be to clearly outline the investment objectives and overall thesis – and how ESG factors align with them and the acquiring and/or investment company's policies regarding ESG performance expectations and overall stewardship. Identifying the motivation for the ESG DD is foundational, and should be consistent with and complement other DD processes. At this stage, it is worth remembering that a growing number of corporate development teams and investors now adopt negative, norms-based or positive ESG-related screens to exclude or include investment in specific companies, geographies (eg, sanctioned countries or protected areas), commodities (eg, thermal coal), or controversial activities (eg, riverine or submarine tailings disposal). These red lines should be established at the outset.

The second essential step is capturing relevant ESG data and information through a failsafe, streamlined and effective DD process. A rigorous, consistent and systematic methodology is vital without defaulting to a box-ticking compliance mindset that some still promote through standardised generic questionnaires. The ability to pose the right questions is the greatest resource for uncovering the reality and gaining unbiased intelligence during ESG-related DD, as there are no right answers to the wrong questions. A codified and structured approach is important but one must consciously avoid complacency and the one-size-fits-all approach – respecting that each transaction counterparty, country and company presents its unique array of interrelated ESG risks and impacts. Good practice involves even-handedness by combining a structured framework with deal-specific deep dives. In addition, the ESG-related DD must be prioritised and properly integrated with all the other DD disciplines, especially the legal and technical teams. This will facilitate a shared consciousness of the entire DD process and ensure that the ESG component fully comprehends the deal rationale; the goals and the plan for achieving those goals; and the drivers of post-investment value creation and any significant hurdles.

As an aside, from an ESG perspective, the approach to DD does vary depending on whether you are a prospective owner/operator looking to acquire, intending to form a joint venture or become a minority investor. When investment will come with management responsibilities, the DD scope must be comprehensive from site to the board. For minority investments, there should be a greater emphasis on evaluating the board's approach to ethics and ESG governance. It involves assessing the effectiveness of their oversight structure to provide confidence in the company's ESG posture and related culture, and determining whether their ESG approach is core to corporate strategy. The DD needs to assess whether the board approaches ESG matters in an ethical, informed and deliberative manner and is capable of demonstrating it. The DD should include assessing governance processes, including board ESG committees, charters and policies; their approach to risk management, oversight protocols, safeguard controls and ethical guardrails; and how they incentivise ESG-related behaviours through executive compensation. It is not surprising that through a robust DD an increasing number of risks are uncovered within 'governance'. This topic encompasses the general oversight and management of ESG within the framework of structured and formalised policies and is growing in prominence. Often, companies that become acquisition or funding targets lack maturity, despite having well-intentioned policies and potentially effective ESG initiatives. They often fall short in formalising and operationalising these actions. ESG-related DD can serve as a tool to help such companies reveal areas where existing procedures can be formalised into site-specific adaptive management plans and standard operating procedures.

The third step requires a risk-based assessment of a wide range of material ESG themes with increased granularity – especially concerning governance and social performance contextualised to the jurisdiction – while proactively looking for and assessing creative ESG opportunities to add societal or environmental value (to support the overall investment thesis). The universe of potential ESG topics is immense (and stakeholder ESG priorities often compete) so effective DD needs to focus the scope on genuine materiality and assess how ESG performance could affect long-term values. A focused scope strikes the right balance between the time and effort expended and the benefits derived. The DD also needs to consider intangible assets including reputation, 'social licence' and stakeholder relationships as well as issues that should be part of the overall price modelling and valuation – such as mine closure financial surety, biodiversity offsetting, decarbonisation or climate change adaptation. Essentially this requires the ability to differentiate between true operational ESG risks, ethical imperatives and impact/innovation opportunities, which could provide an ESG-related strategic advantage. Effective DD should also help distinguish and build resilience against external shocks, regulatory changes and evolving market expectations: it positions a company to adapt to the changing landscape and societal demands, contributing to its long-term sustainability.

At this stage, another key component of a thorough ESG-related DD process is informed benchmarking of ESG performance against appropriate industry peers and the adoption of Good International Industry Practice (GIIP) which helps contextualise the DD findings and pinpoint areas where the company may be underperforming or leading on its ESG maturity journey. This requires having a robust understanding of how ESG standards are selected, operationalised, implemented and ultimately assured. Several such standards and frameworks are used for ESG performance and disclosure in the mining sector, including:

- IFC Environmental and Social Performance Standards;
- Equator Principles (EPs);
- International Council on Mining and Metals (ICMM) – Sustainability Framework and Principles;
- World Gold Council – Responsible Gold Mining Principles (RGMPs);
- Mining Association of Canada – Towards Sustainable Mining (TSM);
- Copper (Nickel, Zinc & Moly) Mark;
- Initiative for Responsible Mining Assurance (IRMA);
- UN Global Compact and Guiding Principles on Business and Human Rights;
- OECD Due Diligence Guidance for Responsible Business Conduct;
- Voluntary Principles on Security and Human Rights (VPSHR);
- International Cyanide Management Code (ICMC);
- ISO 14001 (Environmental Management Systems) and ISO 45001 (Occupational Health and Safety Management Systems);
- Global Reporting Initiative (GRI); and
- Sustainability Accounting Standards Board (SASB).

Any worthy DD should seek to provide a qualified degree of confidence (or lack thereof). Nonetheless what is often lacking in ESG-related DD processes is conducting the assessment through knowledgeable and lived experienced 'operator's eyes' – essential for building operational resilience and mitigating risks associated with climate change, resource scarcity and social instability issues. Therefore, the next (fourth) step requires going beyond the typical pedestrian consultant DD report to help adjudge actual company culture, identifying synergies, potential operational efficiencies, cost savings and integration challenges. It can help objectively evaluate whether ESG commitments are workable and stakeholder expectations manageable and whether the company has the resources and capability to implement and fulfil commitments and obligations. It requires assessing company processes and systems to recognise ESG risks and generate opportunities, measure performance, assess incidents and community grievances and evaluate mitigation measures. This can only be done through site visits and direct engagement and dialogue with company management to unguardedly discuss their approach to ESG issues, their strategies for identifying and managing risks, and their ongoing improvement plans.

Lastly, an effective ESG-related DD requires a knowledgeable interpretation, validated quantification of findings, appropriate candid commentary and recommended post-closing actions that are commensurate with the risk/opportunity and the level of investment and/or ownership and ability to influence. This final and indispensable step in the process links back to the investment thesis. It requires a degree of farsightedness to anticipate the continued uncertainty and evolution of the ESG landscape, especially with the growing attention to critical minerals, and the fast-evolving mandatory corporate ESG disclosure requirements and related securities laws. In combination, this facilitates the proper integration of ESG factors into the investment decision-making process alongside traditional legal, technical and financial analysis. ESG findings and recommendations also need to feed into the deal structuring and financing conditions within the investment package through affirmative covenants and/or contractual obligations in the transaction documents, as well as the relevant indemnities, representations and warranties.

While ESG considerations have been around for a while the practice of conducting systematic ESG DD is still evolving. Different organisations and stakeholders offer competing definitions and priorities resulting in a boundless range of DD approaches. Overall, good ESG-related DD involves a systematic and comprehensive approach to gathering and analysing evidence to make informed decisions, mitigate risks and expose critical insights. ESG issues can have a profound impact on business performance, value and risk. Hence, the reassuring 'compliance' mindset must be avoided as it compromises the integrity and effectiveness of the assessment and fails to support informed decision-making processes. This risks various adverse consequences, including financial losses, legal issues, reputation damage, operational challenges, missed opportunities and a loss of trust. Robust ESG-related DD requires meticulous attention to detail and critical thinking, with multidisciplinary teams and experts collaborating across social, environmental, human resources, security and governance and compliance disciplines. Throughout the process, assiduity, timeliness, transparency and integrity are key principles in ensuring the accuracy and reliability of effective ESG-related DD – remembering it is not a compliance checkbox or controversy filter but a crucial consideration for creating and protecting value.

Key ESG-related DD topics

Responsible business

Does the company apply responsible business practices and appropriate systems of corporate governance and transparency, including the following?

- Establishing systems to secure and proactively maintain compliance with all applicable host country legal requirements, including laws concerning ESG issues, and relevant obligations under the *OECD Guidelines for Multinational Enterprises*.
- Implementing policies and practices with respect to the code of conduct, that prohibit and effectively prevent bribery, corruption and anti-competitive behaviour.
- Ensuring board-level oversight and executive management accountability for ESG performance and disclosure.
- Integrating ESG into corporate strategy and decision-making processes relating to the design, operation and closure of all facilities.
- Integrating ESG into enterprise risk management processes, including assessing environmental and social impacts, risks and opportunities in consultation with interested and affected stakeholders, conducting appropriate baseline and impact assessments, and implementing corresponding risk-based controls.
- Seeking to report annually on ESG strategy, materiality and related performance including with reference to metrics and targets where possible, aligned with host country legal requirements in relation to ESG disclosures, and accepted international standards.
- Publishing annual tax, royalty and other financial payments to governments by country and project and disclosing the value and beneficiaries of any financial or in-kind political contributions whether directly or through an intermediary.

Health and safety

Does the company pursue continual improvement in physical and psychological health and safety performance with the ultimate goal of zero harm, including the following?

- Implementing practices aimed at continually improving workplace physical and psychological health and safety and wellbeing.
- Monitoring performance to eliminate workplace fatalities, serious injuries, psychosocial hazards and prevention of occupational diseases.
- Providing workers with training in accordance with their responsibilities for physical and psychological health and safety and implementing health surveillance and risk-based monitoring programmes.
- Identifying and eliminating or minimising significant risks to the health and safety of local communities related to the company and its activities, including where appropriate emergency preparedness and response.

Human rights

Does the company respect human rights and the interests, cultures, customs and values of workers and communities affected by investments and related activities, including the following?

- Supporting the *UN Guiding Principles on Business and Human Right*s and the *OECD Guidelines for Multinational Enterprises* by developing a public policy-level commitment to respect internationally recognised human rights, undertaking appropriate human rights DD where required, integrating the results of DD into risk management processes, and having an appropriate grievance and remediation mechanism.
- Implementing, based on identified risk, a human rights and security approach consistent with the Voluntary Principles on Security and Human Rights.
- Committing to identifying and proactively addressing modern slavery risks (including direct workforce and supply chain) by considering the ways in which the company and its activities may be considered to cause, contribute to or be linked to modern slavery.
- Respecting the rights of workers by not employing child or forced labour; avoiding human trafficking; not assigning hazardous/dangerous work to those under 18; eliminating all forms of harassment and discrimination; respecting freedom of association and collective bargaining; and providing an appropriate mechanism to address workers' grievances.
- Equitably remunerating workers with wages that equal or exceed the host country's legal requirements or represent a competitive wage within that job market (whichever is higher).

- Avoiding the involuntary physical or economic displacement of families and communities. Where that is not possible apply the mitigation hierarchy and implement actions or remedies that address residual adverse effects to restore or improve the livelihoods and standards of living of displaced people.
- Respecting the rights, interests, aspirations, culture and natural resource-based livelihoods of Indigenous Peoples and Land-Connected Peoples in project design, development and operation.
- Where possible, striving to obtain the free, prior and informed consent (FPIC) of Indigenous Peoples and Land-Connected Peoples where adverse impacts are predicted and capture the outcomes of consultation and consent processes in appropriate benefit-sharing agreements.
- Implementing policies and practices that protect against all forms of discrimination, harassment and behaviours (such as misogyny, sexism, racism, sexual prejudice, ageism, ableism, classism and religious intolerance) that adversely impact employees' participation in the workplace.
- Implementing policies and practices to respect the rights and interests of all workers and seek to foster, cultivate and preserve a culture of workplace diversity, equity and inclusion.
- Encouraging risk-based DD of the supply chain to ensure suppliers, contractors and end users, where possible, operate responsibly and to standards of ethics, safety, health, human rights and social and environmental performance.

Social performance

Does the company pursue continual improvement in social performance and contribute to the social, economic and institutional development of host countries and local and Indigenous communities, including the following?

- Identifying, consulting and engaging in good faith with Indigenous and local communities and key external stakeholders in an open, culturally appropriate and transparent manner.
- Implementing inclusive approaches with Indigenous and local communities to identify their development priorities and support activities that seek to deliver meaningful benefits and contribute to their sustained socio-economic well-being.
- Promoting practices that enable access to, and maximise opportunities for, local procurement and local employment across the project life cycle.
- Seeking broad-based community support while providing local stakeholders and Indigenous Peoples with access to appropriate and

effective mechanisms for seeking resolution of grievances related to the company and its activities.

- Collaborating with the government and, where appropriate, support improvements in environmental and social practices of local artisanal and small-scale mining (ASM).
- Seeking to preserve both tangible and intangible cultural heritage from adverse impacts associated with the company and its activities based on consultation with relevant affected stakeholders and Indigenous Peoples.

Environmental performance

Does the company pursue continual improvement in environmental performance issues, such as water stewardship, energy use and climate change management, including the following?

- Designing and implementing water stewardship practices (usage impacts and risks) that support transparent water governance, effective and efficient management of water and collaboration with relevant stakeholders.
- Designing, constructing, operating, monitoring and decommissioning tailings disposal/storage facilities using comprehensive, risk-based management and governance practices in line with internationally recognised good practices. Managing all high-risk or above-rated dams aligned with the Global Industry Standard on Tailings Management.
- Applying adaptive management (applying a mitigation hierarchy) to reduce noise and vibrations, prevent pollution, manage all forms of hazardous materials, waste and emissions, and address potential impacts on human health and the environment.
- Where appropriate, conducting a climate change impact assessment including qualitative scenario analysis to inform both a mitigation pathway (reduction targets towards net zero), and appropriate adaptation/resiliency plans.
- Implementing measures to improve energy efficiency and where feasible seek to increase the use of renewable energy to reduce total energy consumption and/or energy intensity. Calculating and reporting greenhouse gas (GHG) emissions and reporting the outcomes based on internationally recognised protocols for measuring CO_2 equivalent GHG emissions.
- In the project design, operation and decommissioning, seeking to implement cost-effective measures for the recovery, reuse or recycling of energy, natural resources and other materials.
- Planning and designing for responsible mine closure from the project development stage in consultation with relevant authorities and

stakeholders, implementing surety measures to address closure-related environmental and social aspects, and making appropriate financial provision to fund agreed closure and post-closure commitments.

Biodiversity

Does the company work to contribute to the protection or enhancement of legally protected areas, critical habitats, key biodiversity areas, valued ecosystem components, endangered and threatened species, and ecosystem services, including the following?

- Neither exploring nor developing new mines in UNESCO Natural and Mixed World Heritage Sites and respecting legally designated protected areas (eg, Natura 2000 network) to ensure that new operations or changes to existing operations are not incompatible with the value for which they were designated.
- Assessing and addressing risks and impacts to legally protected areas, critical habitats, key biodiversity areas, valued ecosystem components, endangered and threatened species, and ecosystem services by implementing adaptive management (applying a mitigation hierarchy), with the ambition of achieving no-net-loss, and wherever possible strive to achieve a new positive impact (NPI) on biodiversity.

Mining, minerals and the circular economy in the European Union and the United Kingdom

Kamen Stoilov
CMS Cameron McKenna Nabarro Olswang LLP

1. Introduction

1.1 The concept of the circular economy

With the rise in importance and popularity of sustainability goals in recent decades, the concept of the circular economy has acquired prominence as one of the central pillars of the shift towards sustainable production and consumption models and an important aspect of the combat against climate change and biodiversity loss. While there is no universally accepted definition of the term 'circular economy', in broad terms it is understood to mean "a model of production and consumption, which involves sharing, leasing, reusing, repairing, refurbishing and recycling existing materials and products as long as possible".[1]

Considering its focus on reuse and recycling, repairing and extending a product's lifetime, the circular economy is closely linked with related concepts that are increasingly widely used by regulators, consumers and non-governmental organisations alike. This includes 'zero waste' and slogans such as 'reduce, reuse, recycle', as well as the 'waste hierarchy'[2] as embedded in certain legislation, whereby priority is given to methods of waste prevention and treatment that prolong the use of valuable resources already embedded in finished products via repair, repurposing, recycling and recovery; with products' disposal in landfill or via incineration being a worst-case scenario option to be avoided wherever possible.

1 This is the definition adopted by the European Parliament in its dedicated webpage on "Circular economy: definition, importance and benefits", www.europarl.europa.eu/topics/en/article/20151201STO05603/circular-economy-definition-importance-and-benefits.

2 For example, Article 4 of the EU Waste Framework Directive 2008/98/EC (as amended).

Figure 1. Waste hierarchy

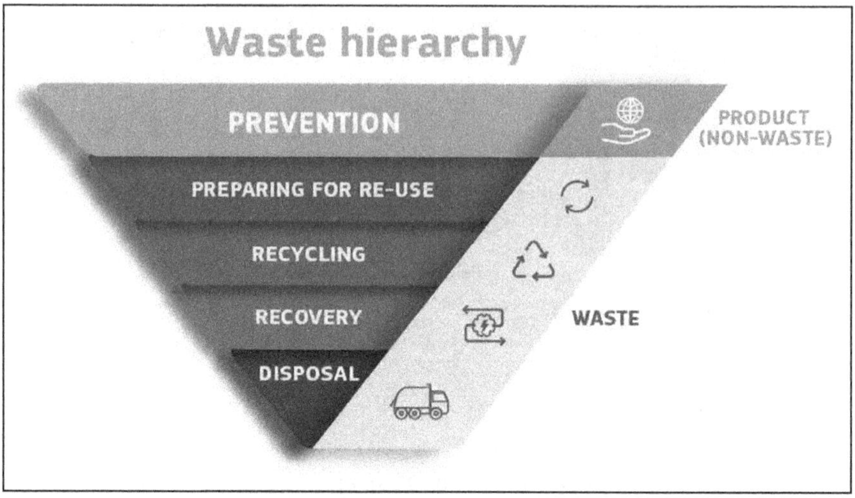

Source: © European Union, 1995–2024, CC BY 4.0.

While not expressly articulated in the definition of 'circular economy' above, the key rationales for the circular economy are two-fold: (i) avoiding the generation of waste; and (ii) minimising the need for the extraction and/or production of new valuable resources. Both of these goals are fundamental to the same overarching objective, which is reducing greenhouse gas (GHG) emissions in order to combat climate change. Apart from the obvious negative impacts of waste generation, which is pollution of the environment when waste is handled improperly and associated costs, the waste industry is responsible for around 3% of global GHG emissions,[3] and it is the fourth largest contributor to climate change in that regard when categorised by industry sectors. Where waste generation, transportation and treatment are minimised, and particularly where disposal of waste in landfills is reduced to a minimum, major emission reductions stand to be achieved. On the flipside, keeping products and the resources embedded in them in circulation for as long as possible reduces the need for the extraction and production of new resources. This is typically very energy-intensive and often involves vast amounts of water being used which in itself is a major contributor to GHG emissions and exacerbates climate change. Additionally, the reduction of the demand for new raw materials correspondingly reduces the need to interfere with the natural environment and disrupt habitats and ecosystems to extract new resources, including by developing new mines and the associated rail, road and other infrastructure. Increased circularity can therefore have a net beneficial impact on biodiversity loss.

3 Based on information from Eurostat regarding GHG emissions from waste from 2020.

Against the backdrop of the exacerbating twin crises of climate change and biodiversity loss, it is therefore not surprising that legislators and regulators across the globe, but particularly in the European Union, have increasingly focused their attention on adopting laws and regulations to promote and indeed mandate the introduction of circular economy goals, strategies and models.

1.2 Circular economy strategies and legislation in the European Union and worldwide

In March 2020, the European Commission unveiled its Circular Economy Action Plan as one of the main building blocks of the European Green Deal, which is the European Union's strategy for sustainable growth and achieving climate neutrality by 2050. The plan contained a strategy for introducing a package of new regulatory measures targeting specific sectors and products with the goal of promoting circularity across the EU economy. In the four years following the communication of the plan, the European Union adopted or is extremely close to having formally adopted (at the time of writing) several transformative pieces of legislation in implementation of its plan to move towards a circular economy.

The EU measures include a new regulation on eco-design for sustainable products focusing on minimum durability, recyclability and repairability of unlimited categories of products, which also prohibits measures leading to premature obsolescence and the destruction of some unsold consumer goods. There are also product-specific revamped regulations targeting packaging, batteries and construction products, to bring those sectors in line with circular economy goals, as well as new rules on the consumers' right to repair and the transboundary shipments of waste (within and outside the European Union). Together, these measures, which have been adopted by the European Union at unprecedented pace, are likely to have a transformative impact on how the bloc's economy will function in the next decades, moving away from linear models and coming much closer to circular models, although of course perfect circularity is impossible to achieve.

The European Union is, without a doubt, a global leader in the promotion of a circular economy, with progress made to date at least with the adoption of relevant legislation, if not actual results in the reduction of waste. However, the importance of the circular economy is becoming recognised globally. The Environmental Protection Agency (EPA) in the United States also has a dedicated webpage about the circular economy detailing the actions already taken by the EPA, as well as those which it intends to take in the near future to promote circularity. Currently, those measures comprise a US National Strategy for Reducing Food Loss and Waste and Recycling Organics, a Draft National Strategy to Prevent Plastic Pollution, and a draft strategy for electronics, which is still being developed. In the United Kingdom, while a country-wide circular economy strategy is still awaited, there have been various initiatives at the level of constituent nations, with each of England and Wales, Scotland and Northern Ireland adopting measures or publishing strategies in that regard. There have been similar initiatives across the world, particularly in developed countries such as Japan (which in some respects is more advanced than the European Union in achieving circularity), New Zealand and others; and across the developed and developing world, the idea is actively being explored.

1.3 Circular economy in the specific context of mining and minerals

The circular economy has relatively recently started to make inroads in the area of mining and minerals regulation, particularly in the European Union, but also abroad. As the fight against climate change has driven a push towards electrification of transport and transition to renewable energy, both industry and state actors have recognised the pressing need to access critical raw materials. Regulators have started to recognise the potential of leveraging well-known strategies for promoting circularity to achieve better security of supply of materials that are of a critical significance, not simply to advance zero waste and net zero ambitions, but more importantly, to ensure sovereignty and independence while transitioning to a modern, low-or-zero emission economy.

Those critical materials include, but are not limited to, inputs that are essential for the production and functioning of modern technologies fundamental to net zero and wider energy transition goals, including wind turbines and electric vehicle batteries. Examples include: lithium, cobalt and nickel (for electric vehicles); boron and rare earths (for wind turbines); and others. Considering that most of these materials are currently imported into Europe from developing countries (primarily China and various African countries), a series of measures has been adopted at the EU level to boost self-reliance in securing access to such materials. In the context of critical minerals, therefore, circularity is driven by slightly different concerns, whereby the security of supply is of primary importance.

2. EU circular economy laws and regulations targeting strategic minerals

While the EU Circular Economy Package of legislation now comprises a dozen statutes, few of them specifically target the issue of supply and circularity in the area of critical raw materials. The two pieces of legislation already in force which are the most relevant in that regard are EU Regulation 2024/1252 establishing a framework for ensuring a secure and sustainable supply of critical raw materials, known as the Critical Raw Materials Act (CRMA); and also EU Regulation 2023/1542 (the Batteries Regulation or EUBR).

2.1 Critical Raw Materials Act

Adopted formally on 11 April 2024 and in force since 23 May 2024, the CRMA is arguably the key piece of EU law that promotes circularity in the European Union of resources vital for the energy transition. Notwithstanding that, the CRMA is not formally considered as forming part of the Circular Economy Package. The reason is set out in the recitals to the CRMA, which are unequivocal on the point that its goal is to ensure access to a secure and sustainable supply of critical raw materials and to safeguard the European Union's economic resilience and strategic autonomy. A secondary goal of the CRMA is environmental protection and ensuring that relevant materials are sourced sustainably. However, the CRMA is not, as such, a piece of EU environmental law.

Within the context of the CRMA, circular economy goals serve the primary function of ensuring the continued availability of raw materials necessary for the European Union's energy transition and other needs. Recycling/recovery targets are imposed with a view to ensuring that raw materials that are already imported into the European Union stay in use for as long as possible, thereby reducing the need for the import of new raw materials, and correspondingly reducing the European Union's dependence on the major global exporters of such materials, enhancing its economic sovereignty. Environmental considerations play an important part in the CRMA, but are not the key driver for the regulation. Indeed, the CRMA modifies some aspects of EU environmental law to facilitate and streamline the process of securing environmental permits for new critical raw materials development projects on EU soil. For example, certain steps in the environmental impact assessment process that is normally required for any type of development are dispensed with, while others are accelerated.

The CRMA sets out two lists of materials. One consists of materials considered to be 'strategic' and the other of materials considered 'critical'. It currently comprises of the following metals and rare earths:

(a) Strategic raw materials

- bauxite/alumina/aluminium;
- bismuth;
- boron – metallurgy grade;
- cobalt;
- copper;
- gallium;
- germanium;
- lithium – battery grade;
- magnesium metal;
- manganese – battery grade;

- graphite – battery grade;
- nickel – battery grade;
- platinum group metals;
- rare earth elements for permanent magnets (Nd, Pr, Tb, Dy, Gd, Sm, and Ce);
- silicon metal;
- titanium metal; and
- tungsten.

(b) Critical raw materials

- antimony;
- arsenic;
- bauxite/alumina/aluminium;
- baryte;
- beryllium;
- bismuth;
- boron;
- cobalt;
- coking coal;
- copper;
- feldspar;
- fluorspar;
- gallium;
- germanium;
- hafnium;
- helium;
- heavy rare earth elements;
- light rare earth elements;
- lithium;
- magnesium;
- manganese;
- graphite;
- nickel – battery grade;
- niobium;
- phosphate rock;
- phosphorus;
- platinum group metals;
- scandium;
- silicon metal;
- strontium;
- tantalum;
- titanium metal;

- tungsten; and
- vanadium.

Apart from measures aimed at incentivising domestic extraction and processing of strategic raw materials and limiting reliance on third countries, the CRMA sets the goal of ensuring that at least 25% of the European Union's annual consumption of strategic raw materials can be produced through recycling of materials already in circulation on the EU market by 2030 and that significantly increasing amounts of each strategic raw material are recycled from waste thereafter. To that end, the European Commission is to adopt secondary legislation setting out recycling capacity benchmarks expressed as a share of the strategic raw materials available in relevant waste streams, by reference to: (i) the current EU recycling capacity; (ii) the extent to which strategic raw materials can be recovered from those waste streams, taking into account technological and economic feasibility; and (iii) targets set in other EU laws relevant to the recovery of strategic raw materials. Those EU-wide targets are to be supplemented by other national level measures to promote circularity and increase the use of secondary critical raw materials, for example, by taking recycled content into account in public procurement award criteria; giving financial incentives for the use of secondary critical raw materials; eco-modulation of fees payable by producers under extended producer responsibility statutes (ie, discounted rates for those using recycled materials); and better collection, sorting and processing of waste with critical raw materials recovery potential.

Some of the circularity measures envisaged by the CRMA target private entities as well. 'Large companies' using strategic raw materials in specific sectors to be identified by the European Commission will be required to carry out a risk assessment of their raw materials supply chain at the latest by 24 May 2025. That assessment must include a mapping of where the strategic raw materials they use are extracted, processed or recycled; an analysis of the factors that might affect their supply of strategic raw materials; and an assessment of their vulnerabilities to supply disruptions. They must then make efforts to address those vulnerabilities. Separately, manufacturers and/or importers into the European Union of some types of products incorporating permanent magnets must, from 2027, disclose various information on the percentage of recycled content incorporated in the magnets, and from 2031 at the latest, but possibly earlier, must ensure that minimum shares of neodymium, dysprosium, praseodymium, terbium, boron, samarium, nickel and cobalt recovered from post-consumer waste are present in the permanent magnets. Finally, the European Commission is empowered to establish rules for the calculation and verification of the environmental footprint of different critical raw materials, and any entity who places raw materials covered by such rules on the EU market will have to publish an environmental footprint declaration. While details are yet to be specified in the required delegated acts, that declaration will likely have to include the raw materials' recycled content.

2.2 Batteries Regulation

In force since August 2023, the Batteries Regulation (EUBR) is the other piece of EU legislation with ambitious recycling and recovery goals targeting critical raw materials. Unlike the CRMA, the EUBR is a key part of the Circular Economy Package and the Green Deal and is fundamentally driven by environmental and sustainability concerns, rather than ones of economic and political sovereignty. The EUBR contains chapters dedicated to sustainability requirements and waste management, the primary goals of which are environmental protection, waste minimisation and sustainability in the broadest sense. Certain aspects of the EUBR, which go beyond the scope of this chapter, are also designed to address concerns around human rights violations in the countries where certain critical raw materials used in batteries are prevalent, imposing an obligation on economic actors to ensure through due diligence that they are not involuntarily complicit in such abuse. This chapter explores solely the main circularity provisions of EUBR.

The EUBR goes a step further than the CRMA because it imposes all the recycling and recovery targets directly on battery manufacturers, rather than primarily on member states and only in rare cases on 'large companies'. Under EUBR, all battery manufacturers regardless of size will be required from 2031 to ensure that their electric vehicle, industrial and starting, lighting and ignition batteries all contain, at a minimum, 16% cobalt, 85% lead, 6% lithium and 6% nickel recovered from battery manufacturing waste or post-consumer waste. The requirement applies per battery model per manufacturing plant, meaning that the targets must be met by manufacturers across their operations. From 2036, these targets are set to go up to 26% cobalt, 85% lead, 12% lithium and 15% nickel for the same battery types. The European Commission has powers to revise the targets up or down based on the forecasted availability of raw materials recovered from waste after 2030, as well as based on technical and scientific progress. Importantly, the requirements do not apply to batteries that have been remanufactured, recycled or repurposed, therefore prioritising the reuse of assembled batteries over the recycling of their raw materials.

Meeting the recycled content targets is a precondition for lawfully selling batteries in the European Union. This means that, unless manufacturers can demonstrate via technical documentation that their recycled content requirements have been met, they would not be able to sell their batteries on the EU market. Further economic actors down the supply chain, for example, importers and distributors, are prohibited from making such batteries available on the market (ie, reselling) where they suspect non-compliance with the applicable targets. This ensures that the primary responsibility for achieving circularity in the field of raw materials used in batteries in the European Union will fall on the private sector, while member states and the Commission will, of course, facilitate the process.

In addition, battery producers are required as part of their due diligence policies to disclose in reasonable detail whether the raw materials present in their batteries are derived from recycling. Since the requirement to publish due diligence statements applies from August 2025, or some six years earlier than the recycling and recovery mandatory targets, this requirement is important as it puts some pressure on actors from a pure publicity and marketing perspective to make at least some progress towards achieving their targets earlier than the date from which they apply.

Additionally, the EUBR embeds the principle of extended producer responsibility whereby the producers of batteries pay waste management fees for the batteries they have placed on the EU market. When determining the amount of those fees, account is taken of secondary raw materials recovered from waste, which aims to further incentivise circularity in the use of critical raw materials in batteries in the European Union. The fees payable would be eco-modulated to reflect the level of recycled content and materials recovered from waste batteries, meaning that higher recycled content results in lower fees. This again goes a step further than CRMA which merely offers to member states the possibility of introducing eco-modulation in their respective domestic laws.

Finally, targets for recycling efficiency and recovery of materials are imposed also on facilities for the recycling and recovery of waste batteries, which are to be reviewed by the European Commission.

2.3 Other relevant EU legislation

Regulation (EU) 2024/1781 on Ecodesign for Sustainable Products (ESPR) entered into force on 18 July 2024. While it does not have raw materials as its primary focus, it references them in the context of the European Union's New Industrial Strategy, intending to support its goal of reducing the European Union's current dependence on imports of raw materials. The EPSR is primarily a piece of framework legislation, meaning that it lays the ground for the adoption of secondary legislation to establish specific eco-design rules and requirements for some product categories. It grants powers to the European Commission to set out the relevant rules in delegated acts. The relevant eco-design criteria are likely to include minimum recycled or recovered content targets, similar to those that already exist for batteries, for other product categories as well. The EPSR states in relation to critical raw materials that they are relevant to a product's 'life cycle' and also its 'material footprint', each of which is listed among the key product parameters in relation to which the European Commission will establish performance requirements that would have to be met for relevant products to be lawfully distributed on the EU market.

Other relevant legislation includes the Waste Framework Directive (as amended) that requires member states to adopt additional measures at the national level to minimise waste in critical raw materials. However, those requirements are not nearly as concrete or ambitious as those of the CRMA or the EUBR. There are related, less relevant, statutes dealing with extractive waste.

2.4 The current UK position

All of the CRMA, EUBR and ESPR entered into force after the cut-off date in the Withdrawal Act 2018 stipulating which EU legislation still applies in Great Britain post-Brexit (as modified). None of them therefore applies in the United Kingdom and there has been no stated intention for them to be replicated in any shape or form in Great Britain. Compared with the European Union, the United Kingdom's recent Conservative government made relatively little progress in promoting the security of supply and sustainability of critical raw materials by way of regulatory intervention or any concrete legislative proposals. That government's efforts were broadly limited to the publication of a Critical Raw Minerals Strategy in 2022, followed by a 'refresh' of that same policy in 2023, neither of which lays out clear steps in terms of regulatory intervention in the area beyond two overdue consultations on potential reforms to the Waste Electrical and Electronic Equipment Regulation and the EUBR. The latter consultation was never published by the outgoing government despite repeatedly announcing its intention to do so. There was also a call for evidence for a new UK Battery Strategy, however a response to it was never published.

3. Looking ahead

The European Union aims to boost its independence in the area of critical raw materials and has set ambitious recovery and recycling targets. Some are directly imposed on private actors and so will have a tangible impact on industry in the not too distant future. Preparation and planning by affected operators must start now for compliance to be feasible within the timeframes that are envisaged. However, the extent to which achieving the European Union's ambitious targets will be met and, if so, how effective that will be in driving down demand for importing new raw materials from countries such as China remains to be seen. While the recycling of raw materials from products already on the EU market will certainly help achieve this, the forecast for an exponential increase in demand for relevant materials means that circularity would be at best moderate and would not fully or even partially eliminate the need to import new materials. That is why the European Union has negotiated a critical minerals deal with Australia, a major lithium producer, and is attempting to negotiate a similar deal with the United States, although that has proven challenging. The European Union has similar non-binding cooperation agreements with a few countries in Asia, Africa and South America. Meanwhile, the United Kingdom is notably lagging behind the European Union in terms of both regulatory and diplomatic efforts to diversify critical raw materials supply and this has become a hot topic in parliament. It remains to be seen how the new Labour government will approach this highly problematic subject.

New mineral frontiers and their ESG challenges

Nabil Abrahams
Ted Rhodes
CMS Cameron McKenna Nabarro Olswang LLP

1. Introduction

The recent focus on critical minerals is a response to the burgeoning demand for resources essential for modern technologies and green energy solutions in the wake of a climate crisis. The environmental, social and governance (ESG) considerations surrounding the extraction of critical minerals present a complex landscape. As the demand for these resources grows, so does the pressure to extract them in a manner that is environmentally sustainable, socially responsible and governed by ethical practices. The World Energy Council initially coined the term 'energy trilemma' to describe the three dimensions to energy supply: energy security, energy equity and environmental sustainability.[1] These factors continue to present serious challenges and prove difficult to reconcile. The world seems less secure now than it has in many years, with renewed geopolitical rivalries giving rise to tensions and conflict, notably in the Middle East and Ukraine. Climate change is no longer just a theory, but being felt in extreme weather events across the world, with resultant property damage, displacement and deaths. We are increasingly speaking in terms of a climate crisis or emergency. As supply shocks, particularly from Russia, have caused energy costs to spike, high inflation has eroded living standards and exacerbated poverty in many countries. That has created a fertile breeding ground for nationalist or isolationist policies aimed at securing supplies of energy and natural resources for domestic markets, often at the expense of other nations.

Against this background, the demand for critical minerals is expected to double by 2030 with prices having been increasingly volatile.[2] Data from Wood Mackenzie suggests that demand for copper – an essential component in electric vehicles – is expected to outstrip supply by 2026.[3] Whether by regulation or strategic investment, governments across the world appear to be responding,

1 World Energy Council, *World Energy Trilemma 2024: Evolving with resilience and justice*, www.worldenergy.org/publications/entry/world-energy-trilemma-report-2024.
2 *Financial Times*, "Higher investment in critical minerals boosts chances of meeting climate targets", 10 July 2023, www.ft.com/content/c51d4601-e2ec-40d2-93d7-fcd7d7ab1310.
3 *Financial Times*, "Miner Rio Tinto to test 'new frontiers' as copper age dawns", 5 August 2023, www.ft.com/content/91c1ae9e-8150-4201-9952-f02efbd60693.

albeit slowly. For example, the European Commission's Critical Raw Materials Act acknowledges that a secure and sustainable supply of critical raw materials is crucial to the energy transition. The US Inflation Reduction Act aims to promote national sources of critical minerals by making eligibility for tax credits on electric vehicles conditional upon a requirement that at least 40% of the value of critical minerals in the batteries was extracted or processed in the United States, or in countries with which the United States has a free trade agreement, or recycled in North America. That percentage will increase gradually to 80% by 2027. Meanwhile, as reported by the *Financial Times* in June 2023, Chinese companies, in 2022, nearly doubled their investments in securing resources essential to clean energy.[4]

This is further complicated by the concentration of critical minerals in certain regions, which have come to dominate certain mineral supply chains, despite the high risk of specific ESG failings. For example, production of cobalt is concentrated in the Democratic Republic of the Congo (DRC), which accounts for about 70% of global production.[5] Meanwhile, Indonesia holds the title of world's largest nickel producer with data from Benchmark Intelligence (as reported in the *Financial Times*) estimating that Indonesia's annual nickel output is expected to grow to 3.02 million tonnes by 2030 and account for 65% of global supply.[6] Lithium is found in Latin America, some parts of Africa, Western Europe, Australia and China. However, different locations contain different forms of lithium, which require different methods of extraction. The World Economic Forum estimates that Latin America holds 60% of the world's lithium reserves, earning Argentina, Bolivia and Chile the title of "the lithium triangle".[7]

Discovering new reserves of these critical minerals, to reduce over-reliance on specific regions and ensure security of supply, has become an economic priority. As the world's population continues to grow and the demand for renewable energy follows suit, supply challenges are likely to grow more acute. But with this global push for new supply will come its own host of ESG challenges, which must be considered and addressed, to ensure a just energy transition. Even with the imperative of meeting demand for renewable energy, it is paramount to ensure that new investments in exploration, development and production meet global ESG standards. As new mineral frontiers are sought, mining companies, investors and society more broadly should emphasise the importance of protecting natural ecosystems and developing less invasive and

4 *Financial Times*, "Higher investment in critical minerals boosts chances of meeting climate targets", 10 July 2023, www.ft.com/content/c51d4601-e2ec-40d2-93d7-fcd7d7ab1310.

5 Cobalt Institute, "Responsible Sourcing", www.cobaltinstitute.org/cobalt-sourcing-responsability/.

6 *Financial Times*, "Indonesia to accelerate nickel output despite low global prices", 29 March 2024, www.ft.com/content/ba1e9856-66aa-4082-b6cd-261b798d050f.

7 World Economic Forum, "Lithium: Here's why Latin America is key to the global energy transition", 10 January 2023, www.weforum.org/agenda/2023/01/lithium-latin-america-energy-transition/.

disruptive technologies. Equally, we should ensure that communities are protected, respected and able to participate in the economic benefits of mineral development.

This chapter will consider emerging and potential future sources of minerals, namely in the polar regions, the deep sea and even space, together with the associated challenges of responsible extraction in these new mining frontiers.

2. Polar mining

In considering potential new mineral 'frontiers', the polar regions – being the areas around the Earth's north and south poles – present increasingly viable (albeit not easy) opportunities for mineral extraction. That said, the applicable regulation, geological potential and ESG challenges vary hugely between the Arctic and Antarctica.

2.1 Arctic

Beneath the tundra and ice of the Arctic lie untouched reserves of oil, natural gas and, importantly, minerals, thought to include gold, diamonds, copper, iron, zinc and uranium.[8] As global warming has reduced the reach of sea ice and permafrost, much of the region has opened up to mineral development, creating what has been dubbed the 'scramble for the Arctic'. However, while resources may be abundant, the climate is still extreme and unforgiving, which often requires increased capital expenditure, higher operational costs and a reduced window for operations. Mine production and construction work may be seasonally restricted and require a higher degree of automation than in more temperate climes.

The Arctic region is generally considered to be the region north of the Arctic Circle, which includes the territory of Greenland (Denmark), Iceland, Norway, Sweden, Finland, Russia, the US state of Alaska and Canada.[9] Each of those countries has sovereign powers to regulate and benefit from mineral extraction and other economic activities on its territory and in, above and below its territorial waters.

The United Nations Convention of the Law of the Sea (UNCLOS) defines territorial waters as generally encompassing the areas within 12 nautical miles from its baselines (ie, normally its coastline at low tide). Beyond that limit, Article 56 of UNCLOS stipulates that a country has sovereign rights for exploring and exploiting, conserving and managing the natural resources of the waters within its exclusive economic zone (EEZ). Article 57 states that the EEZ shall not extend beyond 200 nautical miles from the baselines from which the

8 Jeff Desjardins, "The energy and mineral riches of the Arctic", *Visual Capitalist*, 8 April 2016, www.visualcapitalist.com/energy-and-mineral-riches-of-the-arctic/.

9 *National Geographic*, "Arctic", https://education.nationalgeographic.org/resource/arctic/.

breadth of the territorial sea is measured.[10] That said, it is possible for companies to apply to extend this in accordance with Article 76, for up to 350 nautical miles from the coast.[11] However, the state must collect and analyse certain data to be submitted to the Secretary-General of the United Nations. The United States, Russia, Norway, Canada and Denmark have all made such applications.[12]

Beyond those limits are the High Seas, which cover a large proportion of the Arctic Ocean and are outside national jurisdiction.[13] At least that is what international law says, but international law may be strained by the rivalry of military superpowers. In 2007, four kilometres under the North Pole, Russia planted a titanium flag on the seabed, laying claim to over a million square kilometres of seabed, which it has since extended.[14] China, meanwhile, has also concluded that the resource-rich Arctic presents important opportunities and a 2018 Arctic Policy White Paper outlined plans for a "Polar Silk Road" to increase its influence and economic activities in the region.[15] Many original components of the Polar Silk Road strategy have been delayed or discarded, including the participation of Shenghe Resources in a uranium and rare earths mining site at Kuannersuit, Greenland, which has fallen foul of Greenland's legislature reinstating a near-complete ban on uranium mining.[16] However, it shows that China is not going to let its geography rule it out of Arctic opportunities.

Norway is another example of the pro-mining lobby, and has been a first-mover in its approach to seabed mining, targeting manganese crusts and sulphides on the Norwegian Continental Shelf. In June 2019, the Seabed Mineral Act was adopted to govern commercial exploration and extraction of its deep-sea minerals in Norway. In January 2024, the Norwegian Parliament approved a proposal to allow exploration for seabed minerals on around 280,000 km^2 of its Arctic continental shelf between Jan Mayen Island and the Svalbard archipelago. This decision follows government-sponsored surveys that identified significant amounts of metals and minerals, such as iron, copper, zinc, cobalt and rare earth elements like lithium and scandium, in polymetallic sulphides.[17] Approval will be required from the Norwegian Ministry of

10 United Nations Convention on the Law of the Sea, www.un.org/depts/los/convention_agreements/texts/unclos/unclos_e.pdf.

11 *Ibid.*

12 *Geographical*, "Arctic nations are squaring up to exploit the region's rich natural resources", 12 August 2022, https://geographical.co.uk/geopolitics/the-world-is-gearing-up-to-mine-the-arctic.

13 *Ibid.*

14 *Ibid.*

15 *Ibid.*

16 Kevin McGwin, "Greenland restores uranium ban – likely halting a controversial rare earths mine", *Arctic Today*, 10 November 2021, www.arctictoday.com/greenland-restores-uranium-ban-a-move-likely-to-halt-a-controversial-rare-earths-mine; Marc Lanteigne, "The rise (and fall?) of the Polar Silk Road", *The Diplomat*, 29 August 2022, https://thediplomat.com/2022/08/the-rise-and-fall-of-the-polar-silk-road/.

17 European Parliament, "Norway to mine part of the Arctic seabed", www.europarl.europa.eu/RegData/etudes/ATAG/2024/757616/EPRS_ATA(2024)757616_EN.pdf#:~:text=On%209%20January%202024%2C%20the%20Norwegian%20Parliament%20endorsed,the%20Parliament%2C%20following%20a%20possibly%20long%20exploration%20period%29.

Petroleum and Energy for any production plan, which must include a project-specific impact assessment. However, many environmentalists are worried that this has already opened the door to Arctic offshore mining. Because the technologies are untested and these pristine ecosystems are still relatively unknown, they are concerned that human interference on this scale will always present unacceptable environmental risks, and should be prohibited. Companies from Google to BMW signed a WWF call for a halt to deep-sea mining following the opening of deep-sea mining in Norway.[18]

In fact, there is considerable opposition to mining in the Arctic. For example, a group of Inuit hunters weathered freezing conditions to protest against the expansion of Baffinland Iron Mines' planned expansion to its Mary River site, 520km north of the Arctic Circle on Canada's Baffin Island. This ultimately led to a rejection of the expansion plans after years of uncertainty.[19]

ESG concerns centre on both the unknown environmental damage and arguments that it should be the Indigenous Peoples, including the Sami of Scandinavia, the Inuit of North America and Russian Arctic communities such as the Chukchi and Evenk, that should have first claim on these resources. One potential approach to that concern would be to introduce something similar to the various Aboriginal Native Title regimes found in Australia. Those regimes essentially require the consent of Indigenous Peoples prior to the grant of any mining permit over land on which they have a 'native title' claim. In cases where Indigenous Peoples are receptive to allowing mining activities on these lands, the regime facilitates equitable compensation for access to the land (usually in the form of a royalty or participation interest in the project itself). That may not be sufficient though where Indigenous concerns focus on the potential damage to the ecosystem, and the consequences it may have on their traditional ways of life, including hunting, trapping and fishing.

Other ESG risks concern the rights and working conditions of mine labour, which are thrown into focus by the remoteness and extreme conditions encountered at Arctic mine sites. Although hydrocarbon exploration has a successful track record in onshore areas of Canada, Russia and Alaska, mining presents different challenges, including health risks for the workforce, which may be exposed to extreme cold, risks of mechanical failure and blocking of transportation routes. And while climate change may eventually open up new areas of the Arctic to economic activity, the melting of permafrost can make building infrastructure difficult.

With that said, improvements in drilling and mining technologies suggest that previously inaccessible exploitation may now become accessible. By way of

---

18 *Financial Times*, "Norway should push for a global moratorium on deep-sea mining", www.ft.com/content/2f19e165-5580-4161-addf-bdaff878e787.

19 *The Guardian*, "Canada rejects Arctic mine expansion project after years of fierce protest", www.theguardian.com/environment/2022/nov/17/canada-arctic-mine-expansion-rejected-protest.

example, the University of Alaska is acquiring baseline geological, geophysical and geochemical data to evaluate regions for critical mineral resources. Arguably, machine learning and artificial intelligence could also be used to reduce exploration risk and accelerate mineral development in challenging regions like the Arctic.

Recently, the landmark High Seas Treaty, a significant environmental agreement, was established to safeguard the biodiversity of international waters, which cover nearly half of the planet's surface. The treaty is particularly important for the Arctic, as it aims to create a legal framework for establishing marine protected areas and requires environmental impact assessments for industrial activities including mining. The treaty's adoption is an important step towards preserving the fragile ecosystems of the Arctic, which are critical to global biodiversity, as well as the livelihoods of indigenous communities, while also addressing the challenges posed by the expansion of extractive industries in the region.[20]

Globally, views are very much split as to whether we should accelerate development of the Arctic for its untapped potential to supply critical minerals, including those required for the energy transition, or whether we should respect it as one of the last underdeveloped and underpopulated wildernesses, requiring fierce protection. The familiar tension between developing local economies and protecting habitats becomes more complicated considering the growing need for energy transition minerals in consumer markets many miles away.

2.2 Antarctic

The Earth's southernmost continent, Antarctica, presents similar temptations in terms of a potential wealth of untapped minerals deposits, with scientific expeditions revealing the presence of copper, gold, lead, tin, uranium, zinc, antimony and chromium, to name a few.

At present, the Protocol on Environmental Protection to the Antarctic Treaty (Article 7) provides for a complete ban on mineral resource activities (except for scientific research) in Antarctica, which includes the whole area south of 60°S latitude.[21] This protocol, also known as the 'Madrid Protocol', was signed in 1991 and came into force on 14 January 1998.

The only prospect of this changing would be under a provision allowing parties to request a review in 2048. However, any change would require a majority of the Antarctic Treaty Consultative Parties (currently consisting of 29 countries) and three-quarters of those that were consultative parties in 1991

20 WWF, "Landmark High Sea Treaty agreed – and what it means for the Arctic", 6 March 2023, www.arcticwwf.org/newsroom/news/landmark-high-seas-treaty-agreed-and-what-that-means-for-the-arctic/.

21 Protocol on Environmental Protection to the Antarctic Treaty, https://documents.ats.aq/keydocs/vol_1/vol1_4_AT_Protocol_on_EP_e.pdf.

when the Madrid Protocol was signed (26 countries).[22] Any such change would also need to be ratified by three-quarters of the Antarctic Treaty Consultative Parties, including all of the 26 countries which signed the original protocol in 1991. Any change would also be conditional on agreement on a binding legal regime for Antarctic mineral resource activities.

It seems then that Antarctica is comprehensively protected from commercial exploitation for the foreseeable future, and is perhaps the only place on our planet where economic interests have been effectively subordinated to environmental protection.

3. Deep-sea mining

The High Seas are another area that falls outside national jurisdiction, and has therefore been immune from commercial mining activities to date. However, in this case, that looks set to change over the coming years.

We have known of the mineral potential of the deep oceans for some time. In fact, the existence of polymetallic nodules on the sea floor was discovered as a result of dredging by *HMS Challenger*, a British three-mastered warship, during an expedition in the 1870s. Over the years, researchers have refined their understanding of the locations and composition of these potato-sized balls, which contain important minerals for the energy transition, including copper, cobalt, nickel and manganese, usually in significant concentrations and of unusual purity. Most concentrations of these nodules are located beyond national territorial waters and exclusive economic zones (EEZs) in the deep oceans. One of the most resource-rich areas, for example, is the Clarion Clipperton Zone (CCZ) in the middle of the Pacific Ocean.

The oceans contain other sources of minerals, including mineral-rich crusts on seabed rocks or the flanks of underwater volcanic seamounts. These 'Ferromanganese' crusts precipitate on rocky surfaces and bind other metals. As the name suggests, these crusts are typically rich in iron, manganese and cobalt. Some of the thickest and most valuable crusts can be found in the central-west Pacific Ocean between Hawaii and the Mariana Islands at depths ranging between 800 metres and 2,500 metres. Referred to as the Prime Crust Zone, this area is thought to contain four times as much cobalt and nine times as much tellurium as all known land deposits combined. Sulphide deposits from the discharge of hydrothermal vents in the deep ocean are also known to contain zinc, silver, lead and copper.[23]

The main piece of international legislation governing activities within the oceans is the United Nations Convention on the Law of the Sea (UNCLOS),

22 Antarctic and Southern Ocean Coalition, "Protocol on Environmental Protection to the Antarctic Treaty", www.asoc.org/learn/protocol-on-environmental-protection-to-the-antarctic-treaty/.

23 Prihyanka Runwal, "The deep-sea mining dilemma", *Chemical and Engineering News*, 9 October 2023, https://cen.acs.org/environment/water/deep-sea-mining-dilemma/101/i33.

which counted 168 countries as signatories as of May 2023. As well as demarking national maritime territories, UNCLOS sets out member states' rights and obligations regarding the use of the world's oceans and its resources, and the protection of the marine and coastal environment. Established under UNCLOS and the 1994 Agreement relating to the Implementation of Part XI of UNCLOS (the 1994 Agreement), the International Seabed Authority (ISA), headquartered in Kingston, Jamaica, organises and controls activities (particularly regarding mineral resources) in the international seabed area beyond the limits of national jurisdictions (referred to as 'the Area'). The Area makes up more than 50% of the world's oceans and has been placed under the ISA's authority in order for the ISA to control and supervise activities which are to be "carried out for the benefit of mankind as a whole".[24]

When it comes to mining activities, UNCLOS and the ISA regulate exploration activity under exploration contracts. Since 2001, ISA has entered into 31 15-year exploration contracts in relation to polymetallic nodules, polymetallic sulphides and cobalt-rich ferromanganese crusts, 17 of which cover parts of the CCZ.

While exploration is subject to a regulatory regime, the process to regulate commercial exploitation of mineral resources has suffered from repeated delays and is still not finalised. Since 2014, ISA has started to develop regulations for exploitation, with the last published draft dated 22 March 2019. However, in 2021, the pacific state of Nauru which has expressed its intention to sponsor a commercial mining licence, wrote to ISA stating an intention to apply for approval of a 'plan of work' for exploitation of deep-sea minerals. That letter triggered a sub-clause within the 1994 Agreement which gave ISA Council two years to complete the adoption of the rules, regulations and procedures (RRPs) for exploitation of the seabed. If such RRPs were not adopted, in theory, the ISA Council would consider and provisionally approve such a plan of work based on the provisions of UNCLOS and any rules that ISA Council may have provisionally adopted. The deadline for the two-year rule expired on 9 July 2023.

ISA held its 28th session from 28 June to 28 July 2023. However, ISA Council was unable to adopt the RRPs. Instead, it indicated it would continue to develop the RRPs with a view to their adoption during the 30th ISA assembly in 2025. Nauru has not yet presented a plan of work, and it seems likely that it will await the outcome of the 2025 assembly, pending which there is no certainty as to the rules that will govern seabed mining.

The RRPs will need to consider the requirements of the High Seas Treaty, referred to above, including the requirements for environmental impact assessments (EIAs), restrictions relating to marine protected areas and treaty

24 United Nations Convention on the Law of the Sea, www.un.org/depts/los/convention_agreements/texts/unclos/unclos_e.pdf (see preamble and Article 140).

governance mechanisms, including decisions of the Conference of the Parties. EIAs under the High Seas Treaty are required to take account of the cumulative impacts of multiple human activities affecting the same ecosystem, including the "consequences of climate change, ocean acidification and related impacts".[25] They will be subject to review and recommendations of a new Scientific and Technical Body, and will be made available for public consultation. Although any EIA process established in the RRPs for seabed mining would take precedence over the more general provisions of the High Seas Treaty, there is likely to be considerable pressure to ensure that the RRPs are at least as demanding in this respect.[26]

There is, of course, considerable opposition to the prospect of seabed mining from an environmental perspective. Opponents range from environmental and marine scientists, animal welfare and human rights activist groups, to major corporates (including automotive and electronics manufacturers and technology companies) which are concerned about the reputational risks or risks of disruption to their supply chains resulting from seabed mining.[27] Particular concerns relate mainly to the impact that seabed mining would have on marine life (with species and ecosystem disruption being of critical concern) as well as GHG emissions.[28]

It is clear that seabed mining with the technologies currently proposed would directly impact marine life through the wide tracks of mining vehicles compacting and moving sediments on the seabed, thereby disturbing, or crushing and killing organisms.[29] Deep-ocean mining activities would also introduce noise and light pollution in areas where the absence of light and minimal natural levels of noise are essential characteristics of native ecosystems. The introduction of noise and light pollution could cause long-term species and ecosystem disruption by, for example, disturbing feeding and reproductive patterns for mega-fauna such as whales in these areas.[30] The removal of polymetallic nodules would also amount to the removal of many species' natural habitats, without which such species may face extinction.[31]

Perhaps more concerning is the potential impact of sediment plumes,

---

25 High Seas Treaty, Article 1 (definition of 'Cumulative impacts').

26 High Seas Alliance, "A momentous milestone for the ocean and global diversity", www.highseasalliance.org/wp-content/uploads/2023/06/HSA_Treaty_Factsheet_27June23.pdf.

27 Prihyanka Runwal, "The deep-sea mining dilemma", *Chemical and Engineering News*, 9 October 2023, https://cen.acs.org/environment/water/deep-sea-mining-dilemma/101/i33.

28 Oliver Ashford, Jonathan Baines, Melissa Barbanell and Ke Wang, "What we know about deep-sea mining – and what we don't", World Resources Institute, 23 February 2024, www.wri.org/insights/deep-sea-mining-explained.

29 Daniel Jones, Diva Amon and Abbie Chapman, "Deep-sea mining: Processes and impacts", Natural History Museum, 11 September 2020, https://nhm.openrepository.com/bitstream/handle/10141/622833/NATCAP%20Draft%20Mining%20Chapter%20Sept%202019%20Reviewed.pdf?sequence=3&isAllowed=y.

30 Rob Williams *et al*, "Noise from deep-sea mining may span vast ocean areas", *Science*, 7 July 2022, Vol 377, issue 6602, pp157–168, www.science.org/doi/abs/10.1126/science.abo2804.

31 Lara Macheriotou, Annelien Rigaux, Sofie Derycke and Ann Vanreusel, "Phylogenic clustering and rarity imply risk of local species extinction in prospective deep-sea mining areas of the Clarion-Clipperton Fracture Zone", Royal Society, 1 April 2020, https://royalsocietypublishing.org/doi/full/ 10.1098/rspb.2019.2666.

created either by the direct disturbance of the seabed or when unwanted sediment from mining ships is discharged back into the ocean following initial processing of the ore. These plumes of sediment may smother and suffocate organisms on the seabed while also clogging filtering organs that coral and sponges rely on to strain food from water.[32] Plume sediments are also thought to release potentially toxic substances and reduced metals as well as unstable organic matter, leading to oxygen depletion.[33] Studies estimate that a single polymetallic mining operation would produce approximately 30,000m^3 to 80,000m^3 of sediment per day, which is the equivalent of approximately 4,000 to 10,000 dump trucks of sediment.[34] Wastewater from mining operations are also believed to lead to overheating and poisoning of mining areas.[35]

Supporters of deep-sea mining argue that a direct comparison of the environmental impacts of traditional mining operations with deep-ocean mining, suggests that, overall, deep-ocean mining would have significantly less of a net environmental impact compared to current operations. An argument can be made, for example, that the density of organisms in sediments that would directly be affected by seabed mining operations is much lower than the density of organisms in areas currently affected by deforestation for nickel mining in Indonesia or cobalt mining in the DRC, for example. It is important to note here that comparative studies are industry-funded and, as such, should be considered critically (as all evidence on this topic should be). Notwithstanding, they do provide some persuasive evidence in support of deep-ocean mining from an environmental perspective, as compared to current operations. Additionally, technological advancements in deep-ocean extractive machinery and processes have the potential to mitigate the risks of harm to seabed ecosystems including the resultant dispersion of sediment plumes by the implementation of 'vacuum suction' technologies in extracting polymetallic nodules sitting on the seabed.

Other ESG arguments advanced in favour of deep-sea mining are that energy demands and GHG emissions may be reduced due to the high purity of polymetallic nodules, reducing or eliminating the need for crushing technology and transportation of large volumes of mining waste. Although seabed mining may cause some disruption to coastal and fishing communities, and will have

---

32 Prihyanka Runwal, "The deep-sea mining dilemma", *Chemical and Engineering News*, 9 October 2023, https://cen.acs.org/environment/water/deep-sea-mining-dilemma/101/i33.

33 Walter Leal Filho *et al*, "Deep seabed mining: a note on some potentials and risks to the sustainable mineral extraction from the oceans", *Journal of Marine Science and Engineering*, 2021, 9(5), 521, https://doi.org/10.3390/jmse9050521.

34 Diva J Amon *et al*, "Assessment of scientific gaps related to the effective environmental management of deep-seabed mining", *Marine Policy*, Vol, 138, April 2022, http://dx.doi.org/10.1016/j.marpol.2022.105006.

35 Oliver Ashford, Jonathan Baines, Melissa Barbanell and Ke Wang, "What we know about deep-sea mining – and what we don't", World Resources Institute, 23 February 2024, www.wri.org/insights/deep-sea-mining-explained.

some onshore impacts, those impacts are likely to be much less than those associated with most onshore mining.

However, one persuasive argument against deep-sea mining, at least on an emotional level, is that we should respect and protect the deep ocean as one of the few parts of the planet that are relatively untouched by human interference. We can see the damage wrought by mining on the landmasses of our planet, and should protect the few remaining wildernesses, not least because our understanding of their ecosystems is still so limited.

For those reasons, a number of countries including Canada, Brazil, Ireland, Finland, Portugal and Sweden have called for a precautionary pause on commercial deep-sea mining. In January 2023, France voted in favour of a ban on deep-sea mining in its waters, a position reiterated on a global level at the ISA negotiations held in July 2023. Despite the UK government's sponsorship of two exploration licences in the Pacific Ocean, formal support has been lacking. On the other side of the debate, Nauru, Norway, and other countries such as India and China have expressed their support for deep-sea mining to be approved.

Deep-sea mining will continue to be hotly debated as the race for strategic minerals intensifies. This is likely to come to a head if the ISA is finally required to vote on RRPs at its 30th assembly. Importantly, there are likely to be no clear answers as to whether enough is known about the sector and whether the benefits to humankind outweigh the potential pitfalls. Given widespread resistance, it is likely that any progress towards commercial deep-sea mining will be incremental and require further research into its environmental impacts and optimal technologies.

4. Space

More distant, perhaps, but already being actively explored, is the prospect of mining in space, either on the Moon or on asteroids within our solar system. With commercial space flight slowly coming of age, space exploration no longer seems the preserve of the scientific community, but is coming within reach of the technological and entrepreneurial. Even more so than similar mineral frontiers, the potential of mining in space is held back by very limited knowledge of extra-terrestrial mining conditions and the huge costs of relevant research, let alone the logistics of commercial exploitation.

That said, since the Apollo 15 and 17 missions of the 1970s, multiple studies have confirmed that the Moon has water in abundance – necessary for both operations and sustenance of any crew. In addition, metals such as aluminium, iron and titanium are present on the moon and could be extracted from the oxides in the soil by chemical reduction.[36]

36 Mining Technology, "Mining the Moon", 4 December 2017, www.mining-technology.com/features/mining-the-moon/.

Recent technological advancements, including in AI and automation, have increased international interest in the potential of lunar mining, but it remains in its infancy and faces significant regulatory challenges. Several countries, including the United States, China and Russia, along with private companies like SpaceX and Blue Origin, are actively developing technologies for mining the Moon's resources, such as water ice, rare earth elements and helium-3.

Meanwhile, the regulatory framework for lunar mining is complex and evolving. The Outer Space Treaty of 1967, which most spacefaring nations have signed, prohibits any nation from claiming sovereignty over the Moon, thereby complicating property rights and resource ownership, let alone regulatory responsibility. In response, the United States passed the Commercial Space Launch Competitiveness Act in 2015, allowing US companies to own and sell resources extracted from celestial bodies. Furthermore, in 2020, the United States initiated the Artemis Accords, a series of non-binding bilateral arrangements with other nations (42 as at 30 May 2024) aimed at establishing norms for lunar exploration and resource utilisation. Despite these developments, there is an ongoing debate in the international community about the need for a more comprehensive global framework to ensure the sustainable and equitable use of lunar resources.

From a practical perspective, lunar mining faces major technological and economic challenges, with important ESG consequences. Mining on the Moon would require advanced technology capable of operating in harsh conditions, such as extreme temperatures, high radiation levels, lack of oxygen and low gravity. The next challenge would be to consider processing raw materials *in situ*, as transporting lunar soil back to Earth is unlikely to be feasible. Developing equipment that can efficiently extract, process and transport lunar resources while withstanding these conditions is a major hurdle.

The health and safety risks of transporting mine workers to the moon and accommodating them there are currently unacceptably high. While technological improvements and track record may mitigate those risks, it is likely that mining in space will need to be highly automated to minimise the need for human intervention. While technological challenges are present, they are not insurmountable, given sufficient time and investment. However, it remains to be seen whether that can be done economically and in a manner that makes sense from an ESG perspective.

Many doubt the economic viability of space mining. With current technology, the cost of lunar mining operations is prohibitively high; even more so than deep-sea or Arctic ventures. Even launching the missions needed to explore for minerals on the Moon would require massive investments, which few are likely to fund where there is such uncertainty about the feasibility and cost of establishing mining infrastructure and transporting materials back to

Earth. Ensuring that lunar mining is economically viable, especially in competition with terrestrial mining, is a significant challenge.

Lunar mining would bypass certain ESG risks, such as those associated with local ecosystems and communities at the mine site, and could be presented as a way of mitigating those impacts on Earth. However, it seems complacent to just assume that large-scale human intervention on the Moon will not have detrimental environmental impacts. What might be the effects of changes to the surface of the Moon or the creation of mineral dust in low gravity? We simply do not know at this stage.

What we do know is that it will be necessary to dramatically reduce the climate impacts of transportation to and from the Moon. By way of example, the 1967 Apollo mission rocket used just under 950,000 gallons of fuel (including a combination of kerosene, liquid oxygen and liquid hydrogen). Nowadays, SpaceX estimates that a similar return trip to the moon would require approximately 75,900 gallons of fuel (a combination of kerosene and liquid oxygen).[37] While that is an impressive reduction, it is still equivalent to the average annual gasoline consumption of 175 American cars. Also, soot particles (or black carbon) produced by the fuel required for space travel represent a particularly significant risk to the environment. It is estimated that soot particles emitted in space travel have around 500 times more warming effect than black carbon that is emitted at the surface. This is because pollutants from rockets are released at different layers in the atmosphere where they tend to remain for longer and are able to absorb more of the Sun's heat.[38] In the context of the ongoing climate crisis, many people argue that burning vast quantities of rocket fuel to send a tiny number of people into space exploration is a luxury that the planet cannot afford. It seems impossible to justify consuming such vast amounts of energy to explore the Moon for battery metals, for example, and prospective space miners will have a difficult task in convincing society that the benefits will outweigh the price.

On the legal and regulatory side, the legal framework for lunar mining is still underdeveloped. As noted above, the Outer Space Treaty of 1967 prohibits national sovereignty over celestial bodies, creating ambiguity about property rights and resource ownership. Developing clear international regulations to govern lunar mining activities is essential but will prove complex. Who will have the right to tax mining activities on the Moon? If space mining comes at the expense of government revenues on Earth, as well as terrestrial mining

37 Haley Zaremba, "How much fuel it takes to get to the moon", *Business Insider*, 10 August 2017, www.businessinsider.com/how-much-fuel-it-takes-to-get-to-the-moon-2017-8?r=US&IR=T. Note estimate is as of August 2017.

38 BBC World Service, "The Climate Question: Is space travel a problem for the climate?", www.bbc.co.uk/programmes/articles/24QmpQ0YGGfrB4WxMCFSGBM/is-space-travel-a-problem-for-the-climate#:~:text=According%20to%20Nasa%20Earth%20Observatory,and%20consequently%20more%20global%20warming.

employment and other economic benefits, it is unlikely to gather much societal support.

To build that support, space mining efforts would inevitably require cooperation among governments, private entities and international organisations, to create appropriate regulatory and governance mechanisms, as well as to share technology, knowledge and resources. If we are to avoid an ugly competition for space resources, we should use this opportunity to consider an equitable distribution of opportunities and potential revenues, including to countries which are not in a position to even enter the space race. With lofty ambitions and coordinated efforts on a global scale, perhaps the goal of space mining will one day seem less of a moonshot, but society must maintain the focus on its ESG objectives as well as the economic ones.

The authors would like to extend sincere gratitude to Rachel Strickland for her invaluable contribution to this chapter.

ESG and innovation

Andrew Sullivan
Stantec

1. Introduction

> *Many persons hold the opinion that the metal industries are fortuitous, and that the occupation is one of sordid toil, and altogether a kind of business requiring not so much skill as labour. When I reflect carefully upon its special points it appears otherwise ... There are many arts and sciences of which a miner should not be ignorant.*[1]

Innovation has been constant in mining since its inception as an industry. As problems were encountered, need arose or metals became scarce, people found ways to dig deeper, more productively, and refine poorer grades. The transition from pickaxes and buckets, to bucket wheel and truck and shovel operations has been driven by advances in technology adapted to the needs of the industry. The new technologies enable economies of scale, improve productivities and lower operational risk.

While innovation has typically been spurred on by the need to improve project economics, address the increasing complexities of industry and provide returns to investors, more recently it has also been the focus of the environmental, social and governance (ESG) aspects of mining activities. In this chapter we consider a few important examples of innovation in mining and their ESG impacts, focusing on artificial intelligence (AI), electrification and satellites and visualisation.

1.1 Investment in ESG

It must be noted that investment in ESG initiatives for the sake of the environment or society has recently become politicised and polarising. A panel at the MINEXCHANGE 2023 conference noted that: "[T]here has been a rise in anti-ESG sentiment in the United States. In 2021, Texas became the first US state to pass anti-ESG legislation, and there are several other states proposing or

1 G Agricola, *De Re Metallica* (Dover Publications, 1950).

adopting regulations or legislation to restrict ESG activities."[2] The future of ESG innovation in mining cannot solely rely on a 'do the right thing' approach. Innovation must be tied to company balance sheets. This is the only way that ESG innovation can be achieved, as a purely financial business case, which acts as a successful conduit for advancing technologies. So, where market economics do not align with society's ESG objectives, it is for government to intervene, whether through regulation, taxation, incentives or policies, to ensure that companies are incentivised to innovate in pursuit of those objectives, or at least not penalised for doing so.

2. The use of AI in mining

Current operations' innovations in mining have focused on reducing the footprint of the mine or improving efficiencies. Through these methods they seek to reduce the impact on the environment, while improving economics. Less waste rock mined, means less fuel burned. This helps the bottom line and lessens the environmental impact.

2.1 Surgical mining

Examples of AI use in mining is the surgical mining methods being developed by Novamera. Novamera boasts "[that] unique technology integrates into conventional drilling equipment, making them able to pinpoint, map, navigate and extract high-value narrow vein deposits without the need for costly infrastructure".[3] This technology seeks to use vein mapping technology with a specially designed course correction system. The technology is based on machine learning, "a subfield of artificial intelligence, which is broadly defined as the capability of a machine to imitate intelligent human behaviour".[4] This use of AI technology seeks to minimise dilution and loss while also minimising the footprint needed for mining. Novamera claims that backfilling can begin as soon as the ore has been removed via the drilling and using waste rock produced. Thus, through a surgical approach to mining, enabled by the novel application of recent technological innovations, the need for waste rock storage facilities and standup time are further reduced, while minimising the footprint of disturbed land at the mine.

Reducing the mine's footprint and the need for waste facilities gets to the heart of a looming existential threat for the global mining industry. Closure costs can prove an impediment to new projects, and if calculated wrong can be a huge threat to a company's bottom line. In some of the worst cases this can

---

2 A Goodbody, "The Investment Side of ESG", *CIM Magazine*, 5 April 2023, https://magazine.cim.org/en/news/2023/the-investment-side-of-esg/.

3 Novamera, "Technology – Smart Precision Drilling", https://novamerainc.com/smd-technology/.

4 S Brown, "Machine learning, explained", MIT Sloan School of Management, 21 April 2021, https://mitsloan.mit.edu/ideas-made-to-matter/machine-learning-explained.

result in bankruptcy and insolvency of the corporations which then passes the remaining liability to the public. The impact of the transfer of the liability for mine waste is a major risk for governments. In Canada alone "the official government cost estimates [compiled from official reports] for cleaning up active and abandoned mine waste sites in [the country, to] surpass $10 billion".[5] As these costs may ultimately be passed to the public this negatively affects the view of the industry and can create a barrier to gaining funding for new projects.

If the arguments for reduction in operating costs and bolstering public support are not enough, there is a moral argument to be made as well. That is the long-term consequences mine waste could pose to people and the environment. This can impose closure measures, such as long-term water treatment and management to protect the environment and surrounding communities. The Canadian government states that:

> *some 10 000 orphaned and abandoned mine sites have been identified across Canada, many of which are hazardous and without long-term closure plans ... [but] There is no national inventory of orphaned and abandoned mine sites. Lost mine records and forgotten mine-site locations have left an unknown legacy of problems.*[6]

Some jurisdictions have sought to prevent this sort of liability occurring from future projects. This has already happened in the approach taken in "the Northwest Territories, Manitoba, Yukon, New Mexico, and Wisconsin – where taxpayers and the environment are protected by a simple ban on mining operations that will require very long-term water treatment".[7]

Surgical mining allows us to reduce environmental liabilities, which is good for both companies and the public. This does require a shift in thinking though. Historically, economy of scale has driven many decisions on mining projects, but this new method requires an adjustment of our metrics. By thinking surgically companies can protect their bottom line, find new resources that were previously uneconomic and limit risk.

2.2 Autonomous haulage systems

Another use of AI, if more limited, is autonomous haulage systems (AHS) in open pit mining. AHS technology is focused on improving mines' bottom lines, through improved operational efficiency, reduced labour cost and labour dependency. There are, however, two significant benefits to this technology

5 MiningWatch Canada, "Mine Waste in Canada: A Growing Liability", 5 October 2020, https://miningwatch.ca/blog/2020/10/5/mine-waste-canada-growing-liability.

6 NRCAN, "Programs to Enhance and Sustain Safety and the Quality of the Environment In and Around Orphaned and Abandoned Mine Sites", 2010, https://publications.gc.ca/collections/collection_2010/nrcan/M39-124-eng.pdf.

7 University of Victoria Environmental Law Centre, "BC Mining Law Reform: Water Protection", May 2019, https://reformbcmining.ca/wp-content/uploads/2019/05/BCMLR-Water-Protection.pdf.

that target the environment and society: improved safety performance and reduction of consumables.

AHS helps eliminate the human error factor inherent in a large percentage of incidents involving material haulage. The US National Institute for Occupational Safety and Health (NIOSH) completed "an analysis of 152 fatalities between 1995 and 2014 [and] found that 42% involved loss of control of the haul truck (eg, speeding, backing over a drop-off, drowsiness) and 11% of the fatalities involved berming hazards".[8] Incidents like these may be prevented through AHS technology which doesn't experience fatigue despite continually travelling the same (approved) routes.

Another benefit of AHS technology is its reduced use of consumables. Specifically, AHS uses less fuel and goes through fewer tyres than human operated fleets. In modelling studies "the autonomous mode showed an improvement in fuel consumption Key Performance Indicators (KPIs) of 6.5% for L/cycle and 5.7% for L/t. Tire wear (mm/cycle) also showed an improvement of 7.6%".[9] This decrease in fuel consumption and tyre wear means less crude oil is required to support mining production, which directly results in a reduction of emissions and thereby an overall decrease of the carbon footprint directly related to mining activities.

2.3 AI in exploration and design

(a) *Design*

Mine planning and design are by nature interactive processes. The long-range plan must consider the ups and downs of the market, while the short-range plan must account for today's cost volatility and the geological variability on grade. Truly maximising the potential of any resource requires careful, and sometimes tedious, modelling based on some key inputs like pitwall slope, mining rate and underground mining method.

This process has changed with the introduction of software capable of running automated mine scheduling. Automated scheduling has allowed planning departments to run and see the impacts of multiple scenarios. This type of techno-economic modelling enabled by AI and machine learning offers the next evolutionary step in the mine planning and design process. AI, when paired with high performance cloud-computing infrastructure, can run scenarios much quicker and with fewer errors than humans, allowing for more scenarios to be evaluated and considered. Running multiple scenario iterations allows for early (prefeasibility stage) operations optimisation while optimising

8 Center for Disease Control and Prevention, *Haul Truck Research Roadmap Report 2020*, www.cdc.gov/niosh/mining/researchprogram/strategicplan/haultruckroadmap2020.html.

9 J Parreira, "An interactive simulation model to compare an autonomous haulage truck system with a manually-operated system" (The University of British Columbia, 2013).

physical mine footprints. This means environmental and social concerns as well as cutoff grade and return on investment can all be factored into decision making. Going further, "AI algorithms can optimise the mine planning process, considering environmental factors such as land reclamation and habitat preservation".[10] Having this information allows companies to truly tie closure costs and liabilities to the planning process at all stages. Not only will this help to bolster environmental protections, and consideration, it will also assist in doing so in a way that can be communicated to stakeholders. Often this communication is a weak point in environmental stewardship since it is difficult to quantify on a balance sheet.

(b) Exploration

Given that "99% of exploration projects fail to turn into actual mines",[11] improving a company's ability to find a viable ore deposit creates an advantage and is valuable. AI can assist by using modelling and machine learning to make predictions and decisions more accurately than humans alone. Dr House of the company KoBold, an AI geological modelling company, touts that "[The KoBold AI's] ability to predict the shapes and distributions of subterranean plutonic intrusions ... to make more accurate predictions of the shapes of these intrusions and so suggest the most effective places to drill".[12] AI can suggest better drilling programmes that may ultimately lead to improved definition of an orebody, or tagging thin stringers where a different positioning would have missed them.

AI can be used to optimise drill holes, characterise a deposit, and optimise ore deliveries. GeologicAI even claims a 30% uplift, 400% project acceleration and an 80% decrease in design time. They also claim to be four times faster than manual core logging with a 24–48-hour turnaround.[13] This results in huge cost and time saving for a project and with fewer personnel hours required. This also decreases exposure to risk and is likely to result in fewer injuries and incidents. There are of course challenges with AI tools, and these tools are not always the silver bullet that solve every technical problem.

2.4 AI's challenges

AI use in mine planning is not without its difficulties. Three key challenges must be well understood as we progress in using this technology. The first is the

---

10 D Gleeson, "How artificial intelligence is revolutionising the mining industry", *International Mining*, 23 August 2023, https://im-mining.com/2023/08/23/how-artificial-intelligence-is-revolutionising-the-mining-industry/.

11 "Could AI Help Find Valuable Mineral Deposits", *The Economist*, 1 November 2023, www.economist.com/science-and-technology/2023/11/01/could-ai-help-find-valuable-mineral-deposits?utm_medium=cpc.adword.pd&utm_source=google&ppccampaignID=18798097116&ppcadID=&utm_campaign=a.22brand_pmax&utm_content=conversion.direct-response.anony.

12 *Ibid.*

13 GeologicAI, "Core scanning to mine planning", www.geologicai.com.

hesitance of industry to use these tools. Culturally the mining industry has been observed to be slow to change. This is due to:

> *Mining [having been] traditionally perceived as a risky undertaking with uncertain grades, investment volatility and variable metal prices so every opportunity to reduce risk and stay with the proven methods of operation was encouraged. This risk aversion stifled innovation opportunities and many major operations avoided taking the lead in proving empirical performance of new technologies because the upfront costs and the potential failure or risks involved with bleeding edge innovations was considered unwise.*[14]

To be adopted globally, AI tools will need to prove their accuracy and ability to improve the planning process without unjustified, increased costs.

The second challenge is the accuracy of the tools themselves. While AI removes the human error from calculations, the inputs and results themselves are still potential sources of concern. The inputs, geological data, wireframes, survey data design information, targets etc, need to be vetted by someone with expertise in how to work with the system. The results must also be carefully reviewed for accuracy. Careful verification must be completed because "most AI-driven applications are non-transparent and non-verifiable".[15] Since engineers and data scientists can't debug or check the calculation steps, qualified persons need to vet results for real-world accuracy. This can be difficult since, while human error has been removed, the AI itself may introduce other errors. One example of this is Google's Bard AI, a large language model "[which] got off to a rocky start by making some well-known mistakes and 'hallucinations,' a phenomenon in which AI models make up facts".[16] These mistakes can be costly to a company's bottom line, causing write-offs, and potentially exposing a company to costly litigation. This was the result for "Online real-estate data company Zillow [which] incurred a $300 million write-down because its Offers program couldn't accurately price homes with an AI-driven algorithm".[17] To ensure a mineral resource company can avoid these detrimental results it must have tight QA/QC procedures prior to using these tools. The tools need to be looked at in the same way one would treat a junior designer or engineer where a more experienced senior member of the design team oversees the results.

The third challenge is political. Currently, there is a growing trend of protection of data that could be used by foreign powers against individual countries. Because mining data is tied to the production of everything – from fertiliser to microchips – this raw strategic resource data could be a potential

---

14 Deloitte, *Future of mining with AI: Building the first steps towards and insight-driven organization*, www2.deloitte.com/content/dam/Deloitte/es/Documents/energia/Deloitte-ES-Energia-Futuro-Mineria-Inteligencia-Artificial.pdf.

15 RS Raynovich, "The Top Five Real Risks of AI to your Business", Forbes, 22 June 2022, www.forbes.com/sites/rscottraynovich/2023/06/22/the-top-five-real-risks-of-ai-to-your-business/?sh=68de85481e4a.

16 *Ibid.*

17 *Ibid.*

national security concern. Already countries are studying what materials are strategically important to them. A study of strategic minerals for European defence funded by the Dutch Ministry of Economic Affairs and Climate Policy to the Hague Centre for Strategic Studies found "Forty critical and 'soon-to-be' critical raw materials are deemed strategic for the European defence industry … used across the air, sea and land domains in various military applications and components".[18] The report further calls out that minerals undergo "assessment of probability and impact of supply disruptions, materials are ranked according to their supply risk".[19] Understanding the supply risk of a resource to a country would give an enemy foreign power great insight into how to cripple a country, and incentivises a country to protect its data.

This issue came to the forefront in 2023 with the United States signing into law a bill "to authorize the President to impose certain sanctions with respect to Russia and Iran, and for other purposes".[20] Specifically, Division D of the bill, "Protecting Americans from Foreign Adversary Controlled Applications Act", was specifically set up to target social media. Dubbed the "TikTok Ban" in media, the bill sets out to ensure:

> *PROHIBITION OF FOREIGN ADVERSARY CONTROLLED APPLICATIONS.—It shall be unlawful for an entity to distribute, maintain, or update (or enable the distribution, maintenance, or updating of) a foreign adversary-controlled application by carrying out, within the land or maritime borders of the United States … [p]roviding services to distribute, maintain or update such foreign adversary controlled application … [p]roviding internet hosting services to enable the distribution, maintenance, or updating of such foreign adversary controlled application …*[21]

This legislation sets out, in broad strokes, to block foreign powers from collecting data that could be used to gain advantage on the United States. While Division D of the bill was meant for social media, personal information, and to help prevent anti-US propaganda, it illustrates a policy direction that may have relevance and become important to the resource industry.

The raw materials we, as a society, mine are tied directly to the quality of life of our citizens and the strength of our military. Making the resource data of a country available to a foreign power, specifically one not friendly to us, could have dire economic and national security consequences. Going forward it will

18 The Hague Centre for Strategic Studies, "Strategic raw materials for defence: Mapping European industry needs", 10 January 2023, https://hcss.nl/report/strategic-raw-materials-for-defence/.

19 *Ibid.*

20 118th Congress of the United States Second Session, HR 8038, "To authorize the President to impose certain sanctions with respect to Russia", 17 April 2024, www.congress.gov/bill/118th-congress/house-bill/8038/text#:~:text=Introduced%20in%20House%20(04%2F17%2F2024)&text=To%20authorize%20the%20President%20to,Iran%2C%20and%20for%20other%20purposes.&text=A%20BILL-,To%20authorize%20the%20President%20to%20impose%20certain%20sanctions%20with%20respect,Iran%2C%20and%20for%20other%20purposes.

21 *Ibid.*

be of grave importance that our governments thoroughly understand which companies provide these AI services, understanding the origins and capabilities of the technology. This may slow the evolution of these tools due to lack of international cooperation.

3. Electrification

Electrification is a highly politicised topic in 2024. While some claim it is necessary to meet climate change targets, and is therefore the only moral choice, others claim the technology does not work as required. The two competing arguments raise the question of what is the truth of electric fleets for mining? Are they a technically and economically viable alternative? We know that the industry has to justify technology updates to shareholders and show that it doesn't negatively impact the bottom line. The truth is that "[Battery Electric Vehicles] (BEVs) are generally competitive with Internal Combustion Engine (ICE) (typically +/– 15% on a Total Cost of Ownership), not only for greenfield mines, but also for brownfield operations".[22] With the technology being competitive the mining and resource industry is already moving to electrify.

> *A poll conducted by Mining-Technology.com in April and May 2023 asked respondents to select a period when they expected the greatest change in mobile mining equipment switching from diesel to electric. A quarter of the 348 mining companies interviewed said they were already investing in the switch, but the largest share (34%) expected to start in 2030.*[23]

Mining-Technology.com found the five factors favoring the use of BEVs included "Worker safety, better working conditions, carbon capture incentives, optimizing global mining operations, and long term efficiency".[24] In terms of the operational gains, and outside of the environmental concerns "BEV hourly parts and component costs may be reduced by 20%–30%, and in some applications as much as 40% compared to that of ICE equipment".[25] With the lower component cost and a comparable overall cost, electrification is a viable solution for mining with real environmental benefits.

3.1 Electrification and the environment

Electrification of mining operations is not just important for the efficiency of the mine. It can also have far-reaching environmental benefits, which may also

---

22 Sandvik,"Power at the end of the tunnel – Electrifying underground mining", May 2023, www.rocktechnology.sandvik/en/products/technology/electrification/electrifying-underground-mining/.

23 Mining-Technology.com, "Beyond regulation: What is driving electrification in mining?", 27 June 2023, www.mining-technology.com/sponsored/what-is-driving-electrification-in-mining/.

24 *Ibid.*

25 Sandvik,"Power at the end of the tunnel – Electrifying underground mining", May 2023, www.rocktechnology.sandvik/en/products/technology/electrification/electrifying-underground-mining/.

improve the bottom line. The most obvious advantage being a reduction in greenhouse gas (GHG) emissions. If a mine has access to a renewable resource for power, like hydroelectric, solar or wind, they can greatly reduce their emissions. A study by McKinsey found that "a fully electrified mine with renewable-power sources could have a carbon footprint that is 60 to 80 percent lower, avoiding carbon taxes and capturing potential green-product premiums".[26] This reduction could lead to other competitive advantages for mining companies, such as carbon offset trading being a potential source of income.

As well as reducing GHGs, electrification can eliminate diesel particulates from the burning of fossil fuels. Diesel particulates are small, potentially damaging, particles resulting from the burning of fossil fuels. The EPA states that particulate matter, which includes diesel particulates, can cause environmental damage. The effects depend on the chemical make-up of the particulate matter but may include:

- making lakes and streams acidic;
- changing the nutrient balance in coastal waters and large river basins;
- depleting the nutrients in soil;
- damaging sensitive forests and farm crops;
- affecting the diversity of ecosystems; and
- contributing to acid rain effects.[27]

The elimination of diesel particulates combined with the absence of GHGs means underground mines require less ventilation. A paper authored by Stantec found that "[t]he switch to a fully electric mobile fleet often results in a 40% to 50% reduction in ventilation demands".[28] This reduction in ventilation demand results in a cost savings in both capital and operating expenditures. Less demand means that ventilation infrastructure can be sized smaller, reducing capital costs. It also means lower power consumption, lowering operating costs and lower climate impact. The benefits to the ventilation of underground mines from less pollution being generated are extraordinary, but don't just have implications in terms of operations and capital costs.

---

26 McKinsey & Company, "Electrifying mines could double their electricity demand", 24 April 2023, www.mckinsey.com/industries/metals-and-mining/our-insights/electrifying-mines-could-double-their-electricity-demand.

27 United States Environmental Protection Agency, "Health and Environmental Effects of Particulate Matter (PM)", 23 August 2023, www.epa.gov/pm-pollution/health-and-environmental-effects-particulate-matter-pm#:~:text=Numerous%20scientific%20studies%20have%20linked%20particle%20pollution%20exposure,irritation%20of%20the%20airways%2C%20coughing%20or%20difficulty%20breathing.

28 K Trapani, "As the mining industry pushes for sustainable solutions, it's important to examine the benefits – and potential obstacles – around battery-powered EVs", Stantec, 28 June 2021, www.stantec.com/en/ideas/topic/stantec-era/charged-up-key-considerations-around-electric-vehicle-use-on-mine-sites.

3.2 Electrification and safety

Mining companies have a requirement, legally, to ensure a safe workplace. If they fail to do so, their workers may have cause for a claim against their employer. These claims will have negative consequences financially, and/or reputationally. One area of concern for companies is the diesel particulates from the burning of fossil fuels. A study of the Canadian construction industry found that "[o]verall, 41.6% of samples exceeded the [Finnish Institute of Occupational Health] limit, mostly within underground worksites (93.5%), and 90.6% exceeded the [Dutch Expert Committee on Occupational Safety] limit".[29] While this study was for the construction industry, we can assume a similar trend exists for mining. It has been documented, for particle matter (which encompasses diesel particulates) that numerous scientific studies have linked particle pollution exposure to a variety of problems, including:

- premature death in people with heart or lung disease;
- nonfatal heart attacks;
- irregular heartbeat;
- aggravated asthma;
- decreased lung function; and
- increased respiratory symptoms, such as irritation of the airways, coughing or difficulty breathing.[30]

Socially, as well as from a liability standpoint, the move to electrification makes sense. Improving worker health, and decreasing the liability associated with occupational hazards are two items a company can get behind. When coupled with the competitive cost, environmental benefits and reduction to costly ventilation infrastructure, electrification seems like the wave of the future; provided this is done in an area where the infrastructure can support it.

3.3 Electrification and the grid

The biggest challenge facing electrification is the infrastructure required to support it. It is well known that most countries' infrastructure is not ready to support the electrification that is being proposed by governments. In the United States alone "one estimate of what it would take to reach the Biden administration's goal of 100 percent clean electricity generation by 2035. Transmission capacity would need to more than double in just over a decade".[31]

---

29 Stephanie Ziembicki *et al*, "Diesel Engine Exhaust Exposure in the Ontario Civil Infrastructure Construction Industry", *Annals of Work Exposures and Health*, vol 66 issue 2, March 2022, https://academic.oup.com/annweh/article/66/2/150/6377752, pp150–162.

30 United States Environmental Protection Agency, "Health and Environmental Effects of Particulate Matter (PM)", 23 August 2023, www.epa.gov/pm-pollution/health-and-environmental-effects-particulate-matter-pm#:~:text=Numerous%20scientific%20studies%20have%20linked%20particle%20pollution%20exposure,irritation%20of%20the%20airways%2C%20coughing%20or%20difficulty%20breathing.

The United States isn't alone in this infrastructure challenge: "Reports from the International Energy Agency and the Canadian Climate Institute in 2022 found Canada would need to double or triple its electrical grid capacity by 2050 to reach its net-zero goal".[32] The problem is not only a north American issue either. It is estimated that:

> *Currently, the EU is spending around €23 billion per year on the expansion of electricity distribution networks, with approximately 141 projects regarding transmission networks underway in both the EU and in cooperation between the EU and third countries. However, to sufficiently modernise and expand the grid, EU should increase its investment in grid expansion to at least €38 billion per year by 2030 to meet its climate targets, and up to €100 billion annually by 2050.*[33]

The risk of the state of these national electrical grids poses two considerations for mining companies: rely on the public grids and lobby governments to make the required improvements, or find ways to create, store and distribute their own 'clean' power.

3.4 Small modular reactors

How to generate 'clean' power is a tough problem for the mining industry. Some producers may be fortunate to be in an area that can take advantage of hydroelectric generation, wind farming or solar generation. Some areas, however, do not have these opportunities available. In that case small modular reactors (SMRs) are a potential solution. SMRs "generate power from nuclear fission ... This process creates thermal energy that generates steam to spin a turbine".[34] These reactors offer "energy security [providing] the ability to generate consistent clean power 24 hours a day 7 days a week".[35] This clean power would allow a mining company to take advantage of electrification and reduce their carbon footprint.

There is also an advantage to remote communities who live near to these mine sites. There is an opportunity for them to take advantage of this power generation. Let's look at Canada as a case study, and its First Nations Communities. Many communities are remote and lack access to clean energy. A report by *The Globe and Mail*, on Indigenous communities in Canada, found that as of 2016:

---

31 Nadja Popovich and Brad Plumer, "Why the U.S. Electric Grid Isn't Ready for the Energy Transition", *The New York Times*, 12 June 2023, www.nytimes.com/interactive/2023/06/12/climate/us-electric-grid-energy-transition.html.

32 E Chung, "Will electrifying cars and home heating break Canada's grid?", CBC, 15 August 2023, www.cbc.ca/news/science/electrification-grid-ev-heating-1.6935663.

33 S Kardaś, "Gridlock: Why Europe's electricity infrastructure is holding back the green transition", European Council on Foreign Relations, 26 October 2023, https://ecfr.eu/article/gridlock-why-europes-electricity-infrastructure-is-holding-back-the-green-transition/.

34 J Singh, "Small Modular Reactors: Driving Energy Security with Nuclear Power", Stantec, 26 February 2024.

35 *Ibid.*

Some 200 communities in the country are not connected to an [electrical] grid and must rely on diesel generators for their power. They experience blackouts, fuel spills, and a shortage of capacity that frustrates growth and development plans.[36]

The lack of power stifling the economic prosperity of these communities offers a unique opportunity to mining companies operating in the vicinity of these communities. If they partner with the community to provide clean power to both the mine and the community, they can:

- boost the community economically long term;
- secure a local workforce by providing employment opportunities; and
- create goodwill and buy in to their project from the local community.

To successfully implement this technology, mining companies will need to truly partner equitably with the community. While this case study focused on Canada, it is an opportunity for mining companies globally.

4. Satellites and visualisation

4.1 Leveraging technology to track emissions

Many jurisdictions use disclosure regulation for pollution such as GHG emissions. This methodology is non-interventionist, and thus does not impose expensive enforcement requirements. The methodology relies on naming and shaming polluters where metrics are self-reported. One reason for this manner of tracking emissions is the inability to easily monitor, measure, track and report Scope 1 emissions, "direct greenhouse (GHG) emissions that occur from sources that are controlled or owned by an organization".[37] New technologies may offer governments the ability to change this.

Satellite imagery and monitoring have progressed to a point where they can be used for tasks which were impossible in decades past. MethaneSAT, for example, a research project seeking to provide data freely, is launching a satellite in 2024 to monitor and track methane production. MethaneSAT seeks to quantify oil and gas sector emissions globally. MethaneSAT provides monitoring by processing "observed spectrographic data to calculate quantitative emissions rates, revealing how much methane is emitted and how it varies across landscape … analytics will track emissions based on winds and atmospheric conditions".[38] While they are providing tracking for methane, specifically due to its impact as a GHG, the same or similar technology can be used elsewhere for other pollutants.

---

36 S McCarthy, "Push to End Energy Poverty in Indigenous Communities Underway", *The Globe and Mail*, 23 November 2016.

37 EPA, "Scope 1 and Scope 2 Inventory Guidance", 8 March 2024, www.epa.gov/climateleadership/scope-1-and-scope-2-inventory-guidance.

38 Environmental Defense Fund, "Bridging the Gap", MethaneSAT, www.methanesat.org/satellite.

Satellite imagery can be used to find and report pipeline spills, tailings releases, or encroachment into environmentally sensitive areas. Coupled with AI, this technology offers governments a potentially lower-cost way to set up a command-and-control regime where one didn't exist before or to bolster a weak enforcement regime, based on voluntary disclosure frameworks or one using estimates of emissions rather than measurements.

4.2 Extended reality

Communication is often at the centre of conflict. Often, we have difficulty explaining new ideas and complex concepts. Research into the human brain's ability to handle variables has found that "a structure defined on four variables is the limit of human processing capacity".[39] With this limit in mind the question becomes: How do we explain multi-variable mining models to stakeholders? How do we clearly communicate the impacts of mining projects in a way that allows for open dialogue between companies and the communities they engage with?

One of the best solutions we have for this challenge is to leverage extended reality (XR) technologies, which commonly includes augmented reality (AR), virtual reality (VR) and mixed reality. The benefit of these technologies is "the ability to quite literally see into the future … AR can be used to send interactive virtual 3D models to clients to facilitate real time design reviews".[40] AR allows people to actually step through the design and see it from all views and at different times. Whether this is aiding in design reviews so technical and operations staff can look for potential problems, or communicating to stakeholders, the power of these technologies can't be denied. One company using this mixed media approach, VRIFY, states that the use of a mixed media makes your presentation "65% more memorable … [expands] 10× your reach".[41]

The other benefit of course is that XR can be used to help improve safety. Using "a VR simulation [one] can replicate a mine showing potentially hazardous environments and situations. Employees could then be trained on how to handle these incidents".[42] VR and AR use could potentially save lives, helping people understand how to react when encountering danger, so they aren't trying to figure it out in a panic the first time they see a hazardous condition.

Whether for safety training or communication of ideas, XR technologies are

---

39 Graeme S Halford *et al*, "How Many Variables Can Humans Process", *Psychological Science* 16(1): 70–6, www.researchgate.net/publication/8070322_How_Many_Variables_Can_Humans_Process#:~:text=These%20findings%20suggest%20that%20a,limit%20of%20human%20processing%20capacity.

40 SG Carter, "How VR and AR are Transforming the World of Energy and Resources", Stantec, 2023, www.stantec.com/en/markets/mining/augmented-virtual-reality-energy-projects.

41 VRIFY, "Transforming Mining Communication", https://vrify.com/platform.

42 SG Carter, "How VR and AR are Transforming the World of Energy and Resources", Stantec, 2023, www.stantec.com/en/markets/mining/augmented-virtual-reality-energy-projects.

an important development for the resource industry, truly enabling the next era of communication between stakeholders.

5. Conclusion

Mining and society have come a long way since the ancient days. They have come a long way since Gerg Agricola wrote, concerning the poet Horace and the attitudes of society in his time, that:

> *They contend that inasmuch as Nature has concealed metals far within the depths of the earth, and because they are not necessary to human life, they are therefore despised and repudiated by the noblest and should not be mined.*[43]

While anti-mining attitudes exist, we know our modern lifestyles are directly tied to the minerals and resources we extract from the earth. We now have new technologies to find creative solutions to mining problems. We can reduce our footprint, pollution and impacts. Governments and industry can track and address polluters. We can use technology to solve complex problems and offer solutions quickly. We can do it all without compromising the bottom line by driving investment into the technological innovations required to solve the complex ESG challenges facing the mining industry.

Mining has come a long way since its inception, and I am excited to see what innovations will take this industry into the next century. While the industry has been resistant to change, when it does accept the change, it is with a giant leap forward. Who knows what critical innovation yet to be discovered will next change the shape of the resource industry for the better.

The author acknowledges Cody Ryckman and Resa Furey.

43 G Agricola, *De Re Metallica* (Dover Publications, 1950).

Risk and opportunity in tailings management

Chris Meikle
David Walker
SLR Consulting

1. Introduction

Due to intensified extraction and depletion of higher ore grade mines over the past 40 years, ore yields have declined, leading to a substantial increase in the volume of mine waste and tailings generated. It is estimated that ore yields have decreased by half,[1] effectively doubling the amount of waste produced per unit of ore. It is estimated that the total number of active, inactive and closed tailings storage facilities (TSFs) is in the order of 8,500 globally, comprising around 220 cubic kilometres of waste.[2] Typical contributions of tailings by commodity are:

- 46% copper;
- 21% gold;
- 9% iron;
- 8% coal;
- 4% lead/zinc;
- 2% nickel; and
- 10% other.

In addition, projections for commodity demand suggest that mining activities are likely to increase by a factor of up to 10 by 2060, exacerbating the need for effective mine waste and tailings management. The exponential generation of mine waste is unsustainable and the urgency to address the unique challenge of tailings management in a more sustainable manner is imperative.

Before delving into the risks and opportunities associated with tailings, it's crucial to understand what tailings are and how they are generated. This understanding is necessary to comprehend the magnitude of the problem and the necessity for sustainable management practices.

At a high level, tailings are the wet, slurry-like ultra-fine by-product generated from the crushing, grinding, milling, washing and extraction process

1 Earthworks, *Safety First: Guidelines for Responsible Mine Tailings Management*, 31 May 2022, https://earthworks.org/resources/safety-first/.
2 Global Tailings Review 2021, https://globaltailingsreview.org/.

undertaken at the mine processing plant. They are typically pumped through a pipeline to a dam. Conversely, waste rock is typically the dry coarse cobble-sized material that is bulk excavated from the mine to access the ore and is disposed of in a waste rock dump.

Based on 2016 estimates,[3] 10 billion tonnes of ore were produced globally, based on a total mined volume of ~100 billion tonnes, which resulted in the generation of ~72 billion tonnes of waste rock and ~8 billion tonnes of tailings.

2. A troubled history

The history of mine waste and tailings is marred by numerous catastrophic failures of tailings dams (also referred to as tailings storage facilities, TSFs), with more than 230 major incidents recorded since notable records began in 1915. It is important to consider that many failures go unreported, especially in Asia. Historically, there has been an average of one to two major TSF failures per year, with the past four decades witnessing one 'killer' flow slide every five years, resulting in an average of 50 deaths per event. The financial impact is equally staggering, with environmental cleanup and damage costs reaching millions to billions of US dollars.

Historically, statisticians estimated there might be 11 tailings dam failures between 2011 and 2020. Unfortunately, the actual number was 26 failures, with 13 being major events.

To fully appreciate the scale of these failures, it's essential to understand that mine tailings structures are often massive, sometimes visible from space. Some are so large that they cause measurable micro-seismic events as the Earth's crust buckles and settles under their immense weight.

Several examples illustrate the severity of tailings failures. In 2014, the Mount Polley disaster in British Columbia, Canada, led to the release of 4.5 million cubic metres of tailings slurry and 10 million cubic metres of water. The environmental damage was severe, with significant amounts of lead, arsenic and mercury released into the environment. The failure was attributed to excessive water within the facility, operator error and a weak foundation layer that had been overlooked during investigation, design and construction. The financial cost of this disaster exceeded US$500 million.

Another significant incident occurred in 2015 when the Samarco tailings dam collapsed in Brazil. This disaster resulted in the release of 60 million cubic metres of iron ore tailings, flooding the Rio Doce (ironically translated as the Sweet River) and reaching the Atlantic Ocean. Tragically, 19 lives were lost and the livelihoods of hundreds were destroyed. The financial costs were in the billions, with BHP writing off the asset due to the magnitude of the problem

3 Elaine Baker, "Mine tailings facilities: overview and industry trends", https://globaltailingsreview.org/wp-content/uploads/2020/09/Ch-II-Mine-Tailings-Facilities_Overview-and-Industry-Trends.pdf.

Figure 1: What is mine waste and tailings?

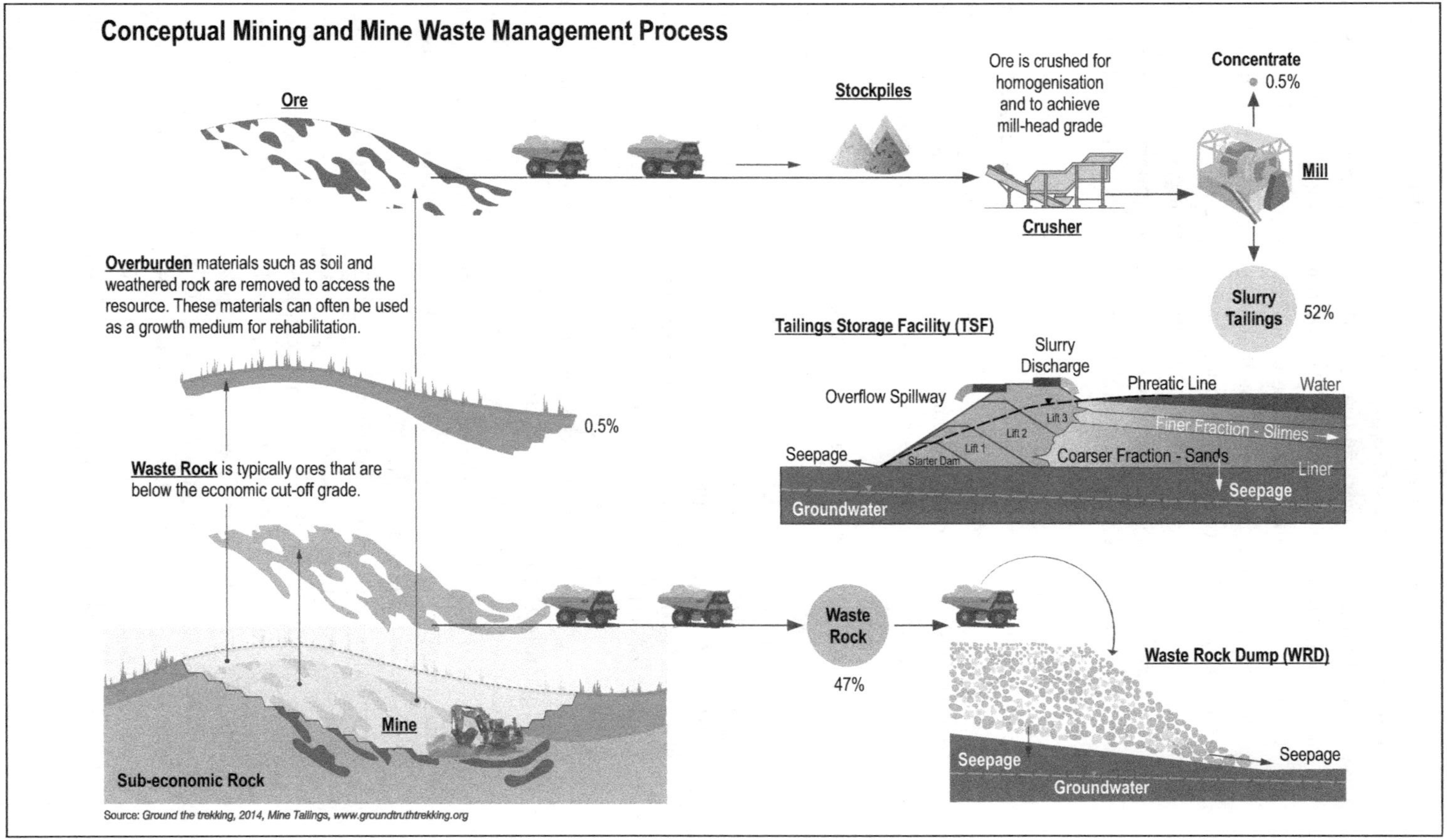

Source: Adapted from Kristina Thygesen, www.grida.no/resources/11415.

and the uncertainty of reopening the mine. In addition to the financial loss, criminal cases were pursued against those responsible.

The Brumadinho dam failure in 2019 was another tragic disaster. The catastrophic failure of the defunct Brumadinho tailings dam at the Córrego do Feijão iron ore mine in Brazil released 12 million cubic metres of waste. The dam, owned by Vale, had been inherited from previous owners in 2001 having been built in 1976. The resulting mudflow destroyed the mine's offices, homes, farms and roads. In total, 270 people were lost as a result of the collapse, of whom 259 were officially confirmed dead, with 11 others reported as missing and whose bodies were never found. The financial costs of this disaster exceed US$5 billion and continues to rise.

Common themes in these failures include operator error, inadequate controls or governance, uncharacterised geotechnical conditions and deficient water management controls. The consequences are catastrophic, often resulting in significant environmental damage, loss of life, social impact and severe reputational harm to both the mine owner and the industry.

3. Legal implications of mine waste failures

The legal landscape surrounding mine waste and tailings is complex, shaped by a myriad of regulations, case law and evolving industry standards. For directors and management in mining and minerals companies, investors and financiers, as well as sustainability professionals, in-house and external counsel or anyone else who is concerned with the environmental, social and governance (ESG) impacts of mining and navigating this terrain, understanding the legal implications of mine waste failures is critical.

When TSF failures occur, the legal consequences can be severe, involving multiple forms of liability. Companies may face civil lawsuits from individuals, communities or other businesses impacted by a tailings dam failure. These claims can include compensation for property damage, loss of income, environmental restoration costs and even punitive damages in cases of gross negligence or wilful misconduct.

In cases where gross negligence or reckless disregard for safety is proven, company executives and managers can face criminal charges. The Brumadinho disaster, for example, led to criminal charges against several Vale executives. Lawyers must be prepared to navigate civil, criminal and administrative/regulatory aspects of such cases.

Risks relating to TSF failures extend to the boardroom, where directors and officers have fiduciary duties to act in the best interest of the company and its shareholders. Failure to adequately oversee mine waste management practices can lead to shareholder lawsuits and other corporate governance challenges.

Figure 2: Causes of tailings dam failures 1915–2016

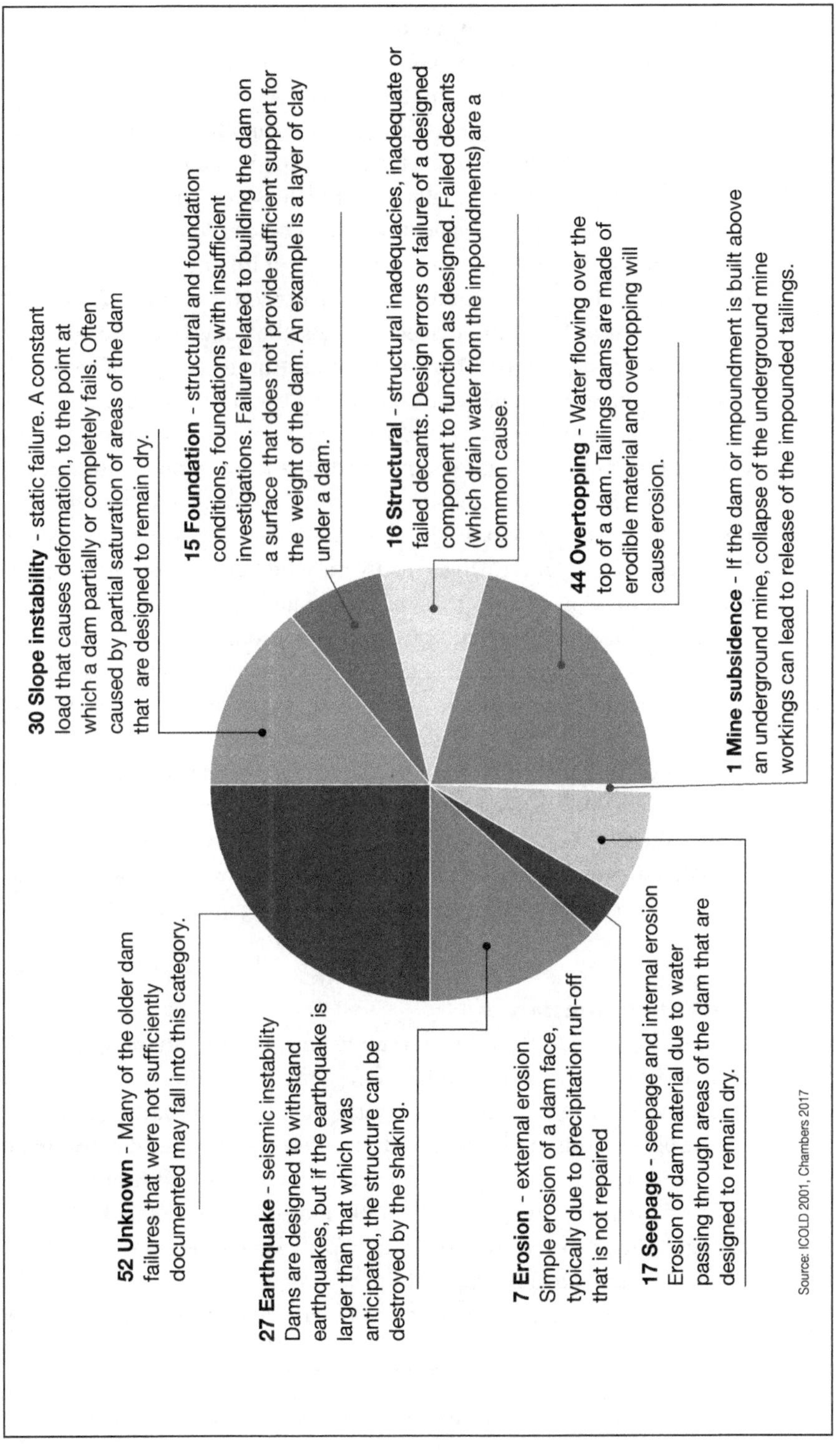

Source: Adapted from Kristina Thygesen, www.grida.no/resources/11415.

4. Insurance and risk management

Management strategies must consider the role of insurance in mitigating the financial risks associated with TSF failures. Asset owners should consider the adequacy of their insurance coverage, particularly in relation to environmental liability policies. Disputes often arise over the scope of coverage, especially in cases involving catastrophic failures with widespread impacts.

Legal counsel and financiers also play a crucial role in risk management by encouraging owners to develop and implement robust compliance programmes. These programmes should not only ensure adherence to legal requirements, but also proactively address the collective risks associated with mine waste management. This approach can significantly reduce the likelihood of legal action and mitigate damages in the event of a failure.

The legal landscape for mine waste management is evolving, with several emerging trends that legal counsel and financiers should monitor closely. As global climate change intensifies, there is growing scrutiny of how mining operations, particularly tailings dams, are affected by extreme weather events. Legal actions may increasingly focus on whether companies have adequately accounted for climate risks in their waste management practices.

There is also a rising trend of framing environmental and mine waste issues within the context of human rights. This perspective emphasises the rights of affected communities to a safe and healthy environment. Asset owners must be prepared to address these arguments in both domestic and international forums.

In addition, investors and the public are increasingly demanding greater transparency and accountability from mining companies regarding their environmental and social impacts. This shift is likely to result in more stringent regulations and a higher volume of litigation, particularly class actions brought by affected communities, non-government organisations (NGOs) or activist groups.

5. Current circumstances

Over the past decade, the mining sector has made significant progress in integrating ESG performance criteria into its strategic and operational decision making.

However, until recently, mine waste management, particularly tailings, has lagged behind this trend. In the decade leading up to 2019, the incidence of very serious and serious failures of TSFs increased significantly compared to historical data dating back to 1950. Projections estimated 18 catastrophic tailings failures between 2015 and 2024, with nine 'very serious' and five 'serious' failures already reported.[4]

It is therefore unsurprising that, following a series of notable failures such as

4 WMTF (World Mine Tailings Failures) (2019). World Mine Tailings Failures – from 1915: Supporting Global Research in Tailings Failure Root Cause, Loss Prevention and Trend Analysis.

Mount Polley in 2014, Samarco in 2015 and Brumadinho in 2019, investors have increasingly demanded that the mining sector disclose details of how it manages its TSFs.

This growing pressure on the mining industry has led to the widespread adoption of enhanced standards and guidelines. As an immediate response to the Brumadinho disaster, the International Council on Mining and Metals (ICMM), the United Nations Environment Programme (UNEP) and Principles for Responsible Investment (PRI) co-convened a multi-stakeholder review that led to the development of the Global Industry Standard on Tailings Management,[5] also drawing on organisations like the International Committee on Large Dams (ICOLD) and the Canadian Dam Association (CDA).

5.1 Global Industry Standard on Tailings Management (GISTM)

The GISTM aims to achieve the ultimate goal of zero harm to people and the environment, with zero tolerance for human fatalities. It requires owners and operators to take responsibility and accountability in the prioritisation of safety throughout all phases of a TSF's life cycle, including closure and post-closure. GISTM is arguably the leading Tailings Governance Framework, presenting performance criteria that address six key topics:

- affected communities;
- integrated knowledge base;
- design, construction, operation and monitoring;
- management and governance;
- emergency response and long-term recovery; and
- public disclosure and access to information.

Across the six key topics there are 15 Principles and 77 Requirements that prescribe the Tailings Governance Framework. They provide a good practice guide, supporting the interpretation and implementation of the standard's requirements and aiding in the fulfilment of commitments under the governance framework without creating additional obligations. Conformance Protocols are also included to support both self-assessment and third-party governance of progress in implementing the standard.

The GISTM also mandates the appointment of key roles and responsibilities for TSF management, across the designer, operations and executive teams. These roles include:

- accountable executive(s) (AE), ultimately responsible for the safety of the tailings facility and reporting directly to the company board of directors;
- engineer of record (EOR), typically an independent engineering

5 ICCM, *Global Industry Standard on Tailings Management*, August 2020, www.icmm.com/website/publications/pdfs/environmental-stewardship/2020/global-industry-standard-on-tailings-management.pdf.

consultancy responsible for confirmation that the tailings storage facility is designed, constructed, operated and decommissioned with appropriate concern for the integrity of the facility, local regulations and international best practice guidelines; and

- responsible tailings facility engineer, who is based on-site, liaises with the EOR and reports directly to the mine management and the owner of the facility on safety, budget requirements and risk management.

The GISTM supports a 'life of mine' (LoM) relationship between the owner's team and the EOR. The owner of the TSF holds ultimate responsibility for the safe operation of the TSF and the safety of the workers, community and environment around the TSF. The EOR supports the owner with any and all aspects of the TSF safety management and is empowered to escalate any concerns to the AE, if and when identified. This requires an advanced level of mutual trust between the owner and the EOR and a relationship that is based on clear and transparent communication.

6. Disrupting traditions

Through increasing industry acceptance of higher standards and duty of care, there is a growing focus on improving the safety and sustainability of tailings storage facilities. GISTM, as described above, includes recommendations for better risk assessment, monitoring and disclosure. The GISTM mandates that an options analysis (as a minimum) be undertaken to identify any alternative solutions to conventional surface tailings disposal. The requirement to consider and/or implement alternative solutions will only strengthen over time.

Some of the prevalent trends in mine tailings management that herald more mainstream thinking for practical alternatives include dry stacking, backfilling of underground mine voids (eg, stopes) and backfilling depleted open cut mine voids. However, it must be recognised that there is no one-size-fits-all solution to this complex problem. There is seemingly unlimited variability in tailings properties, both physically and geochemically, as a function of geology, ore type, processing and metallurgy, climatic, seismic and environmental factors. Simply put, not all tailings are equal and the possibilities of producing the range of tailings types illustrated below varies accordingly.

6.1 Dry stacking

Unlike traditional pumped tailings, dry stacking involves the dewatering of tailings to create a dense, dry material. Dry stack tailings are compacted and stacked in layers, forming a stable solid mass. This method significantly reduces the risk of catastrophic failures associated with tailings dams, as the absence of water minimises the potential for seepage, spills and dam breaches. Additionally, dry stack tailings require less land and offers better long-term environmental and safety outcomes, making them an increasingly considered methodology in mining operations focused on sustainability and risk mitigation. However, the increased cost to produce and place dry tailings can inhibit adoption, depending on the cost model for the operation. In addition, under certain, wetter climatic conditions the effectiveness of dry stacking can be diminished, making it comparable to the risk of a well-run conventional tailings storage facility.

6.2 Co-mingling

Other innovations include combining a slurry, paste or filtered tailings material and co-disposing it with coarse overburden and/or waste rock from the run of mine activities. Co-mingling offers improved stability and an opportunity to encapsulate geochemically unstable or acid rock forming minerals in a way that minimises seepage of contaminates to the surrounding environment.

The example illustrated below is an example of a co-disposal operation at Cerro De Maimon in the Dominican Republic. It combines the co-disposal of potentially acid generating (PAG) tailings and waste rock, some non-PAG waste rock and thickened tailings to facilitate better water management and to allow for co-mingling. The benefits include a smaller overall footprint; simplified water management; more effective seepage controls; lower closure costs; and most importantly a lower risk associated with the improved long-term physical and chemical stability.

6.3 Backfilling mine voids

Backfill mining, which includes tailings as a source of backfill, has several advantages, including the extraction of minerals left in pillars in room and pillar mining, the reduction of the risk of spontaneous rock bursts, the reduction of groundwater contamination when used with binders, and the improvement of mine ventilation. Since 2021, there have been over 62,000 patents filed and granted in the mining industry. In the case of tailings, paste back fill involves the thickening of a mine's tailings and adding cementitious material and pumping it back underground, in so doing creating more stable underground conditions as well as reducing surface tailings quantities. Again, this is arguably more environmentally friendly than traditional surface tailings storage methods and can reduce the size of tailings dams and hence their risk of failure.

6.4 Reprocessing

Tailings reprocessing is the practice of treating and reprocessing mine tailings to extract additional valuable minerals that were not fully recovered during the initial processing and often already disposed of in a TSF. This method leverages advancements in extraction technologies and methods that were unavailable when the tailings were first produced, allowing owners to recover precious metals, base metals and other valuable elements that remain in the tailings.

The process typically involves re-mining the tailings, which may involve dredging or other extraction methods, followed by reprocessing through methods such as flotation, leaching or other advanced separation techniques. The objective is to maximise resource recovery while reducing the environmental impact associated with tailings storage. In addition to extracting valuable resources, reprocessing can reduce the volume of tailings that need to be managed, thereby mitigating the risks associated with tailings dam failures and contributing to the stabilisation and remediation of tailings sites. This approach not only improves resource efficiency but also aligns with sustainable mining practices, addressing both economic and environmental concerns. This dual approach of generating economic value while enhancing safety offers significant sustainability merits.

6.5 Enhanced mine closure and transformation

The GISTM outlines specific requirements for the closure of TSFs focusing on ensuring long-term stability and environmental protection. Closure plans must ensure that TSFs are left in a secure and stable condition, minimising any potential risks to the surrounding environment and communities. This involves measures to prevent contamination, manage water effectively and restore the landscape.

Incorporating natural capital benefits into closure efforts can lead to nature-positive outcomes, such as restoring ecosystems, enhancing biodiversity and improving soil health. Re-vegetation and rehabilitation can create new habitats and contribute to carbon sequestration. GISTM's approach to closure emphasises not just decommissioning but also ensuring that the post-closure landscape provides environmental and community benefits. Mine closure and transformation offer an excellent opportunity to address legacy risk. GISTM sets out several considerations for effective closure, which include:

- preparation, ie, the strategic deposition of tailings to facilitate surface drainage, removing surface water through treatment and discharge and promoting tailings consolidation to enhance structural integrity;
- covering the TSF to reduce dust and metal dispersal, minimise water infiltration, resist erosion and prevent oxygen inflow. Sustainable vegetation may be established to stabilise the site;
- surface water diversion systems to manage water from surrounding areas, directing it away from the TSF to prevent instability, especially during extreme weather events;
- seepage control, using drainage layers and under-drains to collect and remove any seepage, is crucial, preventing contamination of the surrounding environment;

- long-term considerations include access controls and ongoing monitoring to ensure the site remains stable and safe over time; and
- closure cost estimation and provisioning are essential to cover the costs of closure activities and long-term maintenance, ensuring financial readiness for the entire closure process.

7. Forward risk

One of the key areas of risk for tailings management we are yet to fully comprehend is the significance of climate change. Global climate change has the potential to create extremes in wet and dry conditions that may exceed the tolerances of TSF designs, particularly legacy assets that did not contemplate such changes.

Climate change may affect the stability and performance of a TSF in a number of ways.

- Air quality, ie, dust and air quality of mine waste is a challenge, especially in more arid environments or very dry seasonal conditions. Tailings containing heavy metals and other pollutants could be transported further than previously experienced via surface run-off and wind-blown dust due to more extreme weather events;
- Precipitation driven over-topping and impacts to natural water systems, like the Ok Tedi disaster, arguably one of the worst environmental disasters caused by man, as a consequence of the discharge of about 2 billion tons of untreated mining waste into the Ok Tedi River from the Ok Tedi Mine;[6]
- Social challenges, whether it be community access to tailings return water, artisanal miners, or communities at risk from failure events;
- Increased levels of acid mine drainage (AMD) due to increased rates of oxidation of metal sulphides, such as pyrite (iron sulphide), as a result of increased precipitation and/or temperature;
- Similarly, water quality or geochemistry, where acid rock drainage (ARD) can last centuries or even thousands of years. The oldest or most classic example of ARD from ancient mining is along the Rio Tinto, a river in southwestern Spain that rises in the Sierra Morena mountains of Andalusia. Here mining traces its roots back to when the Tartessians and the Iberians started mining in 3000 BC; and
- Structural weakening of dams through increased contraction-expansion cycles caused by more extreme wet-dry periods; erosion and instability of embankment slopes, caused by intense weather events and patterns (eg, rain, wind, hot/humid periods); and potential mass movement of embankment slopes due to increased precipitation, in the form of creep, solifluction and/or landslides.

---

6 Bob Burton, "BHP admits Ok Tedi mine is environmental disaster", *Asia Times*, 17 September 2006.

Allowing for climate change risks includes the consideration of:

- climate change models – using site-specific climate models to simulate possible risks;
- more stringent monitoring (both environmental and geotechnical);
- more stringent storage and water handling capability for extreme weather events;
- increased stringency on layout optimisation;
- more stringent landform and erosion modelling/predictions;
- reduced raw water intake, with maximum recycling (particularly in more arid environments);
- improved seepage controls; and
- adaptation of principles of natural capital, carbon credits, biodiversity offsets and social enhancements.

8. What's next?

Given the significant legal, financial and reputational risks posed by tailings dam failures, it is crucial for the mining industry to continually improve its risk mitigation framework. This framework should encompass legal compliance, operational best practices and crisis management strategies to ultimately eliminate the occurrence of catastrophic incidents and to prepare for effective responses in the less likely event that they occur.

The risks and opportunities outlined here are largely technical in nature and although valid in intent, they do not address the remaining and single biggest change to the governance of the mining sector, which is the ramp up in pressure for increased scrutiny, independent auditing and public disclosure requirements for all stakeholders.

As discussed above, the co-convened model of equal representation from industry, investor and government stakeholders in the formation of the GISTM was designed to give civil society and the public confidence that the initiative would have the necessary level of independence. In so doing, it was also an acknowledgement that no single stakeholder can solve the problem and that community and investor trust in the mining sector needed to be restored.

With the creation of GISTM, it was inevitable that the launch of the Global Tailings Management Institute (GTMI) would follow. Announced in 2023, the GTMI will be an independently chaired, expert panel and informed multi-stakeholder advisory group. It will be an independent institute, which will oversee a process for independent auditing, verification and certification against the GISTM.

The purpose of the independent auditing will be to provide an assessment of the level of conformance for a specific Tailings Storage Facility (TSF) against all 77 Requirements of the GISTM. A Certificate of Conformance will be issued for those TSFs found to comply with the GISTM. It is planned that the process of auditing will include public disclosure of a summary of the audit findings.

While overseeing the assurance programme will be the core function of the GTMI, it will also seek to:

- promote awareness, understanding and adoption of the GISTM;
- facilitate the sharing of experience to improve overall knowledge in tailings management across a range of stakeholder groups; and
- provide transparency by affording stakeholders access to tailings facility details (from disclosures related to Principle 15 of GISTM) and auditing outcomes.

One does not have to become a member of ICMM to become a signatory of the GTMI; it is to be a multi-stakeholder-led organisation with the governance being shared by civil society, affected communities, financial and insurance industries and educational organisations alongside the mining industry. The GTMI will be a fully independent institute with its own board of directors. By becoming a signatory, a company commits to the implementation of the GISTM with conformance assessments being conducted at intervals determined by the Consequence Category of a TSF. Participation in the GTMI will also be open to stakeholders that do not have operational responsibility for a TSF.

The GISTM is particularly focused on the safety of tailings facilities, through all phases of a facility's life cycle, including closure and post-closure. Other more broadly focused mining-related guidelines and standards such as the Mining Association of Canada's Toward Sustainable Mining (TSM) and the Initiative for Responsible Mining Assurance (IRMA) also cover aspects of tailings management. It is encouraging to see that there is increasing alignment and equivalency between the standards and that the GTMI is working to acknowledge and recognise equivalence where applicable.

9. On reflection

ESG principles seek to reconcile the undeniable truth that mining is crucial to sustain modern society with the need to address the environmental damage caused in the pursuit of the technological advances made since our Bronze Age ancestors first discovered the superiority of metal tools over stone.

As the world moves towards decarbonisation in response to global climate change, our future dependence on metals, minerals and rare earth elements will grow exponentially. Mining activities will need to grow by orders of magnitude to meet the material demands of green technologies, such as batteries, turbines, electric vehicles and solar panels.

With advancements in technology, we are now consuming a much broader suite of metals than even a few decades ago. Approximately 60 elements (ie, two-thirds of the periodic table) are now vital to modern society. While significant progress in cleaner technologies and mining practices has reduced environmental harm and increased societal value, there remains a real disconnect in society about where our raw materials come from and their intrinsic value to a greener world.

Recognising that modern society and industry rely heavily on raw materials – captured in the saying "if it's not grown, it must be mined". The challenge is how to carry out mining in a socially and ethically responsible, environmentally sustainable manner such that meets industrial demand while also ensuring a just transition for future generations.

Against this background, it can be difficult for mining companies to navigate what is important and how it should be reported. For each mine this may vary, and a first step will always be to identify the most salient risks and opportunities. To illustrate, the following core subjects are covered by the ESG agenda for the mining industry.

- *Environment:* Tackles questions like do we understand our exposure to climate change related transition; are we capturing all the operational improvements related to a low carbon transition; do we understand the risks or opportunities to biodiversity, ecosystem services, water, mine waste/tailings, air, noise, energy; and do we make use of a natural capital framework to enhance opportunities impacting our effects on climate change (carbon footprint, greenhouse gas), hazardous substances or mine closure.
- *Social:* Asks whether we have considered our risks through a human rights lens; or are we contributing to shared value and measuring our positive impacts on people and planet; and how can we improve labour and working conditions? These together impact plans to address human rights, land use, resettlement, make provision for vulnerable people, gender, labour practices, worker/community health and safety, and security, make room for competing interest of artisanal miners, or address mine closure and the attendant after-use potential.
- *Governance:* Asks do we have appropriate governance, oversight and management systems in place to tackle legal compliance, ethics, anti-bribery and corruption and transparency; it asks whether we are exposed to supply chain risks; and challenges whether we have business ethics policies that support diversity, equity and inclusion.

Within this, mining companies need to consider whether there are environmental, social or governance risks that may affect their ability to: raise capital; obtain permits; work with communities, regulators and NGOs; and/or protect their assets from impairments.

Some key observations noted in this chapter on the risk and opportunities of addressing mine waste challenges include the following:

- Technical, environmental and social issues are inextricably linked.
  - Failures cost money, cost lives, leave legacies for future generations.
- Increased awareness from investors of inherent risks and evaluation thereof is a key driver for change.
  - Linked to standards of best practice (ICMM, ICOLD, ANCOLD, UNEP, PRI, EU Mine Waste Directive, CDA, ie, Global Tailings Standards).
- Improved governance by all, from investors, owners, operators and regulators.
  - Ties together all responsibilities for best possible outcome with least risk.
- Tailings facilities don't generate revenue (except when re-processed), but are usually the single biggest liability in any mining project and remain in perpetuity.
  - Saving money will cost dearly in the long run (lives, livelihood, money, reputation, environment).

Mitigating risks associated with mine waste is essential due to the significant legal, financial and reputational consequences that can arise from tailings dam failures. Directors and management in mining and minerals companies, investors and financiers, as well as sustainability professionals in-house and external counsel and anyone else who is concerned with the ESG impacts of mining, play a crucial role in navigating comprehensive risk mitigation frameworks that should include legal compliance, operational best practices and crisis management strategies.

Beyond regulatory compliance, it is important for all stakeholders to adopt best practices in waste management that exceed minimum legal requirements.

Advocacy for the use of advanced engineering techniques and technologies in the design, construction and maintenance of tailings dams is essential to ensure these facilities can withstand environmental and operational stresses. Owners should also be encouraged to explore innovative approaches to tailings management, such as reprocessing tailings to recover additional minerals or converting waste into materials for other industries, which can reduce waste volumes and generate additional revenue streams.

Financial preparedness is also key to managing risks associated with mine waste. Owners should ensure that they have adequate insurance coverage for environmental liabilities, property damage and business interruptions related to mine waste incidents, with policies regularly reviewed to address potential gaps. Maintaining financial reserves or access to capital that can be quickly deployed in the event of a disaster is essential for covering immediate response efforts, legal fees and compensation claims. Additionally, exploring contractual arrangements with contractors, suppliers and joint venture partners that clearly delineate liability and risk-sharing provisions can help distribute the financial burden in case of a failure and protect the client's interests.

Proactive stakeholder engagement and transparency are crucial to reducing the likelihood of legal disputes and enhancing the owner's reputation. Owners should also build strong, positive relationships with local communities by involving them in decision-making processes related to waste management and ensuring they are informed about potential risks and emergency procedures. Transparency with investors about the risks associated with mine waste and the steps being taken to mitigate them is also important, as this can help maintain investor confidence and reduce the risk of shareholder lawsuits in the event of a failure. Furthermore, maintaining open lines of communication with regulators and seeking their input on waste management practices can lead to more favourable outcomes in inspections or legal challenges.

Finally, all stakeholders should advocate a culture of continuous improvement and adaptation. Every incident, whether at the client's site or elsewhere in the industry, should be analysed for lessons that can improve safety and management practices. Staying abreast of technological advancements and evolving industry standards is also important to enhance the safety and efficiency of waste management practices. Regular reviews and updates of waste management policies and procedures will ensure that they remain aligned with best practices and regulatory requirements, reinforcing the owner's commitment to responsible and sustainable mine waste and tailings management.

About the authors

Nabil Abrahams
Associate, CMS Cameron McKenna Nabarro Olswang LLP
nabil.abrahams@cms-cmno.com

Nabil Abrahams is an associate in the energy and infrastructure team at CMS in London. Nabil holds degrees in law and cognitive neuroscience and specialises in international energy project developments and M&A transactions across the oil and gas, green hydrogen, renewable energy and mining sectors.

María Cristina Alva
Partner, CMS Grau
mariacristina.alva@cms-grau.com

María Cristina Alva is a partner at CMS Grau in the mining practice area. With an extensive background, she has consolidated more than 10 years of experience providing legal advice in the areas of mining, corporate and environmental law. Her strategic vision is geared towards preventing legal contingencies and facilitating crucial decision making in the mining sector, distinguishing her as a results-oriented professional. In addition to her practical experience, María Cristina has a solid academic background. She holds a master's degree in mining management from the GERENS Graduate School in Peru and certifications from renowned institutions such as the University of Toronto Rotman School of Management, where she obtained the Certificate of Inclusion by Design.

Throughout her professional journey, María Cristina played key roles at Compañía Minera Ares (Hochschild Group), including positions such as legal and corporate affairs deputy manager and head of the mining regulation department. She has offered legal advice with a special focus on mining and environmental regulations for various mining units and exploration projects within the group.

Yasmin Batliwala
Chief executive, Advocates for International Development (A4ID)
yasmin.batliwala@a4id.org

Yasmin Batliwala has held a number of significant leadership positions over the years within the public and third sectors. Her portfolios have included HIV/AIDS, drug and alcohol misuse and criminal justice. She has undertaken work for the United Nations Office of Drugs and Crime in this regard. Yasmin has considerable board-level experience, including having been on the board of a large NHS trust, governor of the University of Hertfordshire and serving as a magistrate in the Youth and Adult Courts. She was a recipient of the City of London Woman of Achievement Awards for her work in the public sector. In 2022, Yasmin was awarded an MBE for her work in human rights, rule of law and international development in the Queen's New Year Honours List.

Neal Brewster

Executive director, Elemental Economics
neal.brewster@elementaleconomics.com

Neal Brewster is an expert on economic, market and valuation issues in the metals, mining and energy sectors. He works as an industry consultant and is a visiting lecturer at the University of Dundee. He was chief economist at a leading producer of market intelligence and consulting services in the mining and critical raw materials sectors and has held a number of senior economics, valuation and strategy roles at Rio Tinto, in the United Kingdom and Australia. He also has significant experience working on government policy in the natural resources sector.

Kevin PCJ D'Souza

Founder, KD Consulting
kevinpcjdsouza@gmail.com

Kevin D'Souza is a recognised professional and sustainability/ESG thought leader with over three decades of direct experience in responsible mining. He has experience in a variety of operational, managerial and executive leadership roles that range from remote exploration camps, mine construction sites, operational mines and closure sites to corporate and ministerial offices. Throughout his career, he has amassed direct experience in over 50 countries worldwide working with remote communities and Indigenous groups.

He has worked directly for, or consulted to, numerous mining companies including many of the industry's majors such as Barrick, AngloGold Ashanti, Gold Fields, Rio Tinto, BHP Billiton, Kinross and De Beers. He was most recently the chief sustainability officer for Resource Capital Funds and, prior to that, the VP of security, sustainability and environment for Centerra Gold. Before that, he was senior director community relations and environment for Barrick. He is currently a member of the technical advisory committee for Mining 2030 (Global Investor Commission on Mining) and an advisory board member for International Women in Mining.

Sandra Gogal

Partner, Cassels Brock & Blackwell LLP
sgogal@cassels.com

Sandra Gogal is a partner in the Aboriginal Law Group at Cassels Brock & Blackwell LLP. A strategic thinker and trusted adviser to resource developers, investors, governments and agencies on matters relating to Aboriginal and environmental law, Sandra has a nationally recognised practice with extensive regulatory experience in mining, hydro-electric, nuclear, forestry and oil and gas. Sandra offers a combined 25+ years' experience in-house with the government of Ontario and in private practice – providing strategic legal advice to clients in the resource sector across Canada on matters relating to Aboriginal rights and consultation, environmental assessments, permitting and government relations. An astute negotiator, she has navigated several successful commercial arrangements, settlements, impact and benefit agreements and partnerships between industry and First Nations on major Canadian hydro-electric projects, pipeline and mining projects. For her work, Sandra is recognised as a leader in her field by *Chambers Canada*, Best Lawyers and Lexpert.

Sarah Grenfell
Partner, CMS Cameron McKenna Nabarro Olswang LLP
sarah.grenfell@cms-cmno.com

Sarah Grenfell is a partner in CMS's infrastructure, construction and energy disputes team in London. Sarah specialises in complex, high-value disputes in the energy and construction sectors. Experienced in all forms of dispute resolution, Sarah has a particular focus on international arbitration. Sarah has advised clients on projects around the globe, including in the United Kingdom, Europe, Russia, the Middle East, North and East Africa, Australia and Asia; she has also acted as counsel and co-counsel on disputes governed by English law and the laws of other jurisdictions. Sarah holds an LLB and LLM from the University of Queensland, Australia, is admitted to practise in Australia and England and Wales and is a qualified Solicitor-Advocate.

David How
Associate, Cassels Brock & Blackwell LLP
dhow@cassels.com

David How is an associate in the Aboriginal law group at Cassels Brock & Blackwell LLP, advising on matters across Canada. His practice focuses on Aboriginal rights and title and represents a wide variety of Indigenous, private sector and industry, and provincial and municipal government clients. David advises on and negotiates Indigenous self-governance, the duty to consult, historic claims, modern treaties and impact benefit agreements. David also has experience litigating complex Aboriginal rights and title claims as well as commercial matters. David has a law degree in both the common law and the civil law and is called to the bar in the provinces of British Columbia and Ontario.

Ben Lepley
Senior mining ESG consultant, SLR Consulting
blepley@slrconsulting.com

Ben Lepley is a chartered geologist and practising ESG consultant with over 15 years in the minerals and mining industry. Ben's work involves embedding sustainability and ESG concepts and processes into mineral project development and assisting clients in implementing positive change. He also manages multidisciplinary teams for technical studies, including exploration projects and operational mines, from scoping studies through to feasibility studies. Ben works on behalf of exploration and mining companies as well as financial institutions undertaking due diligence reviews and audits. He has significant relevant experience across base metal and bulk commodities, including copper, iron ore, bauxite and nickel, as well as speciality metals such as lithium and rare earth elements.

Tatiana Londoño Camargo
Counsel, CMS Rodríguez-Azuero
tatiana.londono@cms-ra.com

Tatiana Londoño Camargo is a Colombian lawyer with a Master of Laws (LLM) degree in International Legal Studies from Georgetown University, where she attended as a Fulbright and Colfuturo Scholar. She also holds a master's degree in National Security and Defense from the Colombian Superior War College and a graduate degree in Administrative Law.

She has acted as adviser in human rights and international law in several public institutions, including the Colombian Ministry of Defense, Military Forces Command, National Senate and Inspector General's Office, where, as Inspector General Delegate for Human Rights and Ethnic Affairs, she participated in the creation of Colombia's National Action Plan in Business and Human Rights, among others.

Tatiana is counsel in human rights for CMS Rodríguez-Azuero, prior to which she was partner of LH Law & Consulting advising important companies in Colombia, Guatemala, Mexico, Peru, Ecuador, the United States, Switzerland and other countries in human rights and human rights due diligence. She has also been Public International Law professor at Pontificia Universidad Javeriana's Law School in Bogotá, currently teaches master's degree courses in Business and Human Rights and International Law, and has been invited as speaker for congresses and conferences at several Colombian universities.

Dalia Majumder-Russell
Partner, Cameron McKenna Nabarro Olswang LLP
dalia.majumder-russell@cms-cmno.com

Dalia Majumder-Russell focuses on energy transition technologies and infrastructure projects as part of the energy and climate change practice in the CMS London office.

Dalia specialises in complex process energy projects advising on renewable energy transactions, commercial agreements and the regulatory frameworks within which such projects operate. For over 10 years she has advised governments, lenders and sponsors in Europe, Africa and North America on legal issues arising across the project life cycle. As a core member of the firm's ESG group, her work delves into the ways in which projects best manage their greenhouse gas emissions and meet their ESG commitments.

Dalia is passionate about the decarbonisation agenda across the energy, heat and transport sectors. She leads CMS's carbon capture usage and storage (CCUS) and hydrogen initiatives and champions the firm's thought leadership on the subject, which includes publication of the multi-jurisdictional *CMS Expert Guide to Hydrogen Law and Regulation*.

Chris Meikle
Asia-Pacific mining sector leader and technical director, geotechnics and mine waste engineering, SLR Consulting
cmeikle@slrconsulting.com

Chris Meikle is a chartered engineering geologist with over 20 years' research and applied experience. Chris leads SLR's mining sector representation in the Asia-Pacific region, linking a diverse range of services, including mining advisory, sustainability advisory, geotechnics, tailings, water, environmental assessment, social impact and mine closure. He has a PhD from Newcastle University in the United Kingdom and bachelor's degree in Earth Sciences. His leadership extends across local, national and international networks where he provides input on a diverse range of projects alongside multidisciplinary subject matter specialists. Throughout his career he has undertaken projects across Europe, the Middle East, the United States, South America, Africa, Indonesia and Australia.

Chris is an active technical practitioner, focusing on geohazards and risk assessment and he has previously held the position of Engineer of Record, overseeing the successful implementation of GISTM compliance. He is an advocate for corporate sustainability and routinely contributes to thought leadership on ESG topics.

Eoin O'Shea
Partner and head of corporate crime practice, CMS Cameron McKenna Nabarro Olswang LLP
eoin.oshea@cms-cmno.com

Eoin O'Shea heads the corporate crime practice at CMS. He advises on government and regulatory investigations, corporate crime issues, civil disputes and professional ethics. Areas of particular focus are financial crime, fraud law in all its aspects, anti-corruption, sanctions, legal privilege, regulatory law, public law, competition law and international law. Eoin is a member and former chair of the City of London Law Society Corporate Crime Committee. He is the author of *The Bribery Act 2010: A Practical Guide* (Jordans, 2011), a leading textbook on UK bribery law, and co-author of various books, including the chapter on privilege in the fourth edition of *Banking Litigation* (Sweet & Maxwell, 2017).

Jeff Parshley
Corporate consultant, SRK Consulting (US) Inc
jparshley@srk.com

Jeff Parshley is a professional geologist and corporate consultant with SRK Consulting and served as its global group chairman from 2016 to 2021. A graduate of Dartmouth College, Jeff has more than 40 years of mining industry experience including over 35 years in mine closure.

Jeff has contributed significantly to environmental conservation worldwide, sharing his thought leadership on and knowledge of mine closure well beyond industry consulting to include private and governmental organisations. Jeff's body of work includes best practices, corporate standards, guidance documents, and regulatory policies in support of building ESG frameworks that account for the legal, financial, stakeholder, technical and institutional-capacity considerations within mine closure. In collaboration with the state of Nevada and the US Bureau of Land Management, he authored the Standardized Reclamation Cost Estimator, or SRCE, a public domain tool used around the world to calculate mine closure costs for financial assurance.

Ted Rhodes
Partner, CMS Cameron McKenna Nabarro Olswang LLP
ted.rhodes@cms-cmno.com

Ted Rhodes is the head of the mining and minerals practice of international law firm, CMS. He is a specialist in mining, commodities trading, energy and natural resources projects, having worked on such matters across Africa, Asia, Europe and the Americas. He spent 12 years, from 2009 until 2021, in Brazil, leading CMS's Rio de Janeiro office and the expansion of CMS across Latin America.

Ted advises mining companies, commodities traders and other participants in the minerals supply chain on corporate transactions and joint ventures, project development and commercial contracts as well as regulation, including emerging ESG regulation. He has authored a number of publications on mining and minerals, including a series of articles on the role of mining and minerals in the energy transition.

Kamen Stoilov
Associate, CMS Cameron McKenna Nabarro Olswang LLP
kamen.stoilov@cms-cmno.com

Kamen Stoilov is an associate in the CMS environment team based in London. Kamen has broad experience advising on the full spectrum of environmental and consumer products legislation applicable in the European Union and the United Kingdom, with a particular specialism in circular economy legislation.

During his day-to-day work, he also advises on GHG/F-Gas emissions, non-financial and climate-related reporting, green claims, supply chain due diligence, deforestation regulations, environmental permitting, product safety, right to repair, waste shipments, end-of-life product management and extended producer responsibility.

Andrew Sullivan
ESG lead (Canada Mining, Minerals and Metals), Stantec
andrew.sullivan2@stantec.com

With an engineering and legal background, Andrew Sullivan has a rare perspective on the planning and execution of large resource projects, their legal issues and corresponding regulatory frameworks. He has completed a Master of Laws with a specialisation in energy and infrastructure. Andrew published a paper on the duty to consult in large infrastructure projects in the *Journal of Canadian College of Construction Lawyers*. He has worked on and led teams in the creation of the mine operating budgets and as a project manager has led teams in the creation of NI43-101 reporting, pre-feasibility studies and closure plans. Andrew is currently ESG lead for Stantec Mining, Minerals and Metals in Canada.

Daniela Vergel-Riascos
Partner, CMS Rodríguez-Azuero
daniela.vergel@cms-ra.com

Daniela Vergel-Riascos is a partner in the environmental law and sustainability team, and co-leads the energy and climate change team in the mining sector at CMS Rodríguez-Azuero. She holds degrees in law and has specialised in mining and environmental law and conflict resolutions for over 15 years while based in Bogotá, Colombia.

Daniela is arbitrator and secretary of the arbitration and conciliation centres of the Chamber of Commerce of Bogota and the superintendence of corporations. She has advised different clients on the structuring of environmental and sustainability strategy for projects in diverse sectors, including acquisition of mining titles, compliance of environmental law for all industries, procedures before the mining and environmental authority, among other matters. She has successfully represented clients in litigation disputes and environmental and mining sanctioning processes.

David Walker
Global director, mining and minerals, SLR Consulting
dwalker@slrconsulting.com

David Walker is the global director responsible for SLR's international mining and minerals business, which covers SLR's mining advisory, sustainability, waste and tailings, water, environmental and social and closure offering. David has over 35 years' experience within the mining sector, in both senior management and as an experienced consultant.

Under his leadership at SLR, the mining services brand and recognition by clients and industry peers alike for technical excellence has grown for the nine years in his role.

A keen strategic insight, together with a broad scientific and engineering background, formed by his extensive experience in support of the development, operation and closure of mining projects, has allowed David to develop a deep appreciation of an integrated engineering and environmental approach to projects. In keeping with the evolution of the mining industry, this has come to mean he is a strong advocate of ESG and sustainability and the role that it has in the future of the mining industry.

His own technical specialities and experience covers a range of technical and project work of a geotechnical, hydrogeological and hydrological nature covering all aspects of mine tailings or mine waste and environmental engineering projects. He has extensive experience of working in developing countries, especially in sub-Saharan Africa.

About Globe Law and Business

Globe Law and Business was established in 2005. From the very beginning, we set out to create legal books that are sufficiently high level to be of real use to the experienced professional, yet still accessible and easy to navigate. Most of our authors are drawn from Magic Circle and other top commercial firms, both in the United Kingdom and internationally.

Our titles are carefully produced, with the utmost attention paid to editorial, design and production processes. We hope this results in high-quality publications that are easy to read and a pleasure to own.

In 2021, we were very pleased to announce the start of a new chapter for Globe Law and Business following the acquisition of law books under the imprint Ark Publishing. Our law firm management list is now significantly expanded with many well-known and loved Ark Publishing titles.

We are also pleased to announce the launch of our online content platform, Globe Law Online, which allows for easy access across firms. Details of all titles included can be found at www.globelawonline.com. Email glo@globelawandbusiness.com for further details and to arrange a free trial for you or your firm.

We'd very much like to hear from you with your thoughts and ideas for improving what we offer. Please do feel free to email me on sian@globelawandbusiness.com. Happy reading and thank you for your time.

Sian O'Neill
Managing director
Globe Law and Business
www.globelawandbusiness.com